THE QUEEN'S POOR

THE QUEEN'S POOR
LIFE AS THEY FIND IT IN TOWN AND COUNTRY

M. LOANE

Introduction by
Susan Cohen
and Clive Fleay

Middlesex University Press
London, England

Published by Middlesex University Press
This Middlesex University edition is a reprint of the first
edition published in 1905 by Edward Arnold,
London
Middlesex University Press is an imprint of
Middlesex University Services Limited,
Bounds Green Road, London N11 2NQ

A CIP catalogue record for this book is available from
The British Library

ISBN 1 898253 22 6

Manufacture coordinated in UK by
Book-in-Hand Ltd, London N6 5AH

CONTENTS

INTRODUCTION

by Susan Cohen and Clive Fleay

MARTHA LOANE'S LIFE AND WORK[*]

The Queen's Poor was the first of six popular social commentaries published under the name of M. Loane between 1905 and 1911.[1] For a generation before this work was written there had been a rising tide of social investigative literature, focused largely on the urban poor, which had culminated in the publication of Charles Booth's *Life and Labour of the People of London* (1889-1902)[2] and B. S. Rowntree's study of York, *Poverty. A Study of Town Life* (1901).[3] Booth and Rowntree helped to locate the study of poverty within a new quantitative framework, characterised, *inter alia* by statistical detail and categorical rigour. But Loane — like her contemporaries Stephen Reynolds[4] Mary Higgs[5] and Olive Malvery[6] — belonged to another, more qualitative tradition of British social investigation which was unapologetically subjective and where the emphasis was placed upon the individual experience of deprivation within a wider culture of poverty.[7]

Loane's studies were unlike any other contemporary works of social investigation, for they were all based on the first-hand experiences of a distinguished Queen's (i.e. district) nurse, whose working life involved intimate contact with the 'respectable' urban and rural poor, defined by her as those who managed to keep even the most 'painfully poor and crowded home together'.[8]

Caring for the sick poor in their own homes provided Loane with an unprecedented and unrestricted opportunity

---

[*] We are indebted to Dr M. J. Dedman for commenting on an earlier draft of this introduction

of observing the working-classes in a way denied to other commentators, and this enabled her to reveal a detailed and complex picture of the daily lives of the poor.[9] She made critical assessments of their standard of living and provided penetrating insights into their beliefs, attitudes, language and behaviour. The financial aspects of poverty were carefully evaluated, illustrating how material want dictated the ways people behaved. She debated topical social issues and commented upon legislation which affected the lives of the poor, and throughout the writing was her determination to counter popular prejudice that the poor were a 'race apart'.[10]

M.Loane earned a considerable reputation during her lifetime as an authority on the condition of the working-class poor, but the details of her personal life have remained obscure. Apart from relying on fragments of information revealed in Loane's published work, historians have either ignored her biographical background, or concluded, like Dr Ross McKibbin, that 'little is known about her'.[11] Just how little is evident by the continuing confusion amongst scholars concerning such basic details as Loane's full name. Common, if erroneous, constructions include M.L.Loane,[12] Margaret Loane,[13] Mary Loane[14] and Margery Loane.[15] Mistakes have been compounded by inaccurate British Library catalogue detail and misleading bio- graphical information in *Who Was Who*.[16]

As it happens there is more than the problem of resolving a name. M.Loane was the eminent Queen's nurse, Martha Jane Loane, but *The Queen's Poor*, Loane's other five social commentaries, and much more, were produced by Martha and her half-sister, Alice, in an arrangement apparently overlooked even by their publishers. In the light of this obscure literary partnership and the questions they raise, it becomes all the more pressing to reconstruct the main outlines of Martha Loane's life and career.

Martha Loane (1852-1933)

Martha Jane Loane was born on 7 February 1852 in Plymouth.[17] Her mother, Jane, died soon after she was born, and her father, Jabez, a Lieutenant in the Royal Navy,[18] remarried later that year.[19] Harriet and Jabez Loane had five children. Martha's first half-sister, Beatrice Mary, was born in 1858,[20] and after the family moved to Portsmouth following Jabez's promotion to the rank of Staff Commander in 1863, her other half-sister, Alice Eliza was born.[21] But within a year, Jabez Loane was widowed again.[22]

At the time of her stepmother's death, Martha was a pupil at the newly established Royal Naval School for Females, situated at St.Margaret's, Isleworth, Middlesex.[23] Its object was 'to bestow upon the daughters of necessitous Naval and Marine Officers...a good, virtuous and religious education, in conformity with the principles and doctrines of the Church of England' to enable a girl 'to take her place in the world with a fair prospect of success'.[24] Martha's two half-sisters followed the same educational path, Beatrice being the most academically successful, winning the 'Bruce Scholarship' in 1875.[25] But it was Martha who was to make the greatest impact in the wider world with her celebrated career as a Queen's nurse and authoress.

Martha completed her formal education in 1870, although sixteen years were to elapse before she embarked upon her nursing training and first paid employment. Little evidence of this period of her life has survived but it is possible in the light of her subsequent care of the poor that she was involved in charitable work. And it is probable that Martha spent some of this period travelling on the continent of Europe.[26] What is certain is that in May 1886, at the age of 34, Martha Loane began her training as a nurse. It was an auspicious time for the profession for important changes in attitude were taking place concerning the status of nurses and their role in hospitals and the wider community.[27]

Martha received her initial nursing instruction at Charing Cross Hospital, London, and subsequently took up her first professional appointment as ward sister there in May 1887 under the title Sister Agnes. She remained at the hospital until October 1888, before moving to Shrewsbury as Sister-in-Charge at the Salop Royal Infirmary where she stayed until March 1893.[28]

Again, little information survives concerning Martha's life over the next six months, but in September 1893 she enroled as a probationer with the Queen Victoria's Jubilee Institute for Nurses.[29] The Institute, founded in 1887, was funded by donations collected by the women of England to commemorate Queen Victoria's golden jubilee, and royal patronage conferred upon its members the title of Queen's nurse.[30] The objectives of the Institute were to promote the education and maintenance of nurses for the sick poor in their own houses. It did not employ nurses directly, but trained highly qualified professional women, like Martha, as district nurses. Once qualified, Queen's nurses were then employed by organisations which were affiliated to, and regularly inspected by the Institute.[31]

Martha undertook her preliminary 'district' training of six months at the Institute's headquarters in Bloomsbury Square, London. During this period she also passed the examination of the Obstetrical Society of London, qualifying her to act as a midwife.[32] Her training period completed, Martha spent a further six months working from the London headquarters during which time her status as a Queen's nurse was confirmed: her name was included in the Institute's Roll of Nurses on 10 May 1894 and a few weeks later she was presented with the Institute's distinctive brassard and badge.[33]

Martha's first post as a qualified Queens' nurse was in Buxton, Derbyshire. This was one of the Institute's newly affiliated rural branches[34] covering a district of about two square miles with a population of 10,000.[35] Apart from practical nursing duties, an essential clerical obligation for any Queen's nurse was the maintenance of 'Books of Association' — a case book, a register of cases and a time book.[36] For Loane, these official records had additional importance for they provided a fund of material which Martha and her half-sister Alice could exploit for publication.

There was an interruption to Martha's career in July 1895

when she returned home to be with her dying father.[37] Her
stay at the family home in East Dulwich, London (her father
had lived in retirement there since 1876) coincided with a
brief but portentous correspondence with Florence Nightingale. Accompanying a forty page manuscript, entitled
'Incidental Opportunities of District Nursing', was Martha's
letter dated 30 July 1895:

> Hearing that you are interested in the extension of District
> Nursing, I venture to ask you to read the enclosed M.S and
> I should esteem it a very great favour if you would kindly
> let me know your opinion of it. It is the result of my practi-
> cal experience in the work I had...in Hospitals before
> engaging in District Nursing...[38]

A fillip to Martha's literary ambitions was Miss
Nightingale's encouraging and constructive reply. She had
examined Loane's manuscript with 'the utmost care and
with great interest' approving both its tone and content.[39]
Quite why Loane wrote at this time remains unknown but
it is possible that Alice encouraged Martha to write to this
legendary figure of British nursing. Whether the sisters ever
planned a literary partnership is not clear. It may have come
about by accident as much as design, being facilitated perhaps by Jabez's death and the release of Alice from her filial
duties.

After her father's death Martha resumed her work in
Buxton, and when her period of probation expired in early
1896 she was issued with her official certificate.[40] Although
no details of this appointment have been traced, it is known
that Loane's employers considered her work to be excellent.[41]

1897 was a highly successful year for Martha Loane.
There was the serial publication of her first article in Nursing Notes and promotion to a new post, as Superintendent of
Queen's nurses in Portsmouth.[42] The city, though familiar to
Loane from her childhood years, was in nursing terms a
major contrast to rural Buxton. Her new patients comprised
dockyard workers, soldiers, sailors, labourers, mechanics
and small tradesmen as well as their respective families.
About 160,000 people lived within the two mile radius

covered by the Queen's nurses, and as the official reports
made clear, Portsea, Portsmouth, Southsea and Landport
had their fair share of very poor districts which Martha
would get to know intimately and whose human problems
she would subsequently bring to the attention of her
readers.[43]

Miss Peters, the redoubtable Inspector of Queen's nurses,
was fully assured of Martha's ability, for at the time of her
appointment, with only two nurses at the home, she was immediately entrusted with the training of six probationers. By
late 1903, the total number of nurses, including trainees and
qualified nurses, had more than doubled to fifteen.[44] This
made possible a sizeable increase in the number of poor
people who were able to benefit from the ministrations of the
Queen's nurses in Portsmouth. In Loane's first full year as
Superintendent, her nurses dealt with 448 new cases, and
made 17,990 visits. During 1904, her last complete year in
post, 1,073 new cases were dealt with, involving her nurses
in 26,601 visits.[45]

Loane's responsibilities in Portsmouth should not be
under-estimated. In addition to running the District nurses
home, which she described fully in several articles, she accompanied each of her nurses once a fortnight on a complete
round of duty, 'to ensure the maintenance of correct and efficient nursing procedure'.[46]

The confidence expressed by the Borough of Portsmouth
Association in their new Lady Superintendent at the outset
of her appointment was to be fully justified. Over the ensu-
ing years Martha received nothing but the highest praise
from the local community and its official representatives in
addition to tributes from her own organisation. Its annual
report for 1904 acknowledged Loane's vital contribution —
'the energy and ability displayed by Miss Loane to whom
more than anyone else is due the credit for the high place our
Nursing Association holds in public estimation'.[47]

In Portsmouth Martha demonstrated her didactic skills
and was officially complimented on several occasions 'for the
excellent series of lectures and training she has given the

Nurses'.[48] Her talent for public speaking was put to the test
in 1904 when she was invited to present a lecture on the training of District Probationers at the annual conference of the
Association of Queen's Superintendents for the Metropolitan
and Southern Counties. Loane's lecture was published by the
Association and also appeared in a leading nursing journal.[49]

Martha was actively involved in the financial health of the
Institute.[50] The local Committee and the mother organisation
commended Loane for her 'able and careful management' of
financial matters.[51] During her tenure the income of the
Portsmouth Association rose from £404 in 1897 to £994 in 1904
whilst there was a decline in working expenses.[52] Financial
prudence at the family level absorbed Loane too for she wrote
about it at length in connection with the domestic affairs of
the poor.

Despite her demanding professional responsibilities
Martha's literary career continued to flourish. The name of
M.Loane became familiar to readers of *Nursing Notes*, the
British Journal of Nursing, the newly launched *Queen's
Nurses' Magazine* as well as to a much wider audience in
Contemporary Review. During her time as Superintendent in
Portsmouth Loane published over thirty-five articles and five
nursing handbooks.

Martha's position brought her into regular professional contact with other members of the medical fraternity in
Portsmouth.[53] One highly respected acquaintance was Dr.
Andrew Mearns Fraser, the local Medical Officer of Health
and Honorary Secretary of the Borough Association. Fraser
was widely recognised for his pioneering work in improving
the health of the local inhabitants — which he achieved, in
part by relying on the ability and zeal of the local district
nurses to educate the poor in matters of hygiene.[54] As further
evidence of Martha's rising reputation Fraser agreed to write
the introductory section of Loane's 1905 nursing handbook,
*Simple Sanitation: the Practical Application of the Laws of
Health to Small Dwellings.*[55]

Two letters written to Fraser in connection with this publication have, by good fortune, survived and they provide the

earliest evidence of the literary partnership of the Loane half-sisters. Both letters were written in late March 1905, and were signed, not by Martha, but by Alice Eliza from her home in Pwellmeyric, Chepstow. In the first letter Alice began:

> My sister tells me that you have very kindly promised to write the opening chapter...if we tell you more precisely what it is that we wish to know. I have written down the leading points that we should like the chapter to cover, and enclose the paper...[56]

Three days later, Alice wrote to Fraser again:

> We are extremely obliged to you by your kind promise to answer most of the very numerous questions with which we have troubled you. Only the accuracy of the facts is of any importance but if I cast them into another form you will perhaps be good enough to glance through that portion of the proofs to make sure that I have not let any errors slip in. We know how fully your time is occupied...[57]

The alternating use of the 'we' and 'I' in both letters clearly suggest that the work in question was a joint venture between the two half-sisters, and by inference the earlier and subsequent Loane works as well, with Alice probably casting 'into another form' Martha's material, just as she was offering to do for Dr. Fraser.

1905 was a year of mixed fortunes for Martha Loane. On 11 May her name appeared on the first of several contracts with Edward Arnold for her social commentary, *The Queen's Poor*.[58] The publishers letter, like the correspondence with Dr Fraser, was addressed not to Martha in Portsmouth, but to her at Alice's home in Chepstow.

But less than a month after reaching this important stage in her publishing career Martha became critically ill with appendicitis on 5 June. It was an episode that would change the course of her life. Of immediate concern though was her life itself. Her plight was reported in *Nursing Notes* which poignantly conveyed the deep anxiety felt for such a valued member of the community:

Miss Loane has been nursed by her own staff, and everything has been in her favour except the appalling noise...as
soon as Miss Loane's illness was known "night attacks" and
the time-gun were stopped, while the troops have marched
past the Home without a band...the farewell salutes to the
Spanish ships were rearranged...on her account. Special
police were posted to regulate the traffic during the worst
days...We must all be very grateful to the authorities for
doing everything in their power to help the doctors and
nurses to save so valuable a life...[59]

Martha recovered slowly but ill-health compelled her to
resign from her beloved nursing post in August 1905. In the
Roll of Nurses Miss Peters described Loane as one of the best
Superintendents in the service of the Institute and praised her
abilities in training probationers. Similar tributes appeared in
the nursing press and in the Annual Report of the local Association.[60]

According to a report in the *Nursing Times* in October
1905 Martha had recovered sufficiently to be planning a
move from Southsea to Wales, although her precise movements after retiring remain uncertain.[61] In all likelihood she
stayed with Alice initially but when her half-sister moved to
Dorset in late 1906, Martha decided to live on her own again.
Later, possibly by 1909, the retired Queen's nurse was living
at Newport House, Launceston, Cornwall, as a 'paying lady'
amongst a community of French nuns who had established
a convent and ran a school there.[62] But wherever she was
living, there is every indication that for the first six years of
Martha's retirement the literary arrangement with Alice
continued to flourish. It was during this period that all the
social commentaries were published. Fortunately the contracts for these six important works have survived for they
provide telling evidence of the opaque nature of the Loane
half-sisters' literary partnership.

The contract for *The Queen's Poor* was made with Miss
Martha Loane:[63] those for the remaining titles only included
her surname and initials. Other inconsistencies concern the
signatories to the contracts and the authenticity of the sig-

natures. The contracts for *The Queen's Poor* and *The Ethics of the Poor* (subsequently published as *The Next Street But One*)[64] bear a single signature, 'Martha Loane'. Contracts for the subsequent commentaries *From Their Point of View* (signed on 25 October 1907),[65] *An Englishman's Castle* (signed on 8 October 1908),[66] *Neighbours and Friends* (signed on 19 November 1909)[67] and *The Common Growth* (signed on 9 December 1910)[68] contain the signatures of both Martha and Alice. To complicate matters, there are glaring inconsistencies in the drafting of Martha's signature. Although it has not been authenticated, Martha's signature on the contracts of the first two books bears an uncanny likeness to Alice's handwriting style. Martha's signature on the remaining contracts does appear to be authentic, being consistent with the signatures on letters sent by her from the nurses home in Southsea.[69] At the time the publishers appeared unconcerned with the addition of another party to the contract let alone the apparently forged signature of Martha Loane. However, they did raise questions concerning the authorship of the titles after Alice had died in 1922.[70]

The publication of other material continued undiminished with at least seventy three articles appearing in the period after Martha's retirement. Links were maintained with the nursing profession through articles published in nursing journals, and Loane became a regular contributor to the London *Evening News,* and later to the *Spectator.*

The articles published in the *Evening News* from March 1907 warrant special attention. For reasons which remain a mystery, these were the only contributions which were attributed to 'M.E.Loane'. The newspaper made a point of stressing the authoress's credentials as a Queen's nurse and her published social commentaries, but the use of the initials 'M.E' — clearly no printing error as they appear subsequently — suggest a conflation of Martha's forename and Alice's second name, Eliza. The use of this cryptic device may have been the closest the two half-sisters came to publicly admitting their writing partnership.

Around the same time as the *Evening News* was publishing articles attributed to M.E.Loane, the regular feature, 'Nurses Clinic' dealing with district nursing was appearing in *Nursing Mirror*. Miss M.Loane was already a contributor to the journal,[71] yet payment for two subsequent articles published anonymously was made to a Miss Loane at Buckhorn Weston, Wincanton — the address to which Alice had moved.[72] The decision to publish these later unattributed articles may represent yet further evidence of Martha and Alice's complex literary arrangement.

M.Loane's literary career ended abruptly with an article in the *Spectator* in December 1911 although a paper written for the American Association for the Study and Prevention of Infant Mortality — and presented, in Chicago, Illinois in November 1911 on behalf of M.Loane by Miss Edna L.Foley — was subsequently published the following year in the USA.[73]

In August 1912 Professor Charles Sarolea of the University of Edinburgh received confirmation that Loane was indeed no longer writing. In his capacity as proprietor/editor of *Everyman*, Sarolea sent a letter to M. Loane enquiring about her 'books concerning the lives of the poor'. Writing from Buckhorn Weston,[74] the Loane sister who replied, and who signed herself M.Loane, explained that she had given up 'all literary work more than a year' before. The handwriting style would suggest almost beyond doubt that Alice, not Martha, had penned this letter.

What evidently had ruptured the half-sisters' relationship was Martha's conversion to Roman Catholicism. Martha had had an Anglican education at the Royal Naval School,[75] but throughout her working life as a Queen's nurse she would have been expected to comply with the rule of the Institute that 'there be no interference on the part of anyone connected with the Queen's Jubilee Institute with the religious belief of either officers or patients'.[76]

In *The Queen's Poor*, written when she was still a Queen's nurse and a Protestant, Loane commented on the general indifference, even unconsciousness, of the poor towards religious dogma, adding pointedly: 'Even Roman Catholics have asked for my prayers'.[77]

It is not known what induced Martha's change in religion — the circumstances of her grave illness in 1905 may have played a part — but on 22 March 1910 she was received into the Roman Catholic faith in Plymouth Cathedral.[78] However, according to Martha's half-sister, Beatrice, Alice did not find out about Martha's change of religious denomination until 1912.[79]

The absence of clarification about the precise nature of the writing partnership raises a wider problem. Reviewers and fellow commentators such as Helen Bosanquet,[80] Stephen Reynolds[81] and C.F.G.Masterman[82] as well as modern scholars have taken it for granted that the work attributed variously to M.Loane, M.J.Loane and M.E.Loane was written by the Queen's nurse, Martha Loane. No evidence has come to light which suggests that either Martha or Alice ever made any attempt to dispel this view during their lifetime. So are the views and judgements in *The Queen's Poor* and the other works unquestionably those of Martha Loane? One cannot be certain for it is possible that the Loane half-sisters held increasingly divergent opinions on social questions which contributed to the rift which severed their writing partnership.

It was not until August 1922, six months after the death of Alice, that the publishers, Edward Arnold, wrote to Beatrice Loane, in an apparent attempt to resolve their uncertainty over the authorship of the Loane works published by them between 1905 and 1912. Beatrice was adamant. Martha Loane was not the authoress of any of the titles:

> All the works were written by A.E.Loane and are her sole work. It is true they were published under the initial M.Loane...Miss Martha Jane Loane is A.E.Loane's half sister and her senior by twelve years. In 1912, A.E.Loane finding Miss.M.J.Loane was a Roman Catholic, wrote no more under that initial...[83]

It was understandable that the publishers wrote to the address which Alice had shared with her sister Beatrice because over the years all correspondence concerning the Loane works was directed to Alice. What is less easily ex-

plained is the publishers failure to trace Martha, whose signature — whether genuine or otherwise — appeared on all
six contracts with them. Nevertheless, Edward Arnold must
have been sufficiently satisfied with Beatrice's explanation,
for acting on her statement that she was the sole beneficiary
and executrix of Alice's estate, they agreed to pay her any
royalties which were due on the Loane titles.[84]

Apart from its most contentious assertion, the accuracy of
some of the other information in Beatrice's letter can be
questioned too. For example, a careful examination of the
Loane works reveals that, contrary to Beatrice's statement,
the works were not all published 'under the initial M.Loane'.
The final commentary, *The Common Growth*, published in
1911, was clearly attributed, on the spine at least, to
M.E.Loane, but Beatrice appears to have overlooked this discrepancy.[85]

Beyond this point of detail remains the larger question:
who wrote the Loane works? Beatrice's claim that Alice was
the sole authoress cannot be proven either way but one
should not lose sight of the circumstantial facts. To begin
with there is the incontrovertible evidence of Martha Loane's
distinguished working life as a Queen's nurse. Furthermore,
the M.Loane social commentaries clearly reflect Martha's exclusive, extensive and detailed knowledge of the poor as a
consequence of her professional experiences. Finally, had
the Loane works not been authentic pieces of social investigation it is unlikely they would have escaped the
searching — even destructive — criticism of informed contemporary reviewers.

Martha may not have been the authoress in the strict
sense of the word. Beatrice's statement may have been a partial truth, for Alice could have compiled the text for all the
social commentaries — and much more — using material
provided by Martha, perhaps in the form of diaries. Martha
was, on her own admission, an assiduous note-taker, 'If nurses once realised the use, to themselves and others, of such
a commonplace book, they would not grudge the time spent

in compiling it, and would learn to count it amongst their most cherished possessions'.[86]

The destruction by Beatrice's executors of most of the Loane papers — including valuable manuscripts and other documents — has meant that a definitive resolution of the authorship riddle of the Loane works is now much less likely.[87] But just how dependent the two Loane half-sisters were on each other for their literary success is suggested by the fact that after their estrangement Alice produced only one book and one article under her own name before her solo publishing career petered out.[88]

Martha Loane had a highly respected career as a Queen's nurse. She died on 16 October 1933 at the age of 81, and her funeral took place at the Catholic church of the Holy Cross in Plymouth three days later.[89] She had evidently lived in Plymouth since 1922, for her will was drawn up from an address there just a few weeks after Alice had died. The bequests in Martha's will reflected both her religious convictions and her professional calling. The two beneficiaries were the Catholic Education Council and the Hospital for Women, Soho, London. According to probate records she left £465 8s 3d.[90] And there was another, enduring legacy: her unique contribution as a social investigator in late Victorian and Edwardian Britain.

The Queen's Poor — Methodology, Themes and Highlights

The engaging literary pictures which emerge from *The Queen's Poor* are highly detailed doorstep accounts of the daily trials and tribulations of the respectable poor. Women and children are the dominant subjects of the book, probably because they represented the majority of Loane's patients.[91] The work is remarkably comprehensive, for few aspects of working-class life have been overlooked or ignored although little is said about the leisure activities of the poor or the old-age pensions issue.

Loane's reliance on anecdotal evidence, though praised at the time for enlivening the text with penetrating detail,[92] has recently been the focus of academic criticism.[93] However, in its contemporary context Loane's style of writing was not unusual: anecdotal evidence was widely used by other social investigators.[94] Even so, anticipating scepticism from her readers, Loane was anxious to reassure them that every anecdote, including the apocryphal ones to which she referred, was genuine.[95] There is good reason to believe her for her position as a Queen's nurse secured privileged access to the poor where a climate of trusting relationships could develop. One should not be surprised that her patients spoke so candidly and expansively; nor that Loane preferred the anecdotal form to communicate her poor patients' personal opinions which she valued so highly as authentic and revealing evidence.[96]

Domestic Economy of the Poor

Loane wrote extensively about the financial arrangements of the working-class poor: how they acquired their money and then expended it running a household. But a recurring theme within *The Queen's Poor* is how the exacting challenge of low family incomes defied simple reductive conclusions. On this — and other topics — Loane relied on the depth and detail of her informed observations.

To Loane, the notion of a 'living wage' — a growing subject of debate in Edwardian Britain — was an 'absurdity.' For, she maintained, it was 'not so much a question of what a man earns, as to what his wife can do with the money'.[97] Although she did not specifically study household budgets, she indicated the range of poor men's wages she had recorded, from under twelve shillings[98] to in excess of thirty-two shillings a week.[99] Yet despite her extensive contact with the poor, she could recall 'only three families which seemed in real want of food'.[100] Such knowledge did not endear her to statistics when studying the working poor.[101]

Loane was anxious to demonstrate the complexities of compiling accurate family income pictures of the poor. Apart from the problem of irregular employment, a man's earnings were rarely the only source of income in any one household.

As she pointed out, when questioned, many of the poor omitted to mention other sources of income: the earnings of wives and children, the rent of a room, income obtained in kind such as the produce of a small market garden, or free meals. Loane's awareness of the significance of these other sources of income for the poor led her to criticise well-meaning but unwary investigators and inexperienced do-gooders.[102]

She was in no doubt that within working-class marriages the balance of personal power lay increasingly with the wife.[103] Although most poor wives, had control of the family budget,[104] their ability to run homes efficiently was often compromised by the lack of basic arithmetical and household skills.[105] Even so, Loane did not consider the poor to be inherently improvident and she observed that they could and did save, particularly for funerals and illness. However, even the most prudent amongst them were unable to 'calculate the spending powers of any sum beyond £5.' A legacy, which in theory could resolve a poor family's financial problems, could, Loane thought, prove disastrous.[106]

The Poor, Marriage and Parenthood

Loane's insight into working-class marriage in *The Queen's Poor* was particularly revealing, for she was sure that few well-to-do people realised 'how much self-control and unselfishness' were necessary 'before peaceable lives' could be lived 'in crowded quarters'.[107]

She wrote of the low expectations which poor women had of marriage and of the matrimonial violence which they were prepared to tolerate: all they asked in return was the occasional show of affection or compliment on their cooking.[108] Their often benign acceptance of this status quo baffled Loane, who could not comprehend how, 'in a world so far civilised...any wife need endure active ill-usage'.[109] She commented at length on the effects of drunkenness on the behaviour of men, and passed on advice to young wives on how best to avoid abuse:

> Don't irritate a man, especially if he's tired or hungry or in drink, but never take a blow from him, drunk or sober. If

you make enough fuss over the first you'll never get a second but if you'll stand one beating, men think you'll stand twenty.[110]

There was also the matter of 'husband-beaters': these 'doughty champions of the supremacy of women' were, as Loane admitted, a rarer breed, but it struck her that it was a 'more just arrangement' for a wife to administer retribution when an irresponsible husband returned home 'more foolish' than when he went out, having wasted a large proportion of their meagre week's wages on alcohol, than for him to beat his wife.[111]

Loane wrote of the trends within working-class marriage, of attitudes to courtship and of the discrepancies in the age of partners.[112] She described the relationships which developed between aged couples, and the devotion which enabled them to survive in the face of increasing poverty and ill-health.[113] Her attention to re-marriage amongst the poor enabled her to consider the practical and financial imperatives which underpinned such unions, and of how irrelevant 'the softening halo of romance' was.[114]

In commenting about working-class parents, Loane was at pains to redeem the reputation of both poor fathers and mothers, most of whom she felt were unfairly maligned.[115] She wrote of the affection that fathers showed their children and of their involvement in child-rearing, as well as of the domestic responsibilities which most willingly shared.[116] In matters to do with 'authority...right and wrong' and "manners" Loane described how mothers were considered, by their children, to be superior to fathers, but she was nevertheless critical of most poor mothers and fathers for failing to provide their children with any moral training.[117]

To Loane, the greatest contribution a mother could make was to 'home-keep', and her disapproval of working mothers was unequivocal: women who worked suffered from 'mistaken ideals of duty'.[118] Her strictures on maternal efficiency not only revealed the ignorance of many poor women but enabled Loane to demonstrate the important role of the

Queen's nurse as a 'health missioner' and to reassert her demands for domestic training in schools.[119]

The Children of the Poor

Loane expressed particular interest in the children of the poor, and presented a carefully observed portrait of their lives: her overriding opinion was that their experience of childhood and their health and welfare had vastly improved over recent years.

She was at pains to correct a popular misconception of poor children whose lives were devoid of love and affection, and she wrote of parents who 'rejoiced in their [children's] youth', and who made efforts to protect their innocence and prolong their childhood years.[120] A perceived problem was their often unruly behaviour, and Loane wrote despairingly of the way poor children were indulged by their parents, who then failed to balance this with effective controls.[121]

Despite her general dislike of state interference as a regulating force in social relations, Loane commented on the tangible benefits of compulsory education: she had no doubt that this legislation had 'nearly doubled the years of permitted childhood, and added incalculably to its interest and pleasures'.[122] She described the way in which pupils were acquiring a new range of educational and social skills, and exemplified their widening vocabulary and their interest in literature.[123]

Less successful, Loane argued, was compulsory religious instruction, and the controversy over what doctrine be taught in schools aroused her curiosity.[124] As far as she could judge, in their childhood years most of the working-class were totally unaffected by religious dogma: not only were they perfectly willing to divulge 'their special shades of belief,' but they were also quite happy to attend 'chapel Sunday school in the morning and church Sunday school in the afternoon'.[125]

Nor was Loane entirely convinced of the benefits of the 'Children's Charter', legislation, first introduced in 1889, which was intended to prevent cruelty against children:[126] as

far as she was concerned, the extent of harshness in working-class homes was greatly exaggerated, and more children
suffered from neglect rather than from ill-treatment.[127]

Loane's nursing experience undoubtedly informed her
views about the health of working-class children. She wrote
authoritatively of the unfavourable conditions, the overcrowding, poor ventilation and lack of sanitation which were
commonplace in their homes,[128] which made them so suscep-
tible to a wide range of infectious and potentially fatal
diseases.[129] To Loane, the belief which some held of infant
mortality as 'entirely a loss to the country' was a mistake:
her response, that nearly every young child who died did so
because 'no amount of care would keep it alive,' clearly
reflected the prevailing and popular ideology of Social Dar-
winism and the Eugenics Movement.[130]

On the question of malnourished children, Loane was
equally outspoken: her robust arguments against what she
referred to as 'State-Spread Tables', proposals to introduce
free school meals — a highly contentious political issue at
the time — were based on her opinion that the problem of
under-fed children was a highly complex one, for which there
was no simple solution.[131] Free meals, she concluded, would
not resolve the problem of lazy, ignorant, apathetic or sick
parents who neglected their responsibilities, or of fussy or
overindulged children. Nor would they adequately compen-
sate for the effects of the chronic, substandard living
conditions of the poor.[132]

The Elderly Poor

The plight of the aged poor was all too familiar to Loane:
their lives were generally characterised by 'unbroken
hardship and poverty,'[133] and contrary to popular belief, she
had rarely met any who were sustained by happy recollections of earlier times.[134] The prospects for their final years
were, in her opinion, dismal, for most suffered from infirmity
and poor health which was exacerbated by their poor standard of living.[135]

The financial implications of old age were, as Loane

revealed, especially precarious: she wrote of the need for elderly people to keep on working regardless of their infirmities, of their dependency on others for help, and of the frequent recourse to charitable assistance.[136] Despite the absence of any quantitative survey, Loane's reference to incomes of around nine to ten shillings week was a clear indicator of pecuniary hardship in old age.[137]

Loane was anxious to defend the elderly poor from charges of improvidence, for she was aware that most had never earned enough to save adequately for their old age.[138] The fact that they were willing to make provision for death, rather than life, did perplex her somewhat, but she was forced to accept that such behaviour was a feature of working-class life. In respect of family support, Loane was unsure how much help, financial or practical, the elderly actually received from their adult children, although she suspected that it was minimal, and certainly could not be relied upon.[139]

The last resort for many of the aged poor was the workhouse, where rules and regulations restricted liberty and institutionalised inhabitants.[140] Entry so stigmatised a person that Loane recorded how elderly folk often adopted euphemisms to disguise their demeaning situation, referring to it is as 'the Infirmary' and as a well-managed place to which they had voluntarily retired.[141]

Many of the aged poor were, as Loane discovered, less reluctant to go into the workhouse infirmary,[142] possibly because they believed that entry did not legally pauperise them.[143] However, she was alert to the failings of many institutions, and drew special attention to the poorly trained nursing staff and their unprofessional behaviour.[144] Loane's comments about the aged poor echoed the public and political debates of the day.

Health and the Poor

Since Loane's professional experience was crucial to the content of her literary work, it was appropriate that she should comment on certain aspects of her nursing duties and obligations, and to draw attention to the trials and tribulations of district nursing.

She explained how the ministrations of the Queen's nurse were strictly confined to the sick poor, of the free nature of the service, and of the way it was occasionally abused: some patients made excessive demands on the nurses time, others were hypochondriacs and malingerers, whilst a few unscrupulous well-to-do people tried to get free treatment.[145] The poorest patients tended to be the most generous in displaying their gratitude: small money donations or gifts in kind were not unusual, nor, she recorded, were back-handed references to the nurses as 'Jubilee Tramps'.[146]

The nurse's relationship with the 'medical men' was examined, as was the credulous attitude and indulgence of the working-classes towards 'quack' doctors and their so-called and often expensive remedies.[147] Loane was particularly critical of her Association's rules concerning late night and Sunday calls, which she considered dogmatic and unrealistic. She argued that no Queen's nurse could be expected to cope with the constant and unremitting mental and physical demands of her job day in and day out for eleven months of the year without it having a detrimental effect on her own health, and that of her patients.[148]

Loane had her own ideas for relieving the Queen's nurse of some of her more mundane duties: she proposed the idea of a special assistant, a 'Dark Star', whom she envisaged as a 'well-educated unmarried woman of independent means'. This trustworthy person would act as a companion/housekeeper, and would assist the nurse with non-medical aspects of her work, and be trained to undertake some simple nursing tasks.[149]

In a routine day Loane might expect to encounter patients suffering from epilepsy,[150] pneumonia,[151] and consumption.[152] Conditions such as blindness,[153] paralysis[154] and so-called hysteria[155] were commonplace, as were the innumerable calls she made to the dying.[156] Loane was clearly dismayed that the best she could do for many of the sick poor was to alleviate pain but the fact that she had a vital role to play as an educator and health missioner was certainly a consolation.[157]

Within the homes of the poor, for example, she was able to instruct new mothers in the basic skills of infant welfare and child care,[158] and neighbours and relatives could be shown basic principles of hygiene and health and then entrusted with 'medical responsibilities'.[159] There were, as Loane confirmed, limits to what could be achieved from home visits, so she proposed a number of accessible ways in which information on health and hygiene could be conveyed to the poor. For example, she insisted that better use could be made of mother's meetings, and suggested that Sunday schools and parish libraries should stock copies of illustrated books on hygiene and nursing which they could encourage women and girls to borrow.[160]

Working Class Culture

Loane knew that because the poor were socially distanced from other classes there was a common belief that they adhered to an alien set of moral principles which informed their behaviour. The reality, as she perceived it, was that the poor recognised 'the same virtues as the rich' but they prioritised them differently.[161]

In the matter of working class religious culture, for example, the popular view was of a section of society devoid of belief. Loane refuted this opinion, arguing that deep and true religion was commonly found amongst the poor: however critics were unwilling to accept their religious custom and practice as genuine. She was at pains to stress that the poor did, in fact, have great 'faith in the efficacy of prayer'[162] but chose not to conform to the traditional outward signs of religion such as public worship and observance of the Sabbath.

Cultural differences in the language and speech habits of the working-class poor also marked them out as different, but Loane was convinced that they were making efforts, both consciously and subconsciously, to acquire new literacy skills.[163] Even though many of the conversations of the poor lacked refinement and were often repetitive Loane reported that the use of bad language seemed to be largely confined to their own kind.[164] But certain differences in language still persisted.[165] Loane enumerated these as ' intonation, pronunciation and accentuation, vocabulary, superabundance of negatives and other grammatical errors'[166] — the hallmarks of the language of the poor. Nevertheless Loane noted that the increasing popularity of reading as a pastime contributed towards a widening and more sophisticated vocabulary amongst the poor.[167]

One particular trait which perturbed Loane was the lack of discernment which the working-classes exhibited. Even the 'most superior' amongst them mistrusted any conventional figure of authority on the grounds that they might interfere in their lives.[168] Yet they were nevertheless prepared to invest blind faith in the most 'brazen quack' or fraudster who came their way.[169]

***

As an experienced social commentator Loane had few equals. She was not a trained social investigator but nor were any of her contemporaries, for this was still a profession in waiting. Despite the advances in quantitative methods of social enquiry the favourable reception that *The Queen's Poor* received at the hands of contemporary critics[170] suggested that informed subjective observation remained a valid and respected medium of social investigation in Edwardian Britain. Loane's proposals for resolving numerous social problems of the day did not always meet with approval but she was successful in raising the reading public's awareness of topical issues and of highlighting their complexity.

As a record of the world of the respectable poor in Edwardian England — and before their lives were touched by the post 1906 Liberal welfare reforms — *The Queens Poor* remains an indispensable contemporary literary source.

REFERENCES

1 M. Loane *The Queens Poor: Life as they find it in town and country*, 1st. imp.(Edward Arnold & New York, Longman Green, 1905) New & cheaper edition (Edward Arnold, 1906) 3rd. imp. (Edward Arnold, 1909) 4th. imp (Edward Arnold, 1910) 5th. imp (Edward Arnold, 1914) 6th. Imp.(Edward Arnold, 1919); *The Next Street But One*, 1st. imp (Edward Arnold, 1907) 2nd. & cheaper edition (Edward Arnold & New York, Longman Green, 1907) 3rd. imp (Edward Arnold, 1907); *From Their Point of View: Short Papers on the Life of the Poor* (Edward Arnold & New York, Longman Green, 1908) *An Englishman's Castle* (Edward Arnold & New York, Longman Green, 1909) *Neighbours and Friends* (Edward Arnold & New York, Longman Green, 1910); *The Common Growth* (Edward Arnold, 1911). For a working bibliography of Loane's published work see S.Cohen, 'The Life and Works of M.Loane', unpublished M.Phil Thesis, Middlesex University, 1997.

2 Charles Booth, *Life and Labour of the People in London*, 3rd ed. (London & New York, Macmillan, 1902-3) 17 vols. For a reassessment of Booth's survey see R. O'Day & D.Englander, *Mr. Charles Booth's Inquiry. Life and Labour of the People in London Reconsidered* (Hambledon, 1993). See also M. Bulmer, K.Bales & K.K.Sklar (eds) *The Social Survey in Historical Perspective, 1880-1940* (Cambridge, Cambridge University Press, 1991).

3 B.Seebohm Rowntree, *Poverty: A Study of Town Life* (Macmillan, 1901)

4 Stephen Reynolds, *A Poor Man's House* (John Lane, 1909); *Seems So!* (Macmillan, 1911).

5 Mary Higgs, *The Tramp Ward* (Manchester, John Heywood, 1904), *How to deal with the unemployed* (Brown & Langham, 1904) *Three Nights in Women's Lodging Houses* (Oldham, 1905); *Glimpses into the Abyss* (P.S.King, 1906), *Where Shall She Live? The Homelessness of the Women Worker* (National Association for Womens' Lodging Homes, 1910).

6 Olive Christian Malvery (later Mrs. Archibald Mackirdy)
   The Soul Market (Hutchinson, 1906); *Baby   Toilers*
   (Hutchinson, 1907); *Thirteen Nights* (Hodder & Stoughton,
   1909); *A Year and a Day* (Hutchinson, 1912).

7 In this respect, and as Dr McKibbin has observed in his
   lengthy evaluation of her work, Loane attempted to fulfil
   the conditions of Brandford's 'more intensive survey'. As
   Brandford noted in 1914, 'While the Booth type of survey
   is admirable in giving a picture of the economic and
   material conditions of the family it remains deficient...in
   the difficult task of describing and estimating the family's
   life of leisure, its spiritual condition... Here the problem is to
   discover some methods of observing and recording...the
   thoughts and emotions, the habit of mind and life, of persons
   in their interior relations with one another and with their
   surroundings. The sort of question that this more intensive
   survey has to put before itself is — How can we decipher and
   record people's ideals, their characteristic ideas and culture,
   and the images and symbols which habitually occupy their
   minds.'   V.Brandford,   *Interpretations   and   Forecasts*
   (Duckworth, 1914) as cited in R.I.McKibbin, 'Social Class and
   Social Observation in Edwardian England', *Transactions of
   the Royal Historical Society*, 5th series, vol.28, 1977, p.176 and
   The Ideologies of Class: Social Relations in Britain, 1880-1950
   (Oxford, Clarendon, 1990) p.169.

8 *Queen's* p.27. Loane admitted that she knew 'nothing' of
   those working men who were permanently unable to
   provide the 'necessaries of life' for their children. See
   Queen's, p.139. Rose describes the respectable poor as 'the
   working classes of the artisan type'. See Lionel Rose, *The
   Erosion of Childhood.   Child Oppression in Britain
   1860-1918* (Routledge, 1991) p.190.

9 As *Nursing Notes* stated, 'Miss Loane has made the most
   of the unrivalled opportunities which lie in the path of
   the district nurse, and she tells her tale with abundant
   humour and sympathy.' See *Nursing Notes*, December
   1905, p.179.

10 Social explorers of the Victorian and Edwardian period,
   including Henry Mayhew, George Sims, General Booth and
   Andrew Mearns, adopted the imagery of the poor as a
   'separate nation' as the vehicle for their explorations. For a
   contemporary reference to the poor as an 'unknown' race
   see 'The Life of the Poor', *Daily News*, 13 October 1905, p.4
   and to the poor as an 'other nation' see *The Athenaeum*, 25

November 1905, p.720. See also Peter Keating (ed) *Into Unknown England 1866-1913* (Fontana, 1976) pp.13-15.

11 See McKibbin, Ideologies, *op.cit*, p.170. Dr.McKibbin first included a sketch of Miss Loane in his paper presented to the Royal Historical Society in 1977, at which time he stated that, 'Miss Loane's life (18?-1922) is altogether more shadowy in its outlines and milieu. She was born in Portsmouth, the daughter of a Captain in the Royal Navy, trained as a nurse in the Charing Cross Hospital and then worked as a district nurse in both metropolitan and rural England, before ending her active life where she had begun it — in Portsmouth — as superintendent of district nurses.' See McKibbin, Transactions *op.cit.* p.177. For an important earlier assessment of Loane's work see John Fraser, 'George Sturt ("George Bourne") and Rural Laboring Life', D.Phil thesis, University of Minnesota, 1961, particularly pp.215-21.

12 For a reference to M.L.Loane (sic) see, for example, Standish Meacham, *A Life Apart: the English Working Class* (Thames & Hudson, 1977) p.270. For references to Mrs. Loane (sic) see M.J Daunton, *House and Home in the Victorian City, 1850-1914* (Edward Arnold, 1983) pp.278-9.

13 For references to Margaret (sic) Loane see, for example, Anna Davin, 'Imperialism and Motherhood', *History Workshop*, Spring 1978, 5, pp.9-65, p.52, p.65; McKibbin, Ideologies, *op.cit*, p.24, p.125, p.140, p.169, p.189; David Vincent, *Poor Citizens. The State and the Poor in Twentieth Century Britain* (Longman, 1991) p.9, p.13, p.33, p.254; Geoffrey Finlayson, *Citizen, State and Social Welfare in Britain 1830-1990* (Oxford, Clarendon, 1994) p.418, p.458; Melanie Tebbutt, *Women's Talk? A Social History of Gossip in Working Class Neighbourhoods, 1880-1960* (Scolar, 1995) p.33, p.34, p.36, p.45, p.96, p.178, p.185, p.203.

14 For references to Mary (sic) Loane see, for example, K.Behlmer, *Child Abuse and Moral Reform in England 1870-1908* (Stanford U.S.A, Stanford University Press, 1982) p.164, p.170, p.173, p.176, p.184, p.195, p.215, p.315: V.Henderson, *Nursing Studies Index*, vol.1 (Philadelphia, Lippincott, 1972)) p.114, p.524, p.561, p.584, p.597, p.606, p.615, p.625, p.711, p.725, p.870.

15 For references to Margery (sic) Loane see, for example, Jose Harris, *Private Lives, Public Spirit. A Social History of Britain, 1870-1914* (Oxford, Oxford University Press,1993)

p.65, p.78, p.81, p.84, p.114, p.247, p.280; Jane Lewis, *The Politics of Motherhood. Child and Maternal Welfare in England, 1900-1939* (Croom Helm, 1980) p.143, p.232; Jane Lewis, 'Gender, the family and women's agency in the building of "welfare states": the British case', *Social History*, vol.19, no.1, January 1994, pp.52-3.

16 The British Library Catalogue is inaccurate in its entry for the six Loane social commentaries, as all are listed under the initials M.E.Loane. *Who Was Who, 1916-1928* vol.II (Black, 1962) p.638 and *Who Was Who in Literature, 1906-1934*, vol.II (USA, Gale Research Co. 1979) p.684.

17 Certified copy of entry of birth, 7 February 1852, Martha Jane Loane at 8. North Place, Eldad, Plymouth, Devon. General Register Office.

18 Jabez Loane joined the Navy in 1830, became a sub-lieutenant in 1842, and a lieutenant in 1846. He was promoted in 1870 and appointed Assistant Master Attendant (Staff Captain) at Portsmouth Yard. In 1872 he became Master Attendant and Queen's Harbour Master (Staff Captain) at Chatham Yard. He remained in this latter post until his retirement, at the age of 65, in November 1876. See *Lean's Royal Navy List*, July 1870 & January 1893.

19 Certified copy of entry of marriage, 10 November 1852 at the Chapel of East Stonehouse, in the Parish of East Stonehouse, Devon. General Register Office.

20 Certified copy of entry of birth, 8 January 1858, Beatrice Mary Loane at 7 Melbourne Street, Plymouth, Devon. General Register Office.

21 Certified copy of entry of birth, 23 October 1863, Alice Eliza Loane at 2 Exbury Place, Green Road, Southsea. General Register Office.

22 Certified copy of entry of death, 7 November 1864, Harriet Loane at 2 Exbury Place, Green Road, Southsea. General Register Office.

23 Founded in 1840, the Royal Naval School for Females (henceforth RNSF) was one of the first girls public schools to be established in England. Queen's College, Harley Street was established in 1848, Bedford College for Women in 1849, North London Collegiate in 1850 and Cheltenham Ladies College in 1854. For a general history of the RNSF see Philip Unwin, *The Royal Naval School, 1840-1975* (Kent, Longmore, 1976).Thanks are due to Commander

Sullivan, the school Bursar, for information from the school archives.

24 Unwin, *op.cit.* p.16.

25 For Beatrice's Scholarship see Annual Report of the RNSF 1875, RNSF Archives.

26 For articles which relied upon knowledge of foreign countries see M.J.Loane, 'A Summer Holiday', *Nursing Notes,* August 1897, pp.100-01; M.Loane, 'The Dawn of District Nursing in France', *Nursing Notes,* June 1904, pp.97-8; 'Pas de Vacances', *Nursing Notes,* August 1904, p.127, 'The Dawn of District Nursing in Switzerland', *Nursing Notes,* September 1904, pp.145-6. Loane referred to 'her German governess' in M.Loane, 'The District Nurse's Commonplace Book', *Nursing Notes,* July 1905, p.105 and to the time when she was 'once made to learn a long list of German proverbs' in M.Loane, 'If Nurse had a Little More Tact', *Nursing Times,* 9 September 1905, p.355. For Loane's experiences in Paris see *Queen's* pp.163-5.

27 Brian Abel-Smith, *A History of the Nursing Profession* (Heinemann, 1960) p.17.

28 Roll of Queen's Nurses III, Folio 80, SA/QNI/ J2/1/J3/3, Contemporary Medical Archives, Wellcome Institute for the History of Medicine (henceforth CMA). See also Register of Nurses, Metropolitan and District Nursing Association, Ms. 14,649, no.167,Guildhall Ms. Unfortunately the archives of Charing Cross Hospital relating to the training and employment of nurses post-date Loane's time there. Loane refers to her 'four years [nursing work] in one town' where she was known as Sister Agnes and to having worked 'in a large provincial hospital.' *Queen's,* p.94 & p.137 and to her post as ward sister in M.Loane, *The Next Street But One* (Edward Arnold, 1907) p.6..

29 For details of the establishment of the Queen Victoria's Jubilee Institute for Nurses (hereafter Institute in the text, QVJIN in footnotes) see Mary Stocks, *A Hundred Years of District Nursing* (George Allen & Unwin, 1960) pp. 20-5, pp.40-60 and Monica E. Baly, *A History of the Queen's Nursing Institute. 100 Years 1887-1987* (Croom Helm, 1987) pp. 195-8. The QVJIN owed a great deal to the pioneering work of the Liverpool philanthropist, William Rathbone. Twenty-five years earlier, in 1859, Rathbone, alerted to the neglect of the sick poor by his own wife's illness, had established a charitable scheme which trained qualified nurses as district nurses, their primary role being

to minister to the medical needs of the sick poor in their own homes. Inspiration, encouragement and advice for both the Liverpool scheme and the QVJIN was also provided by Florence Nightingale. For a critical account see Gwen Hardy, *William Rathbone and the Early History of District Nursing* (Lancashire, Hesketh, 1981). For contemporary overviews of other nineteenth century initiatives in charitable home nursing including the East London Nursing Society (est.approx. 1868), Mrs. Ranyard's Biblewomen Nurses and the Metropolitan and National Nursing Association for Providing Trained Nurses for the Sick Poor, see W.Rathbone, *Sketch of the History and Progress of District Nursing,* (Macmillan, 1890), E.Platt, *The Story of The Ranyard Mission, 1857-1937* (Hodder & Stoughton, 1937) and Lucy Ridgeley Seymer, *General History of Nursing*, 3rd.ed. (Faber, 1949). See also Baly, *op.cit.* pp.1-17.

30 As Hardy notes, the Women's Jubilee Offering as it was known totalled £120,000. £50,000 was spent on the Albert Hall [in London], the remaining £70,000 was used to endow the Institute, which was incorporated by Royal Charter in September 1889. See Baly, *op.cit.* pp.18-32.

31 Baly, *op.cit.*p.29. It is possible to argue with Dr. McKibbin's assertion that 'the function of the first generation of district nurses, of whom Miss Loane was one, was never really to bring the wonders of modern medical technology into the slums of England, but to stop people behaving stupidly.' As Mary Stocks explains, the stated aims of the district nursing movement, from William Rathbone's Liverpool experiment onwards, was, primarily, to nurse the sick poor in their homes: the social and reform aspect was a by-product of this work. See McKibbin, Transactions, *op.cit.* pp.184-5 & Ideologies, *op.cit.* p.177, also Stocks, *op.cit.* pp.26-39.

32 For Martha's obstetrical qualification see, *Nursing Notes*, December 1893, pp.164-5. The Society was established in 1826, and started holding examinations in 1872. For an historical background to the Society see J.Donnison, *Midwives and Medical Men* (Heinemann, 1977) p.81 and Betty Cowell & David Wainwright, *Behind the Blue Door. The History of the Royal College of Midwives, 1881-1981* (Bailliere Tindall, 1981). Loane's position *vis-a-vis* midwifery would have changed in 1902, with the introduction of the Midwives Act, 1902 which allowed women with this qualification to continue practising as

midwives, as long as they had been in bona-fide practice for one year when the Act came into force. See 2 Edw 7 c.17, para.2. Midwives Act, 1902. For restrictions imposed on the Queen's nurse in respect of midwifery see Baly, *op.cit.* pp.29-30.

33 For certificate details see Minutes of the Affiliation Committee, 10 May 1894, QVJIN. For badge details see SA/QNI/J3/3. For the history of the brassard and badge see Baly, *op.cit.* pp.35-6.

34 For the background to rural district nursing see O. Stinchcombe, *Elizabeth Malleson (1828-1916) Pioneer of rural district nursing* (Cheltenham, private publication, circa 1990) and Baly, *op.cit.* pp.50-3.

35 Annual Inspectors Reports of Buxton District Nursing Association, 16 October 1891, PRO 30/63/70. The reports for the years 1893-1907 are not included in this file. The only records of the association held by Derbyshire Record Office are the accounts for 1899-1954.

36 *Ibid.*

37 Certified copy of entry of death, 4 August 1895, Jabez Loane at 22 Underhill Road, Lordship Lane, Camberwell, London. General Register Office.

38 Letter of M.Loane to F.Nightingale, 30 July 1895, Nightingale Collection, British Museum, Additional Manuscripts, 45813 f.92. A later publication, M. Loane, *The Incidental Opportunities of District Nursing* (Scientific Press, 1904) although bearing the same title as the articles, was not an exact reprint of the latter. Loane may have been referring to Florence Nightingale's work, *Notes on Nursing for the Labouring Classes,* first published in 1861, which was reissued in 1894.

39 For Miss Nightingale's reply see Miss Loane,'Florence Nightingale and District Nursing', *Nursing Notes*, October 1910, p.239 and reprinted in *The American Journal of Nursing*, February 1911, pp.383-4. For a critical examination of Loane's contact with Nightingale see S.Cohen, 'Miss Loane, Florence Nightingale and District Nursing in Late Victorian Britain', vol.5. 1997, *Nursing History Review* (USA) pp.83-104.

40 Certificate issued 4 March 1896. Roll of Queen's Nurses III, Folio 80, SA/QNI/J3/3, CMA.

41 See Annual Report of the Borough of Portsmouth

Association for Nursing the Sick Poor (henceforth BPA) 1898, p.5, Portsmouth Central Library.

42 For the article see Martha Jane Loane, 'Incidental Opportunities of District Nursing', *Nursing Notes*, 1897, pp.7-8, p.17-19, pp.31-3, pp.46-7, pp.65-6. For Loane's appointment see Roll of Queen's Nurses III, Folio 80, SA/QNI/ J2/1/J3/3, CMA and BPA, 1896, p.5,

43 SA/QN/P4/7/8. CMA. For a corroborative account of the poor areas of Portsmouth, including the slum district of Landport see Robert R. Dolling, *Ten Years in a Portsmouth Slum* (Swann Sonnenschein, 1897).

44 For details of Miss Peters career see Baly, *op.cit.* p.30, p.35. For references to the number of nurses in Portsmouth see *Queen's Nurses' Magazine*, December 1905, p.85; BPA, 1896–1905.

45 Summary of Cases Nursed, BPA, 1898, p.11 & 1904, p.11.

46 K.F.Carpenter, 'Public Health in Portsmouth 1873-1900', p.67, Portsmouth City Records Office. For articles see M.Loane, 'The Duties of a Superintendent in a small Home for District Nurses', Part 1, *Nursing Notes,* October 1903, pp.142-4; Part 2, *Nursing Notes*, November 1903, pp.157-8, subsequently republished as a book of the same title by The Womens Printing Society. Also Miss M.Loane, 'Thoughts on the Final Training of District Probationers', *British Journal of Nursing*, 22 October 1904, p.350; 29 October 1904, pp.349-71, 12 November 1904, pp.390-2.

47 BPA, 1904, pp.5-6.

48 BPA, 1897, p.4; BPA, 1898, p.7.

49 BPA, 1904 pp.5-6, p.9. *Nursing Notes*, February 1905, p.25, contd. April 1905, p.58.

50 Loane addressed this issue in a number of articles. See Miss.M.Loane, 'Thoughts on the Final Training of District Probationers', *British Journal of Nursing*, 22 October 1904, p.350; M.Loane, 'The Duties of a Superintendent in a Small Home for District Nurses', *Nursing Notes,* November 1903, p.158; M.Loane 'The District Nurse and her Connection with the Financial Support of the Local Institution', *Nursing Notes,* March 1905, p.42.

51 BPA, 1899, p.6.

52 BPA, 1897, p.8 & 1905, p.10. In both years receipts and expenditure were perfectly balanced. In 1897 Queen's nurses in Portsmouth cared for 371 cases and made 10,332

home visits. In 1905 the number of cases had more than trebled to 1,162 with 26,601 visits being made. Of most significance was the decline in working expenses: in 1897 the cost per visit was 9¼d, a figure which had dropped to 5¾d by 1899. See BPA, 1899, p.7. *Queen's Nurses' Magazine*, December 1905, p.85.

53 For confirmation of this see BPA, 1904, p.6, which states, 'It is a striking testimony to the efficiency of the Nursing that so large a number of calls should be made upon our Nurses through the agency of medical men.' For Queen's nurses and the medical profession see Baly, *op.cit.* item 5, p.29, pp.79-81.

54 Dr.A.M.Fraser resigned his post as Hon. Sec to the Association after five years. See BPA, 1905, p.6. For his career see, for example, *Portsmouth Evening News*, 26 January 1934; 10 July 1958; 21 July 1958.

55 M.Loane, *Simple Sanitation: the Practical Application of the Laws of Health to Small Dwellings*, with an introduction by Dr A.M.Fraser (Scientific Press, 1905).

56 Letter of A.E.Loane, 20 March 1905, Mearns Fraser Collection, 182A/5/1, Portsmouth City Records Office.

57 Letter of A.E.Loane, 23 March 1905, Mearns Fraser Collection, 182A/5/1, Portsmouth City Records Office.

58 Memoranda of Agreement for *The Queen's Poor*, 11 May 1905, between Miss Martha Loane and Edward Arnold, signed Martha Loane. File 5719, Edward Arnold Archives, Hodder Headline plc (henceforth EAA).Thanks are due to Kevin Stuart, archivist at Hodder Headline plc for his help.

59 'Illness of a Queen's Superintendent', *Nursing Notes*, July 1905, p.105. Contemporary press reports on the activities of the Victoria Association reveal a remarkable decline in the number of visits made by district nurses from a high of 668 in the week before Martha's illness, to a low of 421 in the middle of June, suggesting that Martha's absence from her duties adversely affected the efficiency of the local Queen's nurses in Portsmouth, at least in the short term. For the number of cases attended see, for example, *Portsmouth Times and Hampshire County Journal*, 27 May 1905, p.4; 3 June 1905, p.5; 10 June 1905, p.4; 17 June 1905, p.4; 24 June 1905, p.4.

60 Roll of Queen's Nurses III, Folio 80, SA/QNI/J3/3, CMA; BPA, 1905, p.6; *Queen's Nurses' Magazine,* December 1905, p.85.

61 *Nursing Times,* 7 October 1905, p.438.

62 Loane Papers, Lloyds Bank. The Sisters of the Sacred Heart arrived at Launceston in 1903, having been expelled from France. They established a Convent and school at Newport House, and remained until shortly after the outbreak of the First World War. In 1915, the French government invited the Sisters to return home to undertake the work of nursing wounded soldiers. See H. Spencer Toy, *The Story of St Joseph's Convent School, Launceston* (n.d) p.4. Thanks are due to Sister Eleanora, Archivist for the Dominican Sisters of St. Joseph for her help.

63 File 5719, EAA.

64 File 5719, EAA.

65 File 5720, EAA.

66 File 5721, EAA.

67 File 5724, EAA.

68 File 5726, EAA.

69 See Letters of M.J.Loane to Miss Martin-Loake,16 January 1900, 23 January 1900, SA/QNI/F4/2/60/62, CMA. The handwriting in Loane's letter to Miss Nightingale appears to match these letters. See above, footnote 38.

70 Letter from Miss B.M.Loane to the publishers Edward Arnold, dated 8 September 1922, File 5719, EAA.

71 Miss M.Loane, 'The After-Care of Operation Cases in District Nursing', *Nursing Mirror*, 28 October 1905, p.57; Miss M.Loane, 'Minor Surgery in District Nursing', *Nursing Mirror,* 4 November 1905, p.106; Miss M.Loane, 'The District Nurse and Paralysis', *Nursing Mirror,*2 December 1905, p.131; Miss M.Loane, 'The District Nurse and Prevention of Puerperal Fever', *Nursing Mirror*, 23 December 1905, pp.183-4; Miss M.Loane, 'The District Nurse in Relation to the Treatment of Hip Disease', *Nursing Mirror,* 27 January 1906, pp.213-14.

72 Anon, 'The Nurses Clinic. The District Nurse and Epilepsy', *Nursing Mirror,* 19 January 1907, pp.223-4; Anon., 'The Nurses Clinic. The District Nurse and Discharged Hospital Patients', *Nursing Mirror*, 9 March 1907, pp.337-8. Scientific Press Ledger, Folio 129, Burdett Papers, A/1/11, Bodleian Library. This appears to be the only extant ledger for the Scientific Press, so it is

impossible to be certain whether Loane submitted any more unattributed articles.

73 M.Loane, 'Infant Mortality', *American Association for the Study and Prevention of Infant Mortality, Transactions,* 1912, pp. 319-328. Reprinted in *Nursing Notes,* Part 1, February 1912, p.38, Part 2, April 1912, pp.93-4, Conclusion, May 1912, pp.120-1. Miss Foley, a trained nurse, was on the editorial staff of the *American Journal of Nursing.*

74 Professor Sarolea owned and edited *Everyman* between 1912-1917. For a resume of his career see *Who Was Who,* vol.V, 1951-1960, 2nd. ed (Black, 1964) p.966.

75 It is evident from the official school history that considerable attention was placed upon religious instruction. At prize-giving in 1867, '...Mr. Hales examined the pupils upon the scriptures and the replies he received were given with a readiness which proved careful training.' In 1872, girls under 12 applying for admission to the school were expected to 'know the outlines of Biblical and English History from Pinnock's Catechism.' See, Unwin, *op.cit.* p.30.

76 Stocks, *op.cit,* p.84.

77 See *Queen's* p.31. As an inspection of the extant Roll of Nurses for this period highlights, nurses who admitted to being of the Roman Catholic persuasion were few and far between. For Loane's comments see, for example, *Queen's,* p.36; M.Loane, 'The District Nurse and Dying Patients', *Nursing Notes,* March 1907, p.46; M.Loane, 'Personal Rules for District Nurses', *Queen's Nurses' Magazine*, October 1910, p.127.

78 The Register of Licence to Receive Catechumens, Plymouth Cathedral, 22 March 1910, Plymouth Catholic Archives. Thanks are due to Father Christopher Smith, the Diocesan Archivist, for locating this information.

79 Letter from Miss B.M.Loane to Edward Arnold, dated 8 September 1922, File 5719, EAA.

80 Bosanquet referred to *The Queen's Poor* as Miss Loane's 'beautiful book' and included a number of extracts from the first chapter of it in her own work to support her opinions of the division of responsibility within marriage. Helen Bosanquet, *The Family* (Macmillan, 1906). The extracts appear on pp.199-200 and pp.274-7.

81 For Stephen Reynolds references to Miss Loane see
    Stephen Reynolds, 'Various Conclusions', Chapter 20,
    Seems So (Macmillan, 1911) pp.274-6, p.278, p.283,
    pp.287-8, p.290, p.293, pp.301-02, p.304, pp.307-08,
    p.311-12, p.319. This chapter was previously published as
    Stephen Reynolds 'What the Poor Want', *Quarterly Review*,
    vol.212, Jan-April 1910, pp.152-79.

82 For Masterman's references to Miss Loane see
    C.F.G.Masterman, *The Condition of England*, 1st ed.
    (Methuen, 1909) p.112, p.115, p.308.

83 See above, footnote 79.

84 *Ibid.*

85 The inside pages refer to the authoress as M.Loane.

86 This book was described as being meant 'for constant
    reference' and 'must have a strong binding, and a liberal
    margin should be left all round each page.' See M.Loane,
    'The District Nurses' Commonplace Book', *Nursing Notes*,
    July 1905, p.105.

87 Loane Papers, Lloyds Bank.

88 The book by A.E.Loane, *Shipmates* (Edward Arnold, 1912)
    was described as 'portraits from memory of naval officers
    who were born between 1805 and 1827, and who served
    their country for many years in all quarters of the globe'.
    Publication figures indicate that this was the least
    successful of any Loane title. Six hundred copies were
    originally printed between August and October. Four
    hundred copies were subsequently printed in 1917. See
    Edward Arnold Papers, Guildhall Library, Ms. 29076.5,
    Folio 909. A.E.Loane, 'Country Temper', *Spectator*, 29
    March 1913, pp.528-9.

89 Certified copy of entry of death, Martha Jane Loane, 16
    October 1933 at 22 Woodland Terrace, Lipson, Plymouth.
    General Register Office. For public notice of funeral see
    Western Morning News, 18 October 1933, p.1. Copy of will
    of Martha Jane Loane of 22 Woodland Terrace, Plymouth,
    Devon, 9 May 1922. Principal Registry of the Family Division.

90 Probate was granted in London on 9 April 1933 to her
    executors, William Hayden, Solicitor. Effects totalled £463 8s
    3d. Principal Registry of the Family Division.

91 Loane explained that working-class men tended to enjoy
    relatively better health than their womenfolk. See *Queen's*,
    pp.178-9. As Bell emphasised, good health amongst the

men was vital, for 'even a passing ailment means either a diminution of the weekly income, or else a continuation of work under conditions which may turn the slight indisposition into something more serious.' See Lady Bell, *At The Works*, 1st.ed. (Edward Arnold, 1907) p.85.

92   See, for example, *Nursing Notes,* December 1905, p.179, *The Athenaeum,* 25 November 1905, p.720, *Queen's Nurses' Magazine*, December 1905, p.118.

93   Hugh Cunningham, *The Children of the Poor: Representations of Childhood since the Seventeenth Century* (Oxford, Blackwell, 1991) p.193, p.205, p.212-3.

94   For example, Reynolds, Seems So, *op.cit*. Dr. Cunningham is equally sceptical about the validity of Reynolds conversations with Devon fishermen, but it is important to note that Reynolds was no mere passing visitor, but a working inhabitant of the fishing community. Extant correspondence between John St.Loe Strachey and Reynolds confirms the validity of the anecdotal evidence. See Letter of Reynolds to Strachey, 8 May 1909, Strachey Papers, S/16/3/8, House of Lords Record Office. For a detailed account of Reynolds' life in Devon, see J.D.Osborne, 'Stephen Reynolds, a biographical and critical study.' PhD. London University, 1978, also Harold Wright (ed) *Stephen Reynolds, Letters* (Richmond, L & V Woolf, 1923).

95   See, for example, *Queen's,* pp.75-80, where such apocryphal stories are clearly referred to as 'yarns.'

96   For Loane's defence see *Queen's,* p.112.

97   *Queen's,* pp.154-55 & p.160. The concept of a 'living wage' was later defined by Snowden as 'a wage which will allow the worker to maintain his working powers in the highest state of efficiency, to properly fulfil all his duties as a citizen, and to support his family in decency and health.' See Philip Snowden, *The Living Wage* (Hodder & Stoughton, 1913). The debate should be viewed alongside the pioneering work of Booth who set a notional 'poverty line' and of Rowntree for his definition of primary and secondary poverty. Booth, 1st ed. vol.I, *op.cit*; Rowntree, *op.cit*. pp.170-1. For an historical examination of wages for this period see E.H.Hunt, *Regional Wage Variations in Britain, 1850-1914* (Oxford, Clarendon, 1973) and *British Labour History, 1815-1914* (Weidenfeld & Nicolson, 1981) pp.57-116.

98 *Queen's*, p.158 and for other wage references see *Queen's*, pp.155-60

99 *Queen's*, p.15.

100 *Queen's*, p.161.

101 *Queen's*, p.72.

102 *Queen's*, pp.155-61.

103 Bosanquet asserted that the economic dependency of a wife and children was, in fact, essential to 'secure the family's moral and economic integrity and safeguard the socialization of its children'. See H.Bosanquet, *The Family* (Macmillan, 1906) p.222. For corroboration of this assertion see, for example, Elizabeth Roberts, *A Woman's Place. An Oral History of Working-Class Women, 1890-1940* (Oxford, Blackwell, 1984) p.139.

104 *Queen's*, p.12. Unlike Bell and Reeves, Loane did not undertake detailed surveys of household budgets, but she did state that she corrected her impressions 'by occasionally reading statistics.' See *Queen's*, p.72. Chinn has remarked that, in his opinion, 'M.E.Loane (sic) was one of the few commentators on the lower working-class who realised the considerable influence that this financial control gave to the mothers of the poor'. See Carl Chinn, *They Worked All Their Lives. Women of the Urban Poor in England, 1880-1939* (Manchester, Manchester University Press, 1988) p.52.

105 *Queen's*, p.16, p.139, p.151.

106 *Queen's*, p.98.

107 *Queen's*, p.13.

108 *Queen's*, pp.5-6.

109 *Queen's*, p.4. Loane also drew attention to 'legislation which had done much for women.' See *Queen's*, p.3. As May explains 'the Summary Jurisdiction (Married Women) Act of 1895 expanded the grounds for separation to include persistent cruelty and wilful neglect.' For an overview of legislative change see Margaret May, 'Violence in the Family: An Historical Perspective' in J.P.Martin (ed) *Violence in the Family* (Chichester, Wiley, 1978) p.149.

110 *Queen's*, p.4. Loane also accepted that a wife might have to lie to her husband to keep the peace. See *Queen's*, p.173. The popular view, and one which the NSPCC subscribed to until after the turn of the century, was that alcohol

predisposed men to physically abuse their wives. This same view was expounded by G.B.Cutten in his book *The Psychology of Alcoholism* (Walter Scott, 1907). For an historical account see Behlmer, *op.cit.* p.178. See also A.James Hammerton, *Cruelty and Companionship Conflict in Nineteenth-Century Married Life* (Routledge, 1992) p.46.

111 *Queen's,* p.1. Loane recorded a wife who punished her husband by sewing him up firmly in a stout sheet, and when he was awake enough to know what was going on, she took a stick and thrashed him repeatedly until **she** decided that he had learned his lesson. See *Queen's,* p.306. Whether this remedy for intemperance was actually adopted by the young wife is open to speculation, for as Roberts has recorded, this so-called treatment appears to be based on 'a hoary folk tale' which was commonly recounted in Northern towns. He has suggested that a more authentic cure for intemperance was 'the horse blistering liniment applied regularly by an irate wife to her husband's bare soles as he lay in "swinish sleep".' His was the only case known of a man who gave up drink because it made his feet sore. See Robert Roberts, *The Classic Slum* (Penguin, 1973) pp.121-2. For corroborative evidence of the retribution meted out by wives see E.Ross, *Love and Toil. Motherhood in Outcast London, 1870-1918* (Oxford, Oxford University Press, 1993) p.75.

112 For courtship see *Queen's,* p.221. For age discrepancy see *Queen's,* p.18.

113 *Queen's,* pp.7-11 & pp.307-09.

114 *Queen's,* p.7.

115 *Queen's,* p.20.

116 *Queen's,* pp.20-21, pp.179-80.

117 *Queen's,* pp. 21-2.

118 *Queen's,* p.138. See also *Queen's,* p.267.

119 For the 'health missioning' aspect see *Queen's,* pp.179-80 & p.141. For domestic training see *Queen's,* pp.139-141.

120 *Queen's,* p.48. See also *Queen's,* p.60.

121 *Queen's,* pp.116-17. Cunningham has described Loane's assertions as 'frequent and often contradictory affirmations that the poor were too indulgent to their children, and seemed to see no great harm in theft, idleness at work and lying.' See Cunningham *op.cit.* p.213. However, as other

commentators noted, this juxtaposition of values was commonplace amongst the poor. See, for example, Booth, *op.cit.* Final vol., Notes on Social Influences and Conclusions, pp.42-3 and Roberts, Classic Slum, *op.cit.* p.46. *Queen's*, p.49.

122 *Queen's*, pp.68-9, and as quoted in *The Spectator,* 6 January 1906, p.9. The introduction of Forster's Elementary Education Act of 1870 and subsequent acts played a major role in banishing illiteracy in the generation which followed. For a contemporary outline see W.H.Stuart Garnett, *Children and the Law* (Murray, 1911) pp.76-119 and for an historical examination see J.S.Hurt, *Elementary Schooling and the Working Classes,1860-1918* (Routledge & Kegan Paul, 1979).

123 *Queen's*, p.65. This improvement in children's speech was later confirmed by Thomas Holmes, a police court missionary and Secretary of the Howard Association, who wrote in 1908, in regard to child offenders, 'The change in speech, too, is strongly noticeable; the old blood-curdling oaths and curses spiced with blasphemy are quite out of fashion. Emphasis can only be given to speech today by inter-larding it with filthy words and obscene allusions.' See T.Holmes, *Known to the Police* (Edward Arnold, 1908) p.22-3, as cited in J.J.Tobias, *Crime and Industrial Society in the Nineteenth Century* (Batsford, 1967) p.84.

124 *Queen's*, p.31. For this debate, and a detailed commentary on this Act see, James Murphy, *The Education Act 1870* (Newton Abbot, David & Charles, 1972) with special reference to the religious debate to be found on pp.10-15, pp.54-64 and pp.70-2.

125 *Queen's*, p.32. For confirmation of this view, see, for example, Charles B. Penny, 'The Religion of the Errand Boy', *Contemporary Review*, September 1904, p.406. The exception were Roman Catholic and Jewish children whose 'personal and racial pride' was undermined by petty persecution. See *Queen's*, pp.41-42. For racial prejudice in London Board Schools see Anna Davin, *Growing Up Poor: Home, School and Street in London, 1870-1914* (Rivers Oram, 1996) pp. 201-206. As Jose Harris notes, 'Although racial concepts infiltrated the language of social science and public administration, they did not invariably have the specifically ethnic and exclusionary connotations that a later generation might suppose,' as cited in Jose Harris,

Private Lives, Public Spirit. A Social History of Britain 1870-1914 (Oxford, Oxford University Press, 1993) p.78.

126 *Queen's*, pp.68-69. Prevention of Cruelty to Children Act, 1889; 57 & 58 Vic. c.27; 57 & 58 Vic, c.41; Prevention of Cruelty to Children Act, 1894; 4 Edw.VII, c.15, Prevention of Cruelty to Children Act. 1904. For the Children's Charter and a definitive history of the NSPCC and the battle against child abuse and neglect between 1870 and 1908 see Behlmer, *op.cit.*

127 *Queen's*, p.146 where Loane referred incorrectly to the organisation as the RSPCC. See, for example, NSPCC 8th. Annual Report, Portsmouth, 1896-7, p.5 which recorded that 188 children suffered from neglect, against 37 who were ill-treated. In the 13th. Annual Report, 1901-02, 250 were recorded as neglected, with 32 being ill-treated. NSPCC Archives.

128 For references to overcrowding see *Queen's*, pp.72-3, p.143. For references to poor sanitation see *Queen's*, p.223, p.226, p.235, p.237. For references to poor ventilation see *Queen's*, p.136. For a description of living conditions such as these in Portsmouth see J.Stanford and A.Temple Patterson, 'The condition of the children of the poor in mid-Victorian Portsmouth', *The Portsmouth Papers*, no.21, March 1974.

129 *Queen's*, pp.147-8, pp.168-9. For references to consumption (i.e. tuberculosis) see *Queen's*, p.44; to typhoid fever see *Queen's*, p.43 and to scarlet fever see *Queen's*, p. 227. Queen's nurses were 'not allowed under any circumstances to attend cases of smallpox or scarlet fever.' See, for example, BPA, 1901, p.14. For an historical account see, for example, F.Turner, *Report on Return of Cases of Scarlet Fever and Diphtheria for the three years 1902,1903,1904* (Truscott, 1906) Smith has stated that 'in 1871, scarlet fever claimed the lives of 210 children per million. It dropped to 140 per million in 1881, that is 1,400 deaths a year, to level out in the mid 1890's at 35 per million, or about 4,000 deaths a year.' See F.B.Smith, 'Health' in John Benson, *The Working Class in England, 1875-1914* (Croom Helm, 1985) p.40-1.

130 *Queen's*, p.137. Infant mortality was a subject to which Loane devoted a considerable amount of attention during her years as an authoress and journalist. See, for example, M.Loane, 'Some of the Causes of Infant Mortality', *Point of View*, pp.122-143; M.Loane, London, 'Infant Mortality', *American Association for the Study and Prevention of Infant Mortality; Transactions*, 16-18 November 1911,

pp.319-28; M.Loane, 'The Saving of Child Life', *The Spectator*,11 November 1911, pp.786-7. For the high mortality of infants in Middlesborough, due to 'overcrowding, bad atmosphere, bad air, maternal ignorance and negligence, unsuitable feeding, an inadequate or polluted milk-supply' see Lady Bell, *At The Works* (Macmillan, 1907) p.198. Carol Dyhouse cites the contemporary opinion that the employment of married women was also an important cause of infant deaths. See, Carol Dyhouse, 'Working Class Mothers and Infant Mortality in England, Press, 1981) p.78. For contemporary views of this contention see, for example, F.J.Greenwood, 'Is the High Infantile Death Rate Due to the Occupation of Married Women?', *Englishwoman's Review,* 1901, also Helen G. Bowers, 'A Simple Talk on Infant Mortality', *British Journal of Nursing,* 25 May 1907, pp.387-8.

131   For Loane's chapter on 'State-spread Tables' see *Queen's*, pp.136-65. For some reviews of her comments see *Charity Organisation Review,* vol.XIX, no.113, May 1906, p.261. For other reviews of this chapter see *British Journal of Nursing,* 28 October 1905, p.365; *Nursing Notes*, December 1905, p.180; *Church Times*, 16 April 1906, p.358. For the contemporary argument see *After Bread, Education. A Plan for the State Feeding of School Children'*, Fabian Tract 120 (1905); F.H.Barrow, 'Free Meals for Underfed Children,' *Monthly Review,* no.56. May 1905, pp.1-16. For a comprehensive account of the many other charitable agencies feeding children at this time see L.Andrews, 'The Education (Provision of Meals) Act, 1906. A Study of the Education (Provision of Meals) Act, 1906 against its social, political and economic background,' MA Thesis, Institute of Education, University of London, 1966; J.W. Stewart, 'Children and Social Policy in Great Britain 1871-1909', M.Phil., Goldsmiths, University of London, 1988.

132   *Queen's*, p.136..

133   See *Queen's,* p.237.

134   *Queen's,* p.85, pp.87-8. For a critical reference to this popular ideology see *The Spectator,* 6 January 1906, p.10.

135   *Queen's,* p.235, p.237, p.260. W.Walter Crotch, *The Cottage Homes of England. The Case Against the Housing System in Rural Districts,* 2nd.ed. (King, 1901); E.Gauldie, *Cruel Hab- itations, A History of Working-Class Housing 1780-1918* (George Allen & Unwin, 1974) p.220.

136   Longmate notes that as Unions followed the policy of severity introduced around 1870, the number of people

receiving out-relief fell, and the treatment and amounts they received varied from place to place, and depended on the individual Board of Guardians. See N.Longmate, *The Workhouse* (Temple Smith, 1974) p.258.

137   *Queen's*, p.234 and for the need for the elderly to keep on working despite ill-health see *Queen's*, p. 256-9. For the rates of money wages of ordinary agricultural labourers in the years 1870-1 and 1880-1 see T.E.Kebbel, *The Agricultural Labourer. A Short Summary of his Position* (Allen, 1887)p.18. As Rider Haggard demonstrated in his survey of rural England, agricultural wages varied considerably geographically. In 1906, he recorded that, in Essex, the weekly wage was between 13s and 15s a week, whereas in Warwickshire, in 1902, the ordinary wage for a labourer was 15s a week. See, Rider Haggard, *Rural England,* 1st. ed., vol.1 (Longmans Green, 1902) p.410 and Rider Haggard, *Rural England,* 2nd. ed., vol.1 (Longmans Green,1906) p.443, p.468. See also B.S.Rowntree & M.Kendall, *How the Labourer Lives* (Nelson, 1913) and Hunt, Wage Variations *op.cit.*

138   *Queen's*, p.237. The old were victims of the final stage of Rowntree's so-called cycle of poverty'. See Rowntree, *op.cit.* p.169-71. For his definition of 'primary' poverty see p.117, and for 'secondary' poverty see p.118.

139   How common joint households were is difficult to assess. Jose Harris has calculated from Booth's published material on London households that, in the 1890's, only 3.07% of homes included grandparents and 0.8% other extended kin. See Harris, *op.cit.* pp.64-5. Lady Bell noted that, in Middlesborough, it was rare for an elderly couple to share a home with a married son or daughter, and was generally not a very satisfactory arrangement. Bell, *op.cit.* pp.110-11.

140   *Queen's*, p.211-13.For regulations relating to inmates in the workhouse see W.H.Dumsday, *Workhouse Officers' Handbook* (Hadden Best, 1907) p.42, p.158, p.188 & pp.190-213. According to Longmate, in a population in 1901 of thirty three millions, between half and three quarters of a million were likely to have had recent personal experience of the workhouse. See Longmate, *op.cit.* p.263. Fear of the workhouse existed both prior to and after Loane wrote *The Queen's Poor* as confirmed by witnesses to the Royal Commission on the Aged Poor. See British Parliamentary Papers, *Royal Commission on the Aged Poor*, 1895, XV, Qs.10664, 17592-4, 2338 & 13,352. Later in

the period, Roberts remarked, that, in 1908, 'our elderly
paupers still went to the workhouse — a word that rang
like a knell among us.' See Roberts, Classic Slum,.*op.cit.*
pp.84-5.

141 *Queen's*, p.95, and as cited in K.C. Phillips, *Language and
Class in Victorian England* (Oxford, Blackwell, 1984) p.106.
Phillips notes that both Arthur Morrison, in *Tales of Mean
Streets*, and Flora Thompson, in *Lark Rise to Candleford,*
include comparable euphemisms.

142 For an exception see *Queen's*, p.45.Witnesses to the Royal
Commission on the Aged Poor, in 1895, indicated that the
elderly in particular were far less reluctant to enter the
workhouse   infirmary.   See,   for   example,   British
Parliamentary Papers, *Royal Commission on the Aged
Poor*, XIV, 1895, Qs.2815-16; Qs.14615-16. This was
particularly the case where the infirmary was located in
a separate building away from the actual workhouse, a
situation which was more common after 1880. F.B.Smith,
The People's Health, 1830-1910 (Croom Helm, 1979)
p.390.

143 Smith, *op.cit.* p.390.

144 Workhouse infirmaries had been the subject of much
criticism since the first visitors, members of the Workhouse
Visiting Society, were allowed in during the 1850's and
early 1860's. See Longmate, *op.cit.* p.199 and L.Twining,
Workhouses and Pauperism (Methuen, 1898). In respect of
workhouse nursing, this was less attractive than hospital
or district nursing. As evidence given in the report on Poor
Law nursing, subsequently included in the Royal
Commission on the Poor Law, made clear, unsatisfactory
accommodation, long hours, monotonous work, dislike of
rural life and professional isolation were all mitigating
factors. See *Report of the Royal Commission on the Poor
Law and Relief of Distress*, vol.1., being parts I to VI of the
Majority Report (H.M.S., 1909) Part V, pp.351-2; also *Break
Up the Poor Law and Abolish the Workhouse* being Part I
of the Minority Report of the Poor Law Commission
(Fabian Society, 1909) p.231 ff. A detailed historical account
of pauper nursing and poor law nursing can be found in
Rosemary White, *Social Change and the Development of the
Nursing Profession. A Study of the Poor Law Nursing
Service, 1848-1948* (Kimpton, 1978).

145 *Queen's,* pp.250-2.

146 For the free nature of the service see J.B.Hurry, *District*

Nursing on a Provident Basis (Scientific Press, 1898) p.18 & Baly, *op.cit.* p.94. For donations and letters from grateful patients in Portsmouth see Annual Reports of the Borough of Portsmouth Association for Nursing the Sick Poor, 1897-1905. See also *Queen's*, pp.124-5, p.190 & p.253. For 'Jubilee Tramps' see *Queen's*, p.90, *Nursing Notes*, December 1905, p.179 and 'Queen's Nurses at Portsmouth', *Nursing Times*, 7 September 1907, p.781.

147 As Stocks highlights, there was some professional resentment towards Queen's Nurses. This was, she suggests, dictated by economic fears, for some medical practitioners voiced the concern that, as a result of the nurses ministrations, patients would make fewer calls upon doctors, thus diminishing their income. See Stocks, *op.cit.* p.94 & pp.119-20. For 'quack' doctors see *Queen's*, p.129 & p.186.

148 *Queen's*, p.39 & pp.200-01.

149 *Queen's*, pp.193-7. For an earlier reference to, and article about 'Dark Stars' see M.Loane, 'Dark Stars', *Nursing Notes*, November 1904, pp.177-8. It is evident from Stock's history of district nursing that, from the outset, nurses were often overwhelmed by non-medical demands: one Lady Super- intendent questioned 'whether a young and very highly trained nurse is not thrown away on this branch of the institution.' See Stocks, *op.cit.* p.34.

150 *Queen's*, p.45.

151 *Queen's*, p.178 and for a boy of 15 with pneumonia see *Queen's*, p.124.

152 Consumption, more commonly referred to as tuberculosis, is a wasting disease especially of the lungs. For references to the disease see, for example, *Queen's*, p.44, p.176; For a reference to tuberculosis of the hip see Miss M.Loane, 'The District Nurse in Relation to the Treatment of Hip Disease', *Nursing Mirror*, 27 January 1906, pp.213-14.

153 For references to blind patients see *Queen's*, p.54, p.61, p.260, p.271-5, p.294. For an overview of Homes for the Blind at this time see June Rose, *Changing Focus. The Development of Blind Welfare in Britain* (Hutchinson, 1970) and J.S.Hurt, *Outside the Mainstream. A History of Special Education* (Batsford, 1988)

154 For paralysis brought on 'by worry and overwork' see *Queen's*, p.177 & p.288.

155 *Queen's,* p.185.

156 For visits to dying patients see, for example, *Queen's,* p.33, p. 169, p.171, p.175, p.309.

157 *Queen's,* p.178. Loane's first article dealt with the role of the Queen's nurse as an educator and health missioner. See Martha Jane Loane, 'Incidental Opportunities of District Nursing', *Nursing Notes*, 1897, pp.7-8, p.17-19, pp.31-3, pp.46-7, pp.65-6.

158 *Queen's,* pp.179-80.

159 *Queen's,* p.163 & p.242. It is evident from Lady Bell's study that dependency upon the help of good neighbours in times of emergencies was, in fact, commonplace amongst the working-classes. See Bell, *op.cit.* pp.230-1. For an historical examination of this subject see, for example, Ellen Ross, 'Survival Networks: Women's Neighbourhood Sharing in London Before World War 1', *History Workshop Journal,* 15, 1983, pp.4-28.

160 *Queen's,* pp.141-3. Both Lady Bell and witnesses to the *Interdepartmental Committee Report on Physical Deterioration,* shared Loane's view on the value of mothers' meetings and lectures conducted on simple and practical lines. See British Parliamentary Papers, *Interdepartmental Committee Report on Physical Deterioration,* 1904, vol.XXXII, Qs 5391-5402, 9937-41, 9979-81 and Bell, *op.cit.* pp.24-5.

161 *Queen's,* p.116.

162 *Queen's,* p.29, p.44.

163 *Queen's,* p.113. Jose Harris has described the poor as 'participants in, and contributors to the long drawn out national revolution in the use of language'. See Harris, *op.cit.* p.22.

164 *Queen's,* pp.89-90.

165 *Queen's,* pp.84-5.

166 *Queen's,* pp.112-15.

167 *Queen's,* p.92. Here Loane also noted that the opposite was true of other classes for, 'the rich carefully avoid any bookish tinge.' The increased availability of, and interest in, books and newspapers is confirmed by Lady Bell, who undertook a detailed survey of reading habits in Middlesborough. Lady Bell did confirm what Loane implied, that the poor were deterred from using the Free

library because of the formalities involved. The chapter on reading was originally published as an article in the *Independent Review,* and subsequently reprinted within her book. See Bell, *op.cit.* pp.142-70.

168 *Queen's,* p.127 and as cited in *The Daily News,* 13 October 1905, p.4. See also *Queen's,* p.42, pp.59-60, p.134, pp.142-3, p.146, p.260.

169 *Queen's,* p.129.

170 There were at least fifteen favourable published reviews of *The Queen's Poor,* in the daily national press as well as nursing and literary journals.

SELECTED BIBLIOGRAPHY

Place of publication, London, unless otherwise stated

Brian Abel-Smith, *A History of the Nursing Profession* (Heinemann, 1960).

Monica E. Baly, *A History of the Queen's Nursing Institute. 100 Years 1887-1987* (Croom Helm, 1987).

Lady Bell, *At the Works* (Edward Arnold, 1907. Reprint, with new introduction by Angela V.John, Virago, 1985).

Clementina Black (ed) *Married Women's Work* (Bell, 1915. Reprint with introduction by E.Mappen, Virago, 1983).

M. Bulmer, K.Bales & K.K.Sklar (eds) *The Social Survey in Historical Perspective, 1880-1940* (Cambridge, Cambridge University Press, 1991).

S.Cohen, 'The Life and Works of M.Loane', unpublished M.Phil Thesis, Middlesex University, 1997.

Carl Chinn, *They Worked All Their Lives. Women of the Urban Poor in England, 1880-1939* (Manchester, Manchester University Press, 1988).

Hugh Cunningham, *The Children of the Poor. Representations of Childhood since the Seventeenth Century* (Oxford, Blackwell, 1991)

M.Llewelyn Davies (ed) *Maternity — letters from working women* (Bell, 1915. 2nd.ed Virago, 1978).

Anna Davin, *Growing Up Poor. Home, School and Street in London, 1870-1914* (Rivers Oram, 1996).

D. Englander, & R. O'Day (eds) *Retrieved Riches. Social Investigation in Britain, 1840-1914* (Aldershot, Scolar, 1995).

John Fraser, 'George Sturt ("George Bourne") and Rural Laboring Life', D.Phil Thesis, University of Minnesota, 1961.

Jose Harris, *Private Lives, Public Spirit. A Social History of Britain, 1870-1914* (Oxford, Oxford University Press,1993).

Peter Keating (ed) *Into Unknown England 1866-1913* (Fontana, 1976).

Ross McKibbin, *The Ideologies of Class: Social Relations in Britain, 1880-1950* (Oxford, Clarendon, 1990).

R.O'Day & D.Englander, Mr. *Charles Booth's Inquiry. Life and Labour of the People in London Reconsidered* (Hambledon, 1993).

M.Pember Reeves, *Round About a Pound a Week* (Bell, 1913. 1st.ed reprint, Virago 1979).

Stephen Reynolds, *A Poor Man's House* (John Lane, 1909. Oxford, Oxford University Press, 1982)

Elizabeth Roberts, *A Woman's Place. An Oral History of Working-Class Women, 1890-1940* (Oxford, Blackwell, 1984).

Mary Stocks, *A Hundred Years of District Nursing* (George Allen & Unwin, 1960).

SUSAN COHEN is a part time lecturer at Middlesex University. She has had articles published in *Patterns of Prejudice* and *Nursing History Review*.

CLIVE FLEAY is Senior Lecturer in History at Middlesex University. He has had articles published in the *Historical Journal*, the *Journal of Contemporary History* and *History Today*.

THE QUEEN'S POOR

LIFE AS THEY FIND IT IN TOWN AND COUNTRY

BY

M. LOANE

LONDON
EDWARD ARNOLD
41 AND 43 MADDOX STREET, BOND STREET, W.
1905

(All rights reserved)

THE QUEEN'S POOR

CHAPTER I

HUSBAND AND WIFE AMONG THE POOR

"I CHASTISES my husband like a child," said a patient, who, during my unavoidably long visits, dipped me rather more deeply than I liked in her domestic concerns. Naturally my thoughts turned to "chastise thee with the valour of my tongue," but after being shown the stick it was impossible to put such a gloss upon the text. She was the first avowed husband-beater I had ever met, but by no means the last. As far as I can gather from the statements of these doughty champions of the supremacy of woman, their husbands are beaten for returning home "more foolish than when they went out," and minus an undue proportion of their week's wages. It certainly seems a more just arrangement than that the men should beat their wives on these occasions; and as the delinquents in every case I have observed possess the usual, or even more than the usual, superiority in physical strength, I conclude that they also acknowledge its equity.

I

In a neighbourhood where there was much wife-beating, and little reticence on that or any other point, a husband of twenty-two years' standing, the father of eleven children, told me coolly: "I've never hit my wife, not even when I was drunk, for I know'd if I did she'd hit back again. I don't suppose *that* 'ud ha' stopped me if I'd bin much set on it, for her strength was never much by a man's, but she'd have come on me for all she was worth, and *I didn't want no scrimmage.*" Those few sentences seem to me to sum up the whole doctrine of wife-beating, whether the operator is drunk or sober. First, that there are a few men whom nothing would restrain from cruelty to any weaker creature in their power; secondly, that most of those guilty of ill-treating their wives could very easily be restrained; and thirdly, that this majority, though thinking it no degradation to strike a woman who submits, would be bitterly ashamed to have it said by the neighbours: "Him and his wife gets fighting."

It is true that at the present day there are few men left who would beat their wives, even under considerable provocation, without the excuse of drink; but even if a man were not responsible for being drunk, drunkenness, when one looks closely into the matter, proves a most insufficient defence. If a man ·is completely intoxicated he does not strike anyone; if he is "mad drunk" he does not care whom he kicks,—a policeman on his beat or a sick baby in its cradle;—but how often do men in this condition manage to reach their homes? The average wife-beater is never drunk enough to have lost all power of distinguishing one person from another. Over and over again, children of varying ages have told me, not with the desire to prove any particular point, but with the disjointed impartiality with which most of their voluntary statements are made: " When father's drunk he knocks mother about shameful, but he never hits us a lick." Wives have told me with equal frequency: " He never lays a finger on the children, not even when he has the worst of his turns."

Now, if a man is sober enough to distinguish children, often children as tall as their mother, from that unhappy person herself, why does he invariably choose her for his victim? Because she "nags" at him? The women I mean bear everything, hope everything, and call nothing but their children their own. Because his affection for the children is stronger? Not in the least; he very greatly prefers his wife, but he vents his illhumour on her because he knows from past experience that she will regard it as a venial offence, while to injure one of the children would be unpardonable,—" a thing as he'd never hear the last on."

Legislation has done much for women, and private employers may do more. A certain firm in London, employing a large number of married women, declines to allow them to enter the factory while bearing any sign of ill-treatment. As men of the occasional wifebeating type almost invariably strike at the head, and the women almost as invariably throw up the forearm to break the force of the blow, injuries are usually of a conspicuous nature. A poor woman living in the immediate neighbourhood told me: " It's made a sight o' difference. Men thinks twice before they gives their wife a black eye. when it means a fortnight of her wages gone for nothing."

But, after all, each woman must depend chiefly on herself. The world is so far civilised that it is only in exceptional cases that any wife need endure active illusage. The feminist movement is supposed to date much later than Miss Austen, but one of her heroines, when asked what treatment she expects, sums up an important part of a wife's duties in the gaily confident reply that she expects the very best because she will never tolerate any other. When I see timid young wives likely to slip into the position of ill-treated drudges, I always press on them the advice of experienced matrons in their own class of life: " Don't irritate a man, especially if he's tired or hungry or in drink, but never take a blow from him, drunk or sober. If you make enough fuss over the first you'll never get a second, but if you'll stand one beating, men think you'll stand twenty."

Some years before I began district nursing, I was scandalised by hearing a well-known London clergyman say with reference to wife-beating: " Plenty of women deserve all they get, and more too." After an acquaintance with the poor in their own homes far more intimate though not quite so long as his, I am forced to own that there is some truth in the statement which seemed to me so outrageous. Why then does the sight of bruises on a woman fill me with an ever-increasing disgust and

indignation? Simply because the wives on whom all
the blows and abuse fall are *not* the women who have
deserved them, and who might conceivably be restrained
by them. Is it the woman who keeps her house like a
pigstye, who neglects, starves, and ill-treats her children,
the woman who robs and insults her husband and puts
him to open shame, who is beaten and sworn at?
Scarcely ever. Kicks and oaths are kept for the dull,
patient, timid, uncomplaining drudge, generally a little
—a very little—below the average in intellect, who
toils from morning till night vainly and unskilfully
endeavouring to make fifteen shillings do the work of
twenty-five, while the husband squanders from a third
to a half of his earnings.

Nevertheless, the district nurse learns to understand
how many a woman clings to the husband of whom she
goes in bodily fear every wet Bank Holiday, and who
may have half-killed her three or four times in the
course of their married life, and is far happier than her
neighbour, whose dour, unmannerly master is never
drunk and never civil. There may be hours of fear and
trembling; but ninety-nine times out of a hundred does
he not return from work with a cheery paraphrase of
the greeting that is being uttered in tens of thousands
of civilised homes all over the country: "Well, old girl,
here I am! How's the world bin serving you? The
youngster howling your head off? Come here, you
young beggar, and sit along o' me while your mammy
gets the tea. You're too much like your daddy, that's
what wrong with *you!*" It needs courage to live with

a man who may come back to his family any night like
a raving lunatic? Yes, but it needs more to toil from
year's end to year's end for a man who has never a word
of affection for wife or child, never a jest, never a spice
of humorous exaggeration in his statements, never a
compliment for his wife's cooking, or her management,
or her appearance.

One learns to understand, too, how it is that the dirty,
untidy young wife, who, when her husband returns
hungry and tired from a long day's work, holds up a
smilingly assured face to be kissed, exclaiming, "Gracious!
if I hadn't forgot all about your tea!" and clatters
together an extravagant and ill-chosen meal while she
pours out a stream of cheerful and inconsequent chatter,
is more loved, and dealt with more patiently, tenderly,
and faithfully, than her clean and frugal neighbour, who
has prepared a meal that ought to turn the author of
Twenty Satisfying Suppers for Sixpence green with
envy, but who expects her husband to be eternally grateful because "he could eat his dinner off the boards,"—
when all that the poor man asks is to be allowed to walk
over them unreproached.

Few young husbands appreciate cleanliness as carried
out by a woman in whom it takes the place of art,
literature, social distraction, religion, even love itself;
but elderly and disciplined men are often boastful of
their wife's inhuman devotion to scouring. "You
wouldn't find anyone cleaner than my missus, not high
nor low," said one of these persons to me, hugging his
chains. "Why, she cleans up that theer kettle as we've

a-had ever since we was married, forty-seven years come
next Easter, till it 'ud go to a body's heart to use it.
When we wants a drop o' water for our tea, we just
boils it in a soss-pan in the wash'us, and if," with a
rebellious gleam of humour in his dim old eyes,—" and if
theer *was* anything as could be scrub to a soss-pan, the
missus she'd use it, and I'll warrant that theer soss-pan
'ud be settin' up alongside the kettle as bold as any
ornymint ever you seed!" Having frequently "seed"
fireirons polished and hung on the wall while the fire
was poked up with a stick and beaten down with the
heel of a boot, I have not the smallest doubt that it
would be.

Second and third marriages are very common among
the poor, but even if they occur early in life they are
nearly always regarded as *mariages de convenance*, and
no softening halo of romance or of later tenderness
grows round them. As a child I was often told the
story of a certain post-captain's widow who married
a naval engineer, and kept her first husband's portrait
over the mantelpiece, and addressed stage asides to it
to avenge herself for any supposed shortcomings in his
successor. The old sailor who related it to me always
ended with the comment, "The first time she'd said it
to me I should have smashed the picture, and the second
time I should have smashed *her*"; but although I have
seen this paralleled by many and many a district
patient, these heroic remedies have never been tried.
The photograph of "my first" is constantly found in a
conspicuous place, and his virtues are openly contrasted

with the delinquencies of " my second." The latter are often imperceptible to an impartial onlooker, and sometimes doubting whether, granting all the circumstances, it would be possible for human nature to reach greater heights than " my second," I have made cautious inquiries among old neighbours, and have not seldom elicited facts that went far to prove that " my first" was a drunken bully.

It is much the same with the men; no second wife holds quite the same place as the first, not even if she has a large family and her predecessor was childless. Living or dead, it is rare to hear a complaint against a first husband or wife, while approbation of the second, if ever uttered, is as a rule intolerably patronising. There may be something touching about even this imperfect faithfulness to the love of one's youth, but it is often hard on the legal successor, whether man or woman.

I have recently come across several women genuinely grateful to their second husbands, but they were either persons of exceptionally advanced moral development, or of superior education. A few weeks since we were called to a house where an elderly woman was lying in a perfectly helpless state. " Who nurses you and keeps the house in such order?" I asked.

" My husband, m'm. He waits on me hand and foot. He's better than a woman. I remember when we were coming out of church, I asked myself, ' Do I love him enough?' But he's been so good to me I've never put it to myself again "; and then she went on to speak of "my first love," who "had rats," with a look in her eyes that was never roused by the sight of that good, square, ugly little man waiting anxiously in the kitchen to know if there was anything else that he could do. Another woman, who had married her second husband very late in life, told me: "It's my St. Martin's summer. It's such a blessed rest after the life I've had."

I begin to be puzzled by the frequency with which I learn that deceased first husbands were drunkards, while living first husbands are rarely in that category. Probably the explanation is that we have so much to do with couples who are past the age which a drunkard would be likely to reach.

The relations that grow up between old husbands and wives are often exceedingly tender and beautiful. I remember one powerful man of seventy-five, absorbed day and night in nursing a hopelessly suffering wife. His one unfailing joke was to pretend that she was unkind to him. "Love, you never smile on *me* like that! All the sugar's for nurse, and all the sauce for me. Well, well, my back's broad, and I get a holiday from hard words while nurse is here." "Go 'long with you," the invalid would say reprovingly, "and don't even yourself with them as has been *teached*." One day a clergyman dared to suggest that she would be more comfortable in a Home to which he could obtain her admission. The old man flung out his arm with a magnificent sweep, embracing the room and all it contained. "Sir, there's not a place in all England where my wife would be cared for as she is here!" And indeed I knew of none, attic though it was, with its one window blinking on a street which neighbours struggling on the slippery edge of respectability called "Burglars' Rest."

One day I met a fine well-set-up old man of seventy-three, who had lost his wife a few weeks before, after forty-seven years of life together in a four-roomed cottage. I had been away at the time of her death, and he stopped to speak to me, beginning rather far away from the subject. "D'you remember las' year I told you I was going to thatch them sheds for Mr. Brownlow? Well, the very next day he comes to me and says, 'I've changed my mind about them sheds, John; they'll do as they are.' 'Oh, very well,' I says, but I did feel a bit vexed about it, and I had a kind of feeling against him. The day after the missus was buried I met him in the road; 'John,' he says, 'I'd like you to know how it was about them sheds.' 'Oh, it's no matter, sir,' I says. '*I*'ve no call to ask anyone for work. I've all I can do to get through what I have.' 'Don't be so huffy, John,' he says; 'I only done it to pacify your wife. She came to me in a tearing way, and said she knew you'd break your leg or suthin, and that I wasn't to let you have the work, and I wasn't to tell you why. So I just said I'd changed my mind. But I thought I'd like you to know how it was.' Just to think of her getting behind me like that!" said the man, with a slow, deep laugh of enjoyment, the tears still in his eyes. "The missus never said nothing to me, but in her mind she always thought I'd be the one to go first, and it worried her. She wasn't ill not half an hour. I come back one night very late from work. She seemed just as usual, and gave me my supper. Then she said she'd been house-cleaning and she was tired, and she'd go to bed. She turned round at the door, and said, 'Now, don't you fall asleep there where you sit,' but that's what I *did*. When I went up into the bedroom at last, it must have been near eleven. She was kneeling down by the bed. I thought she'd fell asleep saying her prayers, and I meant to have a joke against her, and not let on I'd been asleep myself, and then all of a sudden something came over me, and I felt frightened. I'm past seventy, but I lifted her up as easy as ever I done in my life. She just give a sigh, and I believe she died that very minute."

Aged husbands and wives seem to live for one another, and are unhappy if separated for even the briefest periods. The women, younger in years and in constitution, are the usual nurses; when neither love nor skill could do any more for the sufferer, I have seen old couples sit hour after hour with hand clasped in hand, drawing comfort and courage from one another's presence. Wives are capable of extraordinary hardness as well as of inexhaustible tenderness. "Another of 'em gone! It's yer fate," was the grim comment made in my hearing when the bandage just removed from the husband's foot proved to contain one of his toes.

Money matters are left entirely to the wife; it is she who decides whether an increased rent can be paid or an article of furniture bought, whether a boy shall be

apprenticed or must take what work he can find, and
what insurance clubs, etc., shall be joined.   The custom
of leaving the management of money to the wife is so
deeply rooted, that children always speak of the family
income as belonging entirely to her, and will constantly
tell you : " Mother has to pay so and so for rent " ; " Mother
is going to try and afford father this or that" ; " Mother
isn't going to let father work for Mr. —— any more,
she says the wages isn't worth the hours."

"The King gave father ten pounds for a present," said
a little boy.

" And what did father do with it ? "

" He gave it to mother."

" Didn't he keep any of it for himself ? "

" No ; mother gave him *what she thought fit*."

How much that was I did not ask ; father's proceedings are open to inquiry and comment, but mother is
infallible.

I can see no justification for the statement that large
bodies of workmen are in the habit of spending a third
of their wages in pleasures in which their families have
no share.   It is impossible to calculate how much a man
spends on himself, unless one knows what articles he is
expected to provide out of the sum he retains.   The
man who only keeps half a crown, but buys nothing
for the family out of it except an occasional paper of
sweets for the little ones, may have had quite as large
a share as the man who pockets ten or twelve shillings,
out of which he has to pay the club subscriptions,
provide all his own clothes and the boys' Sunday suits,

settle the boot bill for the entire family, and save something for the summer holiday. " Mother lets father keep
all his overtime money," I was told by an agricultural
labourer's daughter. It sounded an unusually liberal
allowance, until I learnt that he was expected to " find
hisself in boots " and to buy two young pigs at a cost
of about a guinea each, and pay for all the meal required
as soon as fattening time began.

Among the most needlessly comfortless and unhappy
homes are those where the husband, too soon impatient
and despairing over a young wife's poor management,
degrades her in her own eyes and the neighbours' by
taking the catering into his own hands. " Man alive ! "
exclaimed a worthy old artisan when he saw a younger
comrade preparing to "lay out" his week's wages,
" what's a woman for if she can't spend her husband's
earnings for him ? Let your wife alone ; she'll learn,
and you never will, nor any other man neither. Just
look at the home me and my wife has got together, and
the children we've set out respectable ! When we were
married my wife had been four years in a factory, and
she hardly knew one end of a broom from another, and
she couldn't cut out not so much as a pocket-handker-
cheeve. I don't say but what I mightn't have managed
a bit better than she did at first, me being twenty to
her seventeen, and having had a good mother of my
own, while she hadn't nothing but a stepmother as I
wouldn't have thanked to learn her none of *her* tricks,
and I don't say but what I usen't to lose my temper a
bit over the waste and the muddle, but I stuck to it

through thick and thin that it was *her* business, not mine, and where are we now?—Where you'll never be if you don't see it's just the plain truth I'm telling you."

More practical knowledge of arithmetic would have an inconceivably beneficial effect upon the ways of thought and the habits of the poor. In one excellently managed home the wife told me that she was trying to get regular work for her husband at a guinea a week. I said, much surprised: "I thought your husband's wages were considerably higher than that."

"They call it 32s.," she replied, "but I added it up last year and it averaged 22s. 3½d. We're nine months in this year, and it doesn't fairly make 21s. 9d. Where'd we ha' bin if I'd believed it was 32s. ? Counting all the anxiety and the hanging about wretched when there's no work, we both think we'd be better off at a guinea. My man couldn't see it at first, he's not much of a scholar, though as good a man as you'd find, but I went through it slow for him so's he could follow, and you won't find him go back on it now."

The "tyranny of tears" is known in all classes, but the tyranny of bad language is almost entirely confined to the poor. Many men who would not dream of striking their wives, nor of keeping back a penny of their wages beyond the stipulated sum, are deferred to anxiously in every detail of domestic life, simply from the nervous horror that every decent woman has of being sworn at. Sometimes the tyranny is carried to an extreme of pettiness that has its ludicrous side. A young housemaid singing the praises of her mother told me: "Father can't a-bear nothin' prickly against his skin, so mother she always takes the first wear out of his shirts and socks. Mother 'ud do anything to save swearing!"

Few well-to-do people realise how much self-control and unselfishness are necessary before peaceable lives can be lived in crowded quarters. One of the many little girls who know all their mothers' secrets, and would die rather than reveal them to any of her neighbours, told me, "Mother's chest isn't never really bad except when dad smokes in the kitchen of an evening; but she won't say nothing about it to him, because it's very hard if he can't have a pipe in his own house same as other men does. Sometimes it makes mother feel that queer she has to go to bed, and then dad says: 'Why, what's took you, mother? You've been rampaging round too much. Why don't you let things be? I never take heed of nothing long's I get my meals, and the boys would *rather* be dirty.' Dad's such a stupid, he don't never think it's his smoking as done it. And he'll make her a cup of tea and carry it up to her, and then he tells me to make haste and grow, so's she won't have so much work to do. It *do* annoy me! I don't think I'll let *my* husbin act so silly. But mother says you never know till you get them. He's the biggest baby of the lot."

Owing to the comparative leisure of the years spent in domestic service, and to the constant intercourse with their mistress and her children, labourers' wives are often greatly their husbands' superiors in general education. I have known men who could scarcely count up their wages unless paid in the usual pieces of money, whose wives kept neat account-books; and many men who could not read "so as to find any pleasure in it," married to women who were not merely omnivorous readers, but who showed a decided preference for the best literature obtainable. Superiority of education on the part of the wife never causes any alienation; the man shows no jealousy, the woman no conceit. One scavenger did indeed tell me that he "generally sat outside when the missus began reading," but I think this had some connection with reading improving portions aloud, for he spoke of her "figgering" with enthusiasm. When, on the other hand, this superiority falls to the man in addition to his greater knowledge of the outside world, as occurs in the case of highly skilled artisans, non-commissioned officers in both services, the men who rise in the police force, etc., great estrangement results. The education of these women is not only relatively poorer, but positively so. They have left school at the same age as labourers' wives, or only a few months later, and have then earned their living in ways that gave them little chance of self-improvement. A woman can share her advantages with a man, and a curious gentleness and refinement is often found among labourers who "occupy the seat of the unlearned." Every woman is a possible mother, and therefore to some extent a born teacher, but a man can impart little to his wife. The whole unhappiness of the private lives of "risen" men lies in the inferior education of the women they have married. I call to mind one case where the husband's high wages, never less than four pounds a week, depended largely on his knowledge of French and German, which he was expected to improve to the highest point possible. Lessons of the advanced kind that he required, and which, to save time, had to be given in his own house, could not be obtained for less than four shillings an hour. At first the wife was immensely amused, and used to sit outside the little parlour door doubled up with laughter over "the queer way of talking"; but she soon wearied of this, and endless reproaches over the "waste of money" began and are still going on.

It must be owned that some of the quicker-witted women take a delight in mystifying the simple-minded husbands whom they adore. Not long ago a servant of mine went to tea with a friend who had married a drayman, almost as sleek and ponderous as the splendid team he drove. When the meal was over, the wife sat down with her guest by the fire, and politely requested her husband to wash up the tea-things. In spite of the restraining influence of "company," he declined to do it.

"What!" she exclaimed, in pretended indignation, "isn't it only last week that you promised faithful to honour and obey me?"

"I'm not saying as I didn't," replied the giant cautiously.

"And you're going to break your promise already?"

"I'm not saying as I won't."

2

"Then wash up them tea-things like a dear, and say no more about it."

And Hercules obeyed, while the two women shook with silent laughter.

Husbands and wives are much nearer of an age than is usual among the upper classes, and not seldom the wife is the senior. Strangely enough, far more comment is roused by the sight of a man obviously older than his wife than by the reverse. Only a few weeks ago I overheard a cottager say, "He's old enough to be her father, pretty near," and the neighbour who added, "Yes, a good seven year older'n what *she* is," meant it as a confirmation of the statement, not a correction. "I'd rather have a man younger than me," I was told by a girl of sixteen. "But why?" "So's he'd work for me when I got old," was the uncannily prudent reply. Another girl said: "Father's three years older'n mother, but he don't look it." I gathered from the context that his youthful appearance was in no way a mortification to her mother, but was regarded as an imperfect atonement for daring to be so much her senior.

Unfortunately there are signs of change in this direction, and numerous marriages have recently come under my notice between girls of eighteen and men well over thirty, and even of girls scarcely twenty marrying widowers of forty and more.

One consolation falls to ill-used wives: their children generally love them, and *never* love the father. However indulgent he may be to them, the youngest child cannot be bribed into affection. A little girl scarcely six years old one day drew my attention to an unusually smart garment that she said her father had bought her.

"Lovely!" I said, with the required enthusiasm; "I suppose you thanked him very nicely for it?"

"No," was the determined reply; "I won't never thank him for nothing. He beats my mammy somefin cruel." And her mother assured me proudly: "She wouldn't tell her father anything I didn't want him to know, not if it was ever so!"

"Don't you be afraid, mother," said a little boy of ten, bringing his mother a cup of tea and a crumbly slice of bread and butter that he had cut thin at all hazards; "I don't mean to be like father when I grows up, I mean to be *kind*." Personally the boy had no reason whatever for complaint; the criticised parent was most indulgent to all his six children.

Even when the mother's temper is soured, and some of her misery is wreaked on her children, it is still the same. Little creatures who have scarcely begun to change their first teeth will say with a generous philosophy, learnt one knows not whence: "We hadn't ought to take too much heed of it. Mother has a heap to put up with." One day a grey-haired workman teasingly reminded his mother how, on a bitter winter's morning nearly fifty years before, when he was crying with cold and hunger, she had turned on him where she knelt blowing up a wretched fire of damp sticks, and had knocked him down with the "bellus."

" Garge," she pleaded, her pretty old face trembling
between laughter and tears, " if I'd *killed* you I couldn't
ha' helped it, not at that moment."

" I know you couldn't, mother," he said soberly; " I
knowed it even then."

With the moral indifference of nature, good children
often come to bad parents and find scant appreciation.
A woman, after speaking to me at some length of her
husband, a peculiarly brutal drunkard, who had narrowly
escaped murdering her a few days previously, compared
him with her only son, a steady, well-grown young
fellow who was earning a man's wages at eighteen,
and supplied the very bread that she ate. His kindness
and his unaffected sense of religion had drawn from a
neighbour the admiring comment, " He might have
walked straight out of a track !" but the mother
summed up her opinion of the difference in their
character by saying fervently, " Eh, but his feyther's a
mon !"

The ideal of fatherhood is less developed among the
poor than the ideal of motherhood. The tenderness
lasts for too short a period, and there is rarely any
attempt at moral training. Nevertheless, men of the
working classes are as much libelled as fathers as
working-class mothers are as cooks, nurses, and
managers. In both cases the millions bear the blame
that is only due to a few tens of thousands. Paternal
affection may not be very strong after a boy has
reached his tenth and a girl her twelfth year, but it
is lavished on them at an age when the circumstances

of poor people's daily lives make it almost indispensable for the children's health and happiness. In countless homes, the busy, many-childed mother breathes freely for the first time in the day when her husband returns from work. "They're sure to be hanging round their daddy," she says, and thinks no more of water-butts or motor-cars till the next morning, when the responsible play-fellow vanishes for his ten or eleven hours.

Having spent all my early life among men who were willing to make any sacrifice for children of a reasonable age, but whose first and only idea when a baby cried was, "My dear, do send it up to the nursery," and who showed open aversion even for their first-born, or even for the child of their old age, if he had sticky hands or a spot on his pinafore, I can never get over the surprise with which I see working-class fathers snatch up a grimy, howling baby and walk about with it in their arms, pressing kisses on its cheeks, and crooning lovingly, "What be 'um doin' to 'ee, li'l gal; what be 'um doin' to 'ee, then?"—a form which seems to be a masculine variant of the traditional "diddums was, then?"

The honours of fatherhood are divided. The professional man generally begins to show most attention to his children about the time when the working man's devotion slackens. The working man adores children at an age when the former would not dare to give his candid opinion of them even to a confirmed bachelor.

Fathers are regarded by the children as plainly

inferior to mothers in authority, in knowledge of right and wrong, and above all, of "manners," but they are loved as companions, as abettors of many forbidden practices, and as protectors from the occasional slaps and rather frequent reproofs that the acknowledged ruler of the family deals out for their soul's health and the preservation of their clothes. I had a pathetic instance not long ago of the different moral light in which father and mother are quite unconsciously regarded. An artificer was sitting up at night with his dying son, a manly, intelligent lad of fifteen, suddenly struck down by a mortal disease. As death approached, the relations between the two insensibly slipped back some seven or eight years. Almost the last words uttered by the boy were a refusal to take his medicine : " *You* drink it, dad ! mother won't know the difference." Twice the father drank it in a fond attempt at coaxing, and at daybreak the lad died.

There are so many people who seem totally unable to see the British workman except when he is being ejected from a public-house, or loafing at a street corner, or making an involuntary appearance at the police-court, and in domestic life they are convinced that he is a brutal tyrant. They are completely unaware of the state of tutelage in which he really lives. Talk of the subjection of women !—I doubt if the bare idea of fathers being equal to mothers in rank and authority ever enters the mind of any cottage child under sixteen. From their conversation, all my little friends might be fatherless, except for an occasional dramatic recital of

how dad "went and did" something that mother said
he "hadn't ought to," and the disastrous results of
this untimely rebellion. Father is generally regarded
in the light of mother's eldest child, and disobedience in
him is far more heinous a crime than in *them*, because
" he'd ought to know better than not to do what mother
says." Fathers are, as a rule, perfectly satisfied with
this position, not minding in the least when the youngest
born publicly raises a note of warning : " Mother said as
you *wasn't* to do that, dad ! "

The author of a new " Utopia," and writers on eugenics
generally, seem to lose sight entirely of the fact that the
vast majority of men above the age of twenty-six are
distinctly domestic in their tastes, and have not the
slightest desire to separate themselves from the daily
society of their one wife, nor to abandon the entire care
and upbringing of their children to women who, confined
solely to the society of infants, and occupied solely with
their needs, must rapidly degenerate, first mentally, and
then morally.

I have known men who appeared utterly non-domestic-
ated, but they belonged without exception to the upper
classes. The roughest men I come across in my daily
work have a real preference for family life, although
they only know it under its most trying conditions,
while in the average working man the feeling is extraordinarily strong, and the desire for his " ain fireside "
steadily predominant. I was speaking recently to a
carman who had seen some years active service as a
soldier, and is now engaged in what he considers the

far more dangerous occupation of driving a constantly changed pair of horses all over the county of London. He has been engaged for two years to the youngest of a large family of girls, and is shortly to be married. Telling me of the way in which he spent his leisure, he said: "I have every other Sunday 'off' and half Thursday. Sundays I go with Phillis to see her mother and dad. Thursdays she can't always come, so I go by myself. I haven't got any people of my own. It's just like my own home. I mustn't be five minutes late, but if I am,"—triumphantly—"*they wait tea for me!*"

Now, what was the "home" that this man preferred to anything that London could offer him? Three crowded rooms in a dreary "block," the society of "dad," who is cheerful and sweet-tempered but a chronic invalid, and of "mother," who is a noted grumbler, to whom much is excused because she has lost her only son. One day the ex-soldier found a faded carte-de-visite of the lad, and spent a fortnight's savings in having it enlarged and framed. "Mother cried when I brought it to her," he told me, with deep satisfaction, convinced that he had done the right thing. Four other daughters are engaged or married, and the only difference in the behaviour of these sons-in-law, actual or prospective, is that, having parents of their own, they only pay half as many visits as the six-foot orphan, who might still be enjoying the "illimitable veldt" or whatever else — in theory — delights the masculine soul.

In times of sickness, fathers are often tender and

assiduous nurses. Speaking of a neighbour's neglected children, a young married woman said to me: "Three of us often had abscesses like that, but there was never a mark left to show. Mother wasn't much of a hand at that kind of thing, and we used to kick up a fine row if she tried to touch them, but as soon as ever father come home from work he'd set to and bathe and poultice us by the hour." This is by no means an exceptional case; there are very many homes where district nurses make a point of repeating all their instructions and explaining all the doctor's orders to both parents, and where they would not feel that the treatment was certain of being carried out unless they had done so. I have known men who for months at a stretch did all their own work, waited on a sick wife, and with very little help from the neighbours washed and dressed the children, and gave half Saturday and most of Sunday to house-cleaning. I remember one corporal, who throughout two of the hottest months of a scorching summer did even more. Extra money being sorely needed for the little household, he did the washing for forty men. "And all that time," said his wife, "he kep' me and the children like princesses, and never so much as said he was tired. And only think, when I took up with him I was ashamed to tell my missis he was a soldier. I said he was a dyer."

"But why a dyer?"

"That was his joke for 'dier.' Dier for his country. There was a lot of people used to call them butchers then, but he said dyer sounded better. A long time after I was married I wrote and told her, and she come and see me."

I know one husband, regarded neither as a saint nor as an exception by the neighbours, who for twenty-five years has never failed to rise at six o'clock, light the kitchen fire, make his wife a cup of tea and carry it upstairs to her. One thing only was unusual in this man's conduct: instead of occupying himself on Sunday morning entirely in looking after the children (which of course is pure pleasure!), he used to make the eldest child take them for a walk while he cooked the dinner, " So's your mother can get *one* holiday in the week, anyway."

It is exceedingly difficult for the upper classes to acquire any fair idea of the ordinary domestic relations among the poor, and when they seek for information they too often forget to make allowance for the fact that the chosen teachers are all more or less blinded by their profession. Is it reasonable to ask the club doctor and the district nurse if the lower classes are healthy, to ask the coroner if they are sober and know how to feed their children, the police-magistrate if they are honest and truthful, the relieving officer if they are thrifty, the labour master if they are industrious, the highly orthodox clergyman if they are religious, and then call the replies received, KNOWLEDGE OF THE POOR ? .

CHAPTER II

THE RELIGION OF THE RESPECTABLE POOR

UNDER the title of "respectable poor" I include all persons who, in the expressive phrase so common among them, "keep a home together."

My friends often say to me : "How terrible it must be to work in the slums !" I reply (when I have time): "I do not know exactly what is meant by a slum. I have seen collections of dwellings that seemed to me painfully poor and crowded, but they were homes to the people who lived in them. They even spoke of their 'comforts,' and of not being able to get them anywhere except in their own houses, and meant what they said in a literal way."

"Oh !" (in flat and disappointed tones), "I suppose you have never worked in really bad places ? "

"I have worked in every district of a large seaport town, in an inland town, in the country, and in what are considered the worst parts of London. I have worked—often after dark, and sometimes in the middle of the night—in alleys where I was assured that no policeman dared walk alone in broad daylight. But the people who told me that had such obvious enjoyment in the tale that it was probably an ancient legend.

Bad and sad things often are. Only the other day I picked up an appeal that came from a well-known and very worthy charitable institution, but I was not a little scandalised to find it baited with anecdotes which, though I do not doubt their original truth, are literally the same that made my blood run cold twenty years ago."

"But to go into places where there is no religion, where the name of God is never heard!"

"Ah! I have certainly never been there. I remember one small district, where, in the course of several months, I only once saw anyone go to church or chapel, and then it was a little ballet girl from Drury Lane, leading a still smaller sister; but I have never entered a lane or a court, scarcely a single room, where religion was not to be found."

"Then you have only worked among the respectable poor?"

"I have only worked among the poor whom I respected. It is true that I do not know the homeless poor. A district nurse can, of course, only work where there is *some* kind of a home. She could not, for longer than it would take to fetch an ambulance, nurse a man lying under an archway or by the roadside."

And then my friends turn away disappointed, but exactly why they might find it as difficult to explain as I to understand.

To count up the churchgoers and chapelgoers, compare the resulting number with the population, and then, if there should be a great disparity, argue that the neighbourhood is without religion; or to estimate the

proportion of children and young persons in places of
puplic worship and then say, "religion has no hold on
them when they get older," is a most serious error.   It
is a confusion of formal outward signs and inward
spiritual graces.   Many of the poor rarely attend
church, not because they are irreligious, but because
they have long since received and absorbed the truths
by which they live; while the idea that attendance at
public worship is a duty does not occur to them, and
does not seem credible when suggested.   To put on one's
best clothes, to be surrounded by neighbours in theirs,
to sit in a large, well-lighted, well-warmed and beautifully decorated building, to hear the organ, to join in
the singing, all this differs from anything they are
accustomed to call duty.   It is a pleasure, and, like
most other pleasures, must be left chiefly for the young.
Many, on the other hand, attend regularly because they
have not yet found their Bread of Life, and hunger for
it.   It is acknowledged that there are those in all
classes of life who go to church constantly for reasons
which have no connection with personal religion.   Is it
too difficult to believe that there are those who attend
irregularly, or remain away altogether, not because they
are persons of evil courses, or dead to things of the
spirit, but because their inward religious life is so
strong and so simple that they are independent of any
"assembling of yourselves together"?   A patient whose
life had been one long series of illnesses and troubles,
and who was never seen inside any place of worship,
said to the clergyman who visited her: "I go to the

Fountain Head for strength and guidance; God has always sent it to me in His good time."

To such persons it seems as natural that the young should go to church or chapel, and the middle-aged and old remain at home, as that children should go to school and grown men to the workshop. Often I have seen toil-worn men and women smile with indulgent humour at zealous curates and deaconesses — Nonconformist ministers, I must own, are generally quicker to recognise the signs of spiritual experience—presenting to them the crudest forms of elementary truths, and ask, after they had bidden them a courteous farewell: "Do they suppose that my soul is of so little value to my Maker that I should have been left seventy years waiting in darkness for *them?* Do they think there was no teachers when we was young? Things is changed, but there was always ways o' learning, and there always will be."

We are led too much by words, and our own interpretations of them. I once ventured to say to a vicar, who knew about as much of his poorer parishioners as the typical military governor of sixty years ago knew of his prisoners, that several of the chapels in the town exercised a strong and wholesome influence in some of the most poverty-stricken districts. "How can that be?" he asked. "In all the worst and roughest houses I enter, they tell me, 'we're dissenters,' and I have to clear out before I'm made!" It seemed a revelation to him to learn that Nonconformists are not in the habit of calling themselves Dissenters, but Wesleyans, Baptists, etc., and that the people who had made use of the expression to him meant, in a few cases, " We are unbelievers," and in most, " We don't want you coming in here just whenever you choose. If you had any manners you'd know when to come."

In face of all the controversial bitterness aroused by the Elementary Education Act, it is curious to observe that my patients and their friends, almost without exception, are not so much indifferent to the dogmas of religion, as unconscious of their existence. Even Roman Catholics have asked for my prayers. On the lips of all who are seriously ill I hear but one name, and notwithstanding the strong influence that one would imagine to be exercised on this point by Salvationists, revival meetings, and popular hymns, that name is the First Person of the Trinity. So far from it being possible to detect the special teaching of this or that sect, the phrases that they utter might come with equal propriety from Jew, Mohammedan, Christian, or Hindoo. At other times paucity of language and uncouth expressions exaggerate differences of faith, or create fresh ones. " My religion ain't in these parts," I was told by one very intelligent woman. I listened respectfully, secretly wondering to what strange sect she could belong that found no other adherents in a town of 200,000 inhabitants. I subsequently learnt that the only meaning in the statement was that she had been in the habit of attending the parish church, but having moved beyond walking distance was no longer able to do so.

Few of those who fling themselves into the conflict as to what religious instruction should be given in primary schools, seem to be aware that enormous numbers of children, unblamed by parents, teachers, or ministers, are in the habit of attending chapel Sunday schools in the morning and church Sunday schools in the afternoon, and no doubts or difficulties seem to be roused in the scholars' minds. In many parishes this goes on until the children are of an age to be confirmed, at which period they are expected to cease attendance at one school or the other.

There is a curious anxiety among the least educated of the poor to secure the services of the vicar or rector in times of severe illness, however little they may like him, in preference to those of the curate, however earnest and devoted he may be, and even if he should happen to be considerably older and more experienced. It is partly due, no doubt, to the same feeling that makes a pillow laid in place by a ward sister infinitely more restful than the same pillow arranged by the kindest and most skilful nurse; but there is also some idea of superior sanctity in the office of a beneficed clergyman,—a doubt which, strangely enough, never attaches to the position of pastor, however young he may be, or however obscure the sect to which he belongs.

One obvious superiority of Nonconformist ministers in the eyes of the poor is their trained ability to offer up prayers which are at once full of the soothing and customary religious phraseology, and yet have some clear bearing on the cases in question, a power which is to a great extent developed in all earnest Dissenters, and which is commonly too much neglected by the clergy of the Established Church. I shall never forget the dull hopelessness with which a dying man listened to an excellent clergyman "reading prayers," and the comfort and spiritual joy that shone afterwards on his face when a young barber's assistant, hearing of his hour of need, came in hastily, with his apron still round him, dropped on his knees by the bedside, and uttered a long but simple and heartfelt prayer that at eventide there might be light.

The fear of death endured by this man is very rare among the poor. It is rather the certain hope of death that makes life tolerable to them both in its bitterest moments and in its long-drawn-out struggles against weakness, poverty, ill-health, and sin. Often what is called their callousness to the sight of death should rather be traced to envy of those who are dead and at peace. Have they shed few tears ? For themselves they wish none to fall.

Heaven is something real, almost tangible, to the poor. " Mother," said a little man of six, worn out with more physical suffering than most of us are called on to endure in a life of ten times the length,—" mother, I want to die." " You can't, Willy. There's—there's—no room for you yet." " How can you say so, mother ? Just look how big the sky is !" Yes, the streets were cruelly narrow, the rooms tiny, the gardens a mockery, but mercifully the houses were low, and in the sky he had found his symbol of infinite space and freedom.

3

Here and there the doctrine of hell-fire (for others) is clung to with fierce intensity. I said once to a vigorous and clear-minded though long bedridden woman of seventy-six: "You tell me that your mother was good to you, and that you loved her; you tell me that you are 'saved,' and she was *not*. What happiness, then, can there be for you in heaven?"

"Oh, nurse, when I'm in heaven I shall be so purr-fected I shan't care *where* she is!" This may be religion, but it seemed to me an intensified form of "Every man for himself and the devil take the hindmost."

Old age, with its ample leisure for reflection, generally brings toleration.

"I had a great deal of talk with the vicar yesterday," said another patient, "and I told him I didn't see as the *name* of a religion mattered. They were all roads leading to the same kingdom, and not many of us had the choosing which road we'd start on."

"And what did the vicar say?"

"Nothing,—nothing at all."

I thought it commendable prudence, for even if he had reached that point of view himself, there were many thoughtful persons in that alley who had not, and open agreement with her would have caused them much mental distress.

It is not always possible to make sufficient allowance for weaker brethren, however careful one may be. A friend of mine lent a well-known *Life of Christ* to a man whose reading was entirely confined to religious works. He returned it to her with an air of deep-seated displeasure and injury.

"It says, miss, that Christ wasn't born on Christmas Day."

"Yes, I remember the passage."

"Well, miss," with wrath modified only by satisfaction in his powers as a logician and a theologian, "if Christ wasn't born on Christmas Day, then I don't see where there's any truth in the Bible at all!"

A very respectable old carpenter told me: "I was brought up a Presbyterian, and a Presbyterian I've stayed; but I sometimes think"—his words slow and weighty with unexpressed reasons—"that if I had to begin all over again, I dunno but what I'd be a Piskypalian. I'm getting on for seventy, but I'll tell you what I've never seen, though, mind you, I don't say it ain't to be found. I've never seen a family where three generations belonged to the same kind of chapel. I brought my children up Presbyterians same as I was taught myself, but as soon as they was old enough to choose, every one of them turned to be Piskypalians."

Another patient living with her widowed sister was afraid I might think their difference in religion a flaw in their otherwise perfect friendship, and said apologetically: "You see, m'm, my sister goes where she's always gone, and it's natural she should; but as for me, I feel I must go *where I edify most*."

It appears to me that men are more frequently "converted" than women, who rarely wander far from their early faith, whatever its form. On one occasion we had been attending a woman and a young infant. The family was very poor, and the husband, who was an ardent Salvationist, gave every farthing that could be spared to the support of the Army. The wife consented gladly to these sacrifices, for some of its members had redeemed him from the curse of drunkenness, and she felt that she could never repay the debt of gratitude that she owed the association. When the child was a few weeks old, she rejoiced her husband's heart by allowing it to be " passed under the flag." Not knowing of this, I asked her soon after: " Has baby been christened yet ? "

" Yes, lady ; he'd been 'under the flag,' but I've little heart with such ways, and so, unbeknown to my husband, I took him to church. The stifficate is hid behind that there picture frame. My husband must never know it."

It has always seemed to me that the seed of natural religion which I believe to exist in every heart needs, owing to individual differences in intellect and character, a variety of soils if all natures are to develop in full strength and beauty, and that therefore the ministers of every form of faith should be welcomed. The special dogmas of this or that sect may seem repellent or grotesque, but nevertheless they are the only forms in which strength and peace can be conveyed to certain hearts.

The desire for a different religious atmosphere sometimes shows itself strangely early. I was speaking recently to two poorly-dressed boys of eleven and six.

The elder, a dreamy-looking child, told me he was in the choir of a certain church that I knew to be Roman Catholic. I turned to his brother, and asked him if he also was being trained for the choir. "*Me!* I'm a *Protestant.*"

It may seem incredible, but although these boys were at an age when normal children take no genuine, independent interest in religion, I believe that each had already adopted the form that corresponded to his inward need, and would probably hold to it throughout his life.

The following story presents a branch of the vestments question in as ludicrous a form as its worst enemies could wish. An acquaintance of mine, the wife of a west-country vicar, was making arrangements for the annual school treat, and interviewed a Punch and Judy man. Hours and terms had been settled, and she turned to go, when he said—

"Beg pardon, mum, there's one question I'd ought to ask. Is the treat High Church or Low Church?"

"But what difference *can* that make?"

"It makes *this* difference, mum," with an air of stiff reproof for her culpable ignorance, "If it's Low Church, Judy's pall has to be plain black, but if it's *High* I always use one with a violet border."

As I never introduce the subject of religion, I hear little of it from children, but one day a child told me—

"Everyone's got to be good, Caff-licks and Proddy-stans too."

"Where did you learn that?"

" At school."

I thought that if that was a fair specimen of the religious instruction given, we could well afford to pay for it. "Conscientious objectors" can have very little conception of the feebleness and inefficiency of most of the teaching in Sunday schools of every denomination, and the misdirection of a large percentage of the more skilled and zealous instruction. To know the first, one need only scan the list of teachers, listen to a few of their lessons, or take temporary charge of one of their classes.

The following may perhaps be an extreme instance of misdirection, but will show what is meant better than a less glaring example.

A London clergyman had a large class of boys, and one Sunday about nine years ago, when clerical feeling was running rather high on the point, he made them a vehement and impassioned address upon the validity of Anglican Orders and the attitude taken by the Pope. The lads had some liking for him, and maintained a decent pretence of listening. Finally he appealed to them for their " opinion." The star of the class tried to rise to the occasion.

" Father says, ' Never take no orders excep' from the boss.' He says he lost his job once juss through doing it."

The only extenuating circumstance is, that unless that eager Anglican had related the story himself, no one could ever have known it.

Sabbatarianism still forms a strong feature in the less

spiritual forms of religion.   Quite recently we were very short of nurses, and I went myself one Sunday morning to see a woman whom I knew to be in urgent need of attendance of a kind that could not possibly be given by her relatives.

"What! do you work on Sundays?" was her scandalised question.

"We do, when it seems necessary."

"You haythan! Have you never been taught? I'd die before I did it!"

Another woman, who was entirely confined to one room, was speaking to a visitor about the duty of strict observation of the Sabbath, and the lady asked her how she marked the day, considering that she was obliged to do what was really necessary for herself Sundays and week-days alike, and never had strength to do any more, and read the church service and the Bible every morning and evening of her life.

"Do you see that geranium on the windy-sill, miss? It wants a lot of water, it do. Well, I never gives it none of a Sunday."

The association to which I belong is strictly un-sectarian, but as a rule the name of a patient's religion is entered in our books. We can generally learn it without asking any question, but in one house the nurses were totally unable to decide the point, although they had been in constant attendance for many weeks. No minister of any denomination had entered the place, no religious books of any kind were visible, no opening was ever given that would supply an excuse for a question on the subject. The patient was a man of notoriously bad character, but he had always behaved quietly and decently, and naturally they were unwilling to do anything that might annoy him.

At the termination of the case I called at the house, and, after casting round in vain for any clue to his nominal religion, I asked—

" Are you a Roman Catholic ? "

" Sooper," he replied with unction, " I'm the same religion as yerself. I goes about doing good to everyone, and no harm to myself."

I will not say under which heading I entered him.

In popular history the Roman Catholic Church is the one and only persecutor, and among a large section of the English poor it is greatly feared, and any supposed approach towards its practices is viewed with shrinking disapprobation. " Mind you," said a woman to me a few months ago, almost blocking the doorway, " I wouldn't never let none of you in, not if you had no religious ambles."

" Quite right, quite right," I said vaguely, as I slipped quickly in to the invalid, for fear closer scrutiny should reveal anything unsatisfactory in my gait. In the process of attending to her manifold needs, it suddenly dawned upon me that the things deprecated were *emblems*.

At the same time, the Roman Catholics are the one religious body in England to which members ever fear to own their allegiance. The Anglican, the Jew, the Salvationist, the Bible Christian, the Christadelphian, the Catholic Apostolic, hasten to inform me of their special shades of belief; but if I see reason to think that any poor person is a Roman Catholic, I dare not put a direct question for fear of meeting with a hasty denial. When it is necessary to know, I have to ask some question that takes the leading fact for granted. "How long is it since Father L. was here? Is it Father Z. who visits in this parish?" We pride ourselves on being a tolerant nation, but such timidity looks like the result of very recent persecution. I have lately been told by a lady working in a large midland town: "My experience is the same as yours. Several times when I have seen things that led me to believe that poor people were my co-religionists, I have asked the question, and received an evasive reply. When I say, 'I am Roman Catholic myself,' they acknowledge it readily."

Two cases of petty persecution and its effects have come under my notice. A young Jew said to me: "If Jews were not persecuted, I do not at all know that I should be a Jew; but as long as they are, what choice have I but to remain one?"

A little boy of a slightly superior class, who had suffered much at the hands of his schoolfellows, told me—

"I hate being a Jew."

"Oh, you must be proud of your ancient race."

"Ancient race?" scoffed the child,—"all the more time to learn our beastly old tricks!" and he pretended to slip the tablespoons up his sleeve. I knew that in a

few years' time he would probably reach the same point
as the elder lad, but it was sad to see personal and racial
pride undermined.

A curious story of his early childhood was told me by
a young French Jew. " When I was five years old, a
neighbour died, and I asked who had killed him, for I
had no idea of death except as a thing caused by
soldiers. I was told that it was God's doing. I said
nothing, but I was horrified. I went into the kitchen
and took the carving knife to kill God, because He had
killed that man. I had been told that God was "everywhere," so I drove the knife several times into the outer
side of the front door. I felt satisfied that I had
performed a good action, that I had very well frightened
God, and He would do so no more."

Detailed criticisms of sermons are rare, but a rather
keen-witted woman, who had been in service before her
marriage, said to me one day : " Mr. —— never preaches
but of two things, money and death. We haven't got so
much money that anyone need be troubled about it, and
we're none of us afraid to die " ; while of another clergyman she remarked : " We like him very much, but I
should think he'd preached to pore people all his time :
he talks so loud."

Few things are more touching, and at the same time
more encouraging to all really capable and zealous
instructors of the young, than to find how the lessons
learnt at Sunday schools and Bible classes are remembered and valued in later life. Quite recently an
old woman wrote down for me from memory a religious

poem which had been taught to her nearly seventy years before, and which she said she "had always thought of." Her recollections of what she wore, and what the teacher wore, were so keen that I can picture exactly the bright-eyed, spasmodically attentive little creature she was, and what small hope the teacher had that she was doing anything more than temporarily and imperfectly "keeping her out of mischief."

"Lady Sister, will you read to me?" said a merchant seaman dying a lingering and painful death in a London hospital. I asked what I should read. "Read 'There's a Friend for little children.'" I knew something of a sailor's life, and the experiences that probably lay between him and the days when he repeated "Hymns for the Young," but for him all that intervened had been swept away.

A year or two ago I said to a mother, four of whose children had been removed to hospital suffering with typhoid fever, while the three youngest were being nursed at home with the same complaint: "You are having a terrible time of work and anxiety, and it seems to me to make it all the worse to know that the disease was contracted at the factory. You have always kept their home so beautifully for them." "Yes," she said simply, "it's been a hard time, but I've had much comfort in my own mind. Many of the things that I learnt at school, and which had no great meaning to me then, all come back to me now, and it's been a wonderful help." Not long since I met an old woman in the street and inquired after her grandchild, a girl of fourteen, who had developed rapid consumption, and was told that she had died a few days previously. She mentioned the special reasons that the mother had for regretting her loss, the child's beauty and intelligence, the only girl in the family, and just of an age to begin to be useful, adding that the poor woman had recently had a severe internal operation which made the necessary work for husband and sons a heavy burden. Her sole comment at the end, and I thought it a beautiful one in its courageous resignation, was : " Ah, her mother has all she can do to *keep herself above it*."

One day a speechless and paralysed lodging-house keeper pointed to her prayer-book, and signed that she wished me to read to her. I held the volume before her, while with the one hand over which she retained some control she found the portion she wished to hear. It was the *Benedicite Omnia Opera*. As she lay there in the pretentious " best-bedroom " of the house she had so laboriously furnished, it seemed to me an even greater triumph of faith than that of another bedridden sufferer in a wretched cottage on a wind-swept moor three miles away, often left half the day while her feeble old husband toiled into the town to fetch their few necessaries, but who told me with solemn gladness : " I am never alone."

Faith in the efficacy of prayer is very strong among the poor. Recently, at the end of a historic commission, a petty officer, distinguished among brave men for quiet, instinctive heroism, said to his mother, one of my patients : " I served Long Thomas all the time, and I never got a scratch. Were you praying for me? I _knew_ you were." And I was equally certain that the mother's faith in prayer was of such a nature that it would have been no whit shaken if at the end of one of those terrible days her son had been counted among the dead.

I speak of spiritual religion among the poor, merely to imply that it has little need of outward ceremonies, for it is a religion which takes not only the form of submission, or the nobler one of fortitude, but of every-day effort and selflessness throughout a lifetime of poverty, suffering, toil, and deprivation. It is a religion which makes devoted parents say to one another over the deathbed of their only child, " It is the will of God "; a religion which enables a woman of eighty-four years, filled with hardship and good works, to bear a death of slow agony with unbroken sweetness and serenity; and a religion which made the landlady and her husband, though she could only pay them a tiny pittance, wait on her day and night, absolutely refusing to allow her to be removed to the workhouse infirmary.

For six years I have watched the unfailing patience and courage of a woman who, during the whole of that time, has been nursing a paralysed and unconscious husband, has been responsible day and night for an epileptic step-daughter, whose conduct is so violent that we dare not leave our cloaks in the room with her lest she should tear them to pieces, and who has had to eke out their scanty means by poorly paid sewing. I do not know of a single outward pleasure or relief that she has enjoyed. It was only last week that she told me for the first time the source of her strength to fulfil an unceasing round of repulsive duties. She said: " Every one of my trials is sent to me by God. It is my duty to bear them and do the best I can." There are people who do not hesitate to class her as irreligious because she never enters a church, and immoral because there are doubts as to the validity of her marriage, and it is probable that neither the paralytic nor his afflicted daughter has any legal claim upon her.

Many years' experience of the poorest of the respectable poor have convinced me that deep and true religion is commonly found among them, the chief tenets of which are: The existence of a Supreme Being intimately concerned with the life of men, and best served by loving faithfulness to the homeliest duties; the spiritual efficacy of prayer, and triumphant faith in the immortality of the soul.

CHAPTER III

THE CHILDREN OF THE POOR

"A CHILD exists not for the very poor as any object of dalliance; it is only another mouth to be fed, a pair of little hands to be betimes inured to labour. It is the rival till it can be the co-operator for food with the parent. It is never his mirth, his diversion, his solace; it never makes him young again with recalling his young times. The children of the very poor have no young times. It makes the very heart bleed to overhear the casual street-talk between a poor woman and her little girl, a woman of the better sort of poor, in a condition rather above the squalid beings which we have been contemplating. . . . It is of mangling and clear-starching, of the price of coals or of potatoes. The questions of the child, that should be the very outpourings of curiosity in idleness, are marked with forecast and melancholy providence. It has come to be a woman before it was a child. It has learned to go to market; it chaffers, it haggles, it envies, it murmurs, it is knowing, acute, sharpened; it never prattles. Had we not reason to say that the home of the very poor is no home?"

I had been reading these words of Charles Lamb,

and others yet more poignant, when I met a woman whose husband earns on an average rather less than a guinea a week, and who has seven children, five of them wholly dependent on their parents, and one of them a hopeless invalid. Without any leading up to it on my part, she repeated some remarks that had been made by the two youngest girls with the keenest appreciation of their unconscious humour.

The following instance of naïveté was related to me with great delight by a former patient. A few days previously she had told her little boy, aged five, to say "Not at home" if anyone called, and then retired to take a bath. Soon after, the fire insurance agent knocked at the door.

"Mother at home, sonny?"

"No, sir; mother's not at home."

"When will she be at home?"

"I'll run and ask her, sir," said the little fellow obligingly, and, trotting down the passage, he tapped at the kitchen door, inquiring: "Mother, please when will you be at home?"

The agent laughed, and passed on to his next client without waiting for a reply.

This is only a typical case; most of my little friends are young, and their parents rejoice in their youth, shield it, and try to prolong it. The point of all the stories related to me by poor parents is never precocity, but almost invariably naïve ignorance. In fact, I am constantly struck by the babyishness of the children of artisans and the better class of labourers as compared with the children of professional men.

There is scarcely a home so poor that no one in it rejoices over the birth of a child; scarcely a family so poverty-stricken that every child in it cannot tell you its birthday, and does not expect some little gift, or at least some sign of favour and indulgence, on the anniversary.

"I shall be nine on Toosday," said a little girl who often bestows her companionship on me.

"And what will happen then?"

"Well, nothing don't happen, not *gen'ally*. You see, twelve is such a many of us; it's one a month! But when it was Chris's birfday mother give him a piece of tart to his tea; so perhaps"—

She would not tell me her expectations, but for once reality outsoared imagination, for I heard the following week that the "happenings" had been, "a silver thrup'ny and a penny and a halfpenny and a doll what isn't dressed, not yet, and a piece of cake." Moreover (it seemed to rank next the thrup'ny in her estimation), "Mother had let her off a hiding," which, to judge from her own account, was tolerably well deserved. But although she is a moderately truthful child, I find it necessary to swallow many grains of salt both with tales of her peccadilloes and of the swift recompense with which they meet. Set midway between half a dozen obstinate and turbulent boys, and being by nature timid and orderly, she can only keep up a proper sense of her courage, importance, and general unmanageableness

4

by making the most of any small sins that she plucks up heart to commit, or of any stray slaps that fall to her share.

It must be remarked that in all fairly well regulated homes the father may not strike any of the children without the mother's consent, and it is rarely given except in the case of boys above the age of eleven or twelve. "Where is Tom this morning?" I asked his little sister. "He's doing a day in bed. Father told him to do some weeding yes'day, and he told mother he'd done it, so mother let him go out to play. And then when father went to look this morning, he found none of it wasn't done, so he give him a clump on his head and pulled his clothes off and put him to bed. Mother was very angry with father. She said father might have knocked him silly slapping him on the head; he'd ought to have took a stick to him and put it about his back. But she's going to make him do another day in bed to-morrow if he doesn't do the weeding same as father told him. He's a dreadful one for cheek."

It will be noted that the boy's deliberate falsehood to suit his own ends drew no remark from his sister, and presumably none from his parents. It is a sad fact that "cheek" heads the list of childish sins, and that the acknowledgment of a fault comes under this heading. Not only ignorant parents, but often persons of whom one might fairly say that they ought to know better, will roar angrily at a small culprit: " Do you dare to tell me that you did it?"

Indirect checks are sometimes put upon tne father. "Gertie wont get the first prize at the Sunday school, not this year," said an affectionate elder sister regretfully.

"How is that?"

"She was cheeky to mother, and she's been locked up in the children's bedroom all day, so she missed an attendance. When I go to bed I shall tell her it wasn't none of mother's doing, not *reely*. Mother would have let her off easier, but being Sunday father was at home, and he heard what she said, and mother locked her up to keep father from thrashing her. Mother don't mind their being beaten a *little* when they deserve it, but she says father's hand is too heavy, and he don't know when to leave off. Mother doesn't hold with frightening them, and if they once gets *hardened,* she says the more you beat them the more you may. But I shall let on to Gertie as it wasn't her doing, for it's almost certain to lose her the prize, and she'll be in an awful taking about it."

One day of unusual leisure I told the story of Red Riding Hood to two little sisters aged four and six, belonging to a class slightly above most of my patients.

"Have you telled it to me *all?*" asked the elder when I had finished,—"then tell it again."

I did so; there was deep silence for a few seconds, and then the younger one drawled out slowly—

"What betame of the poo-er old 'oolf?"

"He died."

"Did they eat him?"

"No; people do not eat wolves. I think they buried him."

"Did they put flowers on his gwave?"

"No, no; he was a very bad old wolf; everyone was glad when he was dead; he ate the poor old grand-mother." The elder child looked at me regretfully, "*Weren't there any more old grand-mums?*"

I tried to explain that things could not be valued strictly according to their scarcity, but to the end of her days (ah, how short!) she regretted the 'oolf's untimely fate.

Another child of four was fascinated by the tale of the Three Bears. Every time she saw me I was begged to repeat it. Noticing that during the almost daily recital she kept her eyes fixed on a picture of some boys playing football, I wondered what connection there was in her mind between the two, and finally asked her, "What are bears?" With the level tones of a person perfectly sure of her facts, she replied, "Bears is little boys."

It is always a mistake to push one's inquiries too far. An elderly relative of mine asked a little boy, the son of an artificer, if he were not sorry for the recent death of his sister, a child a year younger than himself. Un-fortunately she was so much pleased with his fervent "Yes" that she continued the conversation.

"And why are you so sorry?"

"She used to eat the crusts, and I've got to do it now!"

One day in Paris a little girl of four was brought to

see me by her young parents. I knew that she could
not possibly wish to come, for there was a merry-go-
round of leaping white rabbits in an opposite direction
which possessed her entire heart for the time being, and
I produced several little presents as a small consolation.
On leaving, the mother asked her pointedly—

"Are you not glad that you came to see
mademoiselle?"

"Oui, maman," replied the poor little mite dutifully,
but with a most excusable lack of enthusiasm.

"And why are you glad?" prompted the proud
father.

She turned mutinous under the cross-fire—

"*Parce qu'il—parce qu'il fallait.*"

I am sorry to add that the mother shook her and the
father roared at her until she consented to mutter the
correct formula: "Because mademoiselle is always so
kind." It was a lesson in hypocrisy, and I trust she
forgot it.

Increasing refinement of manners among the poor
leads to stories of a kind that used to be told many
years ago of those considerably above them in position.
A woman with half a dozen young children asked a
friend to tea, and for the first time placed a complete
set of china on the table, including a slop-basin. The
children stared to see the use to which it was put, and
presently one of them so thirsted for information that
she was obliged to ask: "Mammy, why don't you throw
the grouts in the grate, same as you always does?"

I often try to extract definitions from my little friends,

but as soon as they have reached a self-conscious age it is extremely difficult to obtain any. Hearing two children of five and seven using the word " dead," I asked : " How do you know what is dead and what is not ? "

" Because you *do !* " said one impatiently, but the elder had more pity on my ignorance, and replied—

" When you do things to things and they do nothing to you, *then* they're dead."

Another little girl, possibly ten, who certainly can never have heard of the infinite divisibility of matter, told me that she had been thinking for a long time, and that she had discovered that "you could cut things into two pieces for ever and ever, because the half of *something* can't be *nothing*."

I found a child of four seriously puzzling herself over the cause of bodily heat. She had observed that either thick bedclothes or the fire made *her* feel warm, and was astonished to find that only the latter affected her doll. She drew the attention of a slightly younger cousin to the mystery, and piled clothing on the doll to prove to the latter that it could not be warmed in this way.

Another girl of seven afforded me a curious instance of confusion between cause and effect. She asked me why a certain old person was blind. I hesitated, not knowing what reason to give her, when the child suddenly exclaimed : " *I* know why ! She's blind because she can't-walk well. I knew a blind man before, and *he* walked like that, all slow and shuffly."

In a town which shall be nameless, fond fathers are in the habit of teaching their sons not merely to fight, but to kick, and I have often seen babies of twenty months overbalance themselves in carrying out the paternal instructions. One day I witnessed a struggle between a boy of three and one perhaps eight or ten months younger, but unusually warlike. It began in play, but the vigorous junior struck too hard, and the elder had raised fist and foot to "give him what for," when a boy of five or six left off munching his bread and jam to say pityingly : "Don't kick him, Jimmy ! He's got no father."

Jimmy vaguely understood that this was an appeal for generosity, dropped his heavily booted little foot and turned away, but the enraged baby evidently interpreted the words as an unusually effective threat, for he followed his adversary up until he reached a corner beyond which he dared not go, uttering truculent yells of "Is got no farver, no *farver !*"

I am often struck by the girlish gentleness of many boys to their younger brothers and sisters. Not long ago I saw two little fellows, the eldest can hardly have been six, walking together on a very windy day. The younger one's hat was fastened by an elastic under his chin, but had blown to the back of his neck. The careful brother observed it, and, backing to the wind with his legs very wide apart, he rearranged it, saying sweetly : "Billy, I can *always* put your hat right. Mind you tell me *always* when you want things done."

A boy of ten had been living for three years with his German grandmother, who had supplied him with a wardrobe which his poor mother could not afford to throw away when he returned to her, whatever the child suffered from the jeers of his school-fellows. The hats were, as always, the chief points of offence, and during many weeks of bitter mortification he had been saving laboriously earned pence to buy himself a cap of the orthodox shape. Returning from school one day, he found his mother in tears, and anxiously asked what had happened. She told him that "the School Board man" had called, that his two sisters would have to enter their names on the following Monday, and that she did not even know how she could get decent pinafores to cover their shabby little frocks. Without an instant's hesitation the boy fetched his money-box and emptied it on her lap, saying, in his grave German-English: "I need it not, mother. Kitty and Bessi eare young and small, and I would not that anyone should mock at them."

Unhappily the end of the story, if such a generous action could have an end, is that the worthless father entered at that moment, and confiscated the money, telling the little lad roughly: "I give your mother plenty. She can get your sisters all they want."

There are equally hard hearts to be found. A London boy of fourteen, reproved for too openly enjoying himself at the heavy meal that followed his father's funeral, replied in self-justifying tones: "I don't get a beano like this every day."

Although beauty is rare, the average of good looks among poor people's children is high, and under the increasingly favourable circumstances in which the majority of them live, they tend to retain their good looks much later than they formerly did.

I remember being told by an Englishman who had lived thirteen years in China: "Chinese children are just as pretty as any others. It is not until they are eleven or twelve that they turn ugly." I often think of this with reference to the children of the very poor, for by that time bad boots, insufficient clothing, innutritious food, strong soaps and neglected teeth have generally undermined their original claims to beauty.

The poor as a rule seem insensitive to all forms of personal beauty except the most ordinary childish prettiness. I was looking at a baby one day, and its mother said: "It's not old enough to look very nice to anyone but me just yet." I replied: "Oh, it will be as pretty as the other two before long." She exclaimed in genuine surprise: "You don't call Gladys pretty, surely? Now Rosie I *do* think pretty, but Gladys has such a funny little face."

Rosie, as it happened, was just the ordinary tow-headed, pale blue-eyed, snub-nosed, rosy-cheeked type that one sees in every street by the dozen; while Gladys, with her upright figure and graceful movements, her dark grey eyes, exquisitely modelled features and delicately tinted complexion, was a child of the rarest loveliness. The lack of appreciation sprang from no want of affection on the mother's part, for though convinced that she was plain, if not ugly, she dwelt constantly on the child's daring, cleverness, and charm.

Another beautiful child of the dark-haired olive

complexioned type spent a large part of her time in lying in wait for me, and then trotting by my side as I went from one case to another. In the poorer parts of the town she never attracted even a passing glance, but in the wealthier quarters every third or fourth head was turned to look at her, and people often crossed the road to observe her more closely.

This extreme insensitiveness to personal appearance has often made me feel pangs of doubt when I hear that this or that prisoner has been "identified" by women of the poorer classes and condemned, chiefly on their testimony, to penal servitude. These persons have no lack of words, and if utterly unable to describe what they expect to see, how can we believe in their power to recognise it when they see it? As an example of their usual inability to describe appearance : I had often heard of a certain man, and had repeatedly asked poor women who knew him well, and who were by no means wanting in general intelligence, to tell me what he was like. The only definite ideas that they gave me were that he was taller than themselves—not one of my informants being above five feet two—"and not just what you might call young." I concluded that he must be one of the many persons of whom it is said, "he would pass in a crowd." At last he was pointed out to me by a friend, and, to my astonishment, I found that he was .extraordinarily tall and thin, bolt upright and a very rapid walker, that he had eyebrows on which a marble might have rested, was completely bald except for a narrow fringe of dark hair, and in addition he was weirdly ugly. Not one of these features had made the smallest impression on these women, or on their husbands and brothers. How then could they have been reasonably expected to discern the difference between one commercial traveller and another six months after a single interview ?

I once visited a patient who was not seriously ill, and was most certainly in full possession of all her faculties. I remained about half an hour, making necessary arrangements, and on leaving told her that I should send a nurse in the course of the afternoon to give the attendance of which she was in need. It happened that no nurse was available, and I went myself, dressed in precisely the same clothes that I had worn in the morning. To my bewilderment, I was given a detailed, and on the whole accurate, account of the visit that " the superintendent " had paid her. An observant child shyly whispered, " It's the same lady," but the mother scouted the notion. " The superintendent was far and away taller, and she's very nice looking, and has such a superior voice. That's a thing I always take note of. I hope she's kind to you, miss ? Of course, people isn't always as pleasant as you'd think, first seeing them." I assured her that I had no special reason for complaint.

Policemen are the usual bogeys for little boys, and are generally regarded as implacable, deaf to the entreaties and pie-crust promises that so soon soften a mother's anger, but one small district friend of mine evidently thought he had plucked the heart out of their mystery. His response to his mother's time-honoured threat, " I shall call in the policeman, and what'll you do then ? " was the cheerful and confident assertion, " I'll say, Mr. Peeseman, have a nice dint of bee-ar ? "

At the present day the ordinary speech of even the poorest children is wonderfully free from all blasphemy and coarseness. Strangely enough, when one hears oaths they come from the lips of mere babies. A few weeks ago a child of scarcely three lisped some words which were quite unintelligible to me until a nine-year-old sister gave the key by angrily shaking her by the arm and saying threateningly : " Don't you get swearing where I am ! "

Even in the worst neighbourhoods many children are brought up in great innocency. I have known mothers who, contrary to the usual custom of poor people, put all their children to bed at six so that they might be asleep " before the language begins." At an astonishingly early age they learn to distinguish what words may and what may not be repeated. The mother of a child of three told me, " She often swears in her sleep until I don't know whether to laugh or cry," but in her waking hours no little lady in the land could have been more precise.

" What do you think Florrie done to me one day ? " said a little girl who frequently tacked herself on to me in the street; " she asked me if I could spell ' mad ' backwards, and I *did !* "

I tried to look intelligent, but I had so obviously missed the point of the tale that she explained, " And so she had made me spell a bad word, but I hadn't *said* it."

One thing that makes it easier than it used to be for children to avoid bad language, is the increase in their vocabulary. I saw five or six little ragamuffins playing together in a London park. " Let's cross that rustic bridge," said one, and they clattered over. I could not help wondering what adjective would have been used by children in their position a few years previously.

One of the most pitiable sights I ever saw was a boy of four, born and bred in a very low street, and suddenly attacked by incurable blindness. The unhappy child was convinced sometimes that he was blindfolded, sometimes that he was in a dark room, and would implore his mother to uncover his eyes or to light the lamp; presently the entreaties would turn to a storm of rage, and all the oaths and foul language that had ever fallen on his ears were poured out with horrible fluency. It was heartrending.

Great are the struggles of respectable mothers with bad next-door neighbours. " I shall have to move, whatever it costs, if *they* don't," said one of these. " I can't tell you how often I didn't have to slap baby last week for the things she was saying; just what she catches up like a parrot when she hears 'em quarrelling, as they'll do sometimes by the hour together. It do seem a shame, but how else can I learn her ? And there's Victoria, too. Last Friday when she come home from school I had to take and give her a real good whipping, a thing I don't do once in a blue moon. I'm sure it's three years since I'd laid a finger on her, if it was a day. Poor little soul, I don't believe she knew a bit what she was saying, not any more than Alexandra does, but at nine years old she'd ought to have some *feeling* for words, so I give her something to remember. I smacked her arms till she fair danced. But it's very hard on the children, and it's hard on me too. Her little arms was boiling hot an hour after."

Fathers, even when hasty tempered (a failing less common among manual labourers than in the professional classes) are as a rule careful in the language they use before their children. "Father has the gout dreadful bad," said a daughter of eighteen, "but he never swears, not before the younger ones, I mean." She was one of those rare girls both of whose parents are always right, and something in her tone impossible to reproduce implied that to hear him was a privilege of which the little ones were not yet worthy.

This restraint is not always exercised towards the wife. A girl of about the same age, wishing to express what very bad language a groom had used to her mother when she had transmitted an unwelcome order to him from his master, said: "Mother hadn't never heard such language. Why, father wouldn't have used it to her!"

The children's manners are often surprisingly good. A small boy calling by invitation at my house was attacked with great noise and well simulated fury by a mischievous fox-terrier. I was trying to console him for his fright, when, with lips still trembling with nervousness, he said, " Oh, lady, he's a *lovely* house dog." Could any practised courtier have done more ?

In comparing elder brothers and sisters among the poor and among the middle and upper classes, I notice one great difference : instead of reproaching the younger ones with the greater indulgence with which they are treated, they are nearly always convinced that their own childhood was happier. " Although mother and father is such a sight better off than they was when me and Lizzie and Tom was young, the little ones don't get a scrap more than we used to have, and they haven't a book or a toy except what me and Lizzie have given them. Father often brought us home things, and took us out summer evenings a lot more than he does them."

Again : " I can't think what's come to mother. She took the copper-stick to Janey to-day. Of course she's tiresome, but we was all that, but I can't remember her ever taking anything worse than her hand to us. We didn't mind that, we thought it hurt her too ; but a stick doesn't seem fair."

Another girl told me : " I used to cheek mother dreadful myself, 'spesh'ly over having to mind Lily. Lily is a lot better with the little ones than ever I was. Some takes to babies and some doesn't. If ever mother aims to give one of the little ones a slap, they'll always run behind Lily. Mother always makes the eldest at home mind the youngest. Now, Aunt Maria she has two big girls, and one of them hates children, so Aunt Maria always lets her do nothing but housework.

Mother says it isn't right of her, because they'll all have children one day, and they'd ought to learn; but Aunt Maria says: "If Louie's going to make *her* children miserable, that's no reason why she should smack *mine*, and sour their tempers as well as hers.' But of course it's all how you look on it."

The younger the children in charge, the greater their faith in "smacking." A little boy of about eighteen months one day threw a stone at me, and was promptly slapped by his sister of nine. "He *is* wicked," she said, "he's so hardened; but we smacks him, and he do get better. There *is* them as don't smack 'em, but it don't never answer." Perhaps she knew her business, for five minutes after he made me a voluntary peace-offering in the shape of a green leaf which he picked and pushed into my hand.

Another little girl offered to sing me "The Pilot," and wandered rather wildly from the tune. "If you sings out of tune at school you gets hit with the pointer," she remarked parenthetically. "That is rather hard measure." "Yes, but it gets you on with your singing."

I saw two little boys gazing at a board recently put up in the forecourt of a school of the type that exists in neighbourhoods where people will pay ninepence or a shilling a week for their younger children, considering the Board School too rough for them until they are seven or eight.

"What does it say?" asked the most unlettered. His companion began boldly, but "Preparatory School for

Young Gentlemen" was too much for him, and he abandoned the effort. "Smack school; that's what it *means*!" he said succinctly.

Compulsory education has had a great effect on the vocabulary of the poor, and has swept away many differences of pronunciation, but errors in grammar are perhaps as frequent as ever. Outside two of the oldest Board Schools in England, situated more than a hundred miles apart, I have heard the following and many similar phrases: Us be going. Her don't belong to we. I seed father, but father didn't saw I. Her know'd I.

Mistakes of this kind are no doubt stereotyped by the home teaching.

" See they flowers !" cried a little village girl.

" They flowers !" mocked the mother tenderly; " you'd oughter say '*them* flowers,' same as like what I does." The child, much abashed, repeated the amended form.

There are strange gaps in the vocabulary of town children. I once took an intelligent little boy of nearly seven, the son of an artisan, into a public park. He gazed with silent rapture at three white ducks swimming over the lake, and then suddenly plucked my dress and shouted: "Look at that angel over there, he's tucking his leg under his wing !" He had been a regular attendant at Sunday school, and had never seen any bird but a sparrow. He knew no word for garden, and when I spoke of a hill he evidently had not the faintest idea where to look, nor what he should see.

A few months earlier, his elder sister, who had

5

reached some giddy height in " Standards," was telling
me the results of a recent examination.

" *We* had one too ! " he broke in jealously.

" Oh, for shame, Tom !—you *are* a story ! What was
it in, I'd like to know ? "

" It was a zamynation in sitting still."

Any deliberate attempt to collect the opinions and
sayings of children in order to use them to pierce the
hearts or open the purses of the unwilling generally
has poor results. A friend of mine who was much
interested in a Fresh Air Fund for the London poor was
asked by a celebrated preacher to speak to some of the
little ones on their return from their holiday, and try
and elicit an account of their doings, some expression of
gratitude, or some touching tale of contrast between
town and country life. My friend greatly loved
children, and was thoroughly accustomed to them, but
she talked, questioned, and cross-questioned utterly in
vain. For the twentieth time she asked: What did
you like best in the country ? "

" Chasin' th' ole pig when he got out of his house."

" Who let him out ? "

There was an appreciative grin at the quickness of
her apprehension.

" Me," said her one witness to the moral efficacy of
" being brought into touch with nature, if it were but
for one fortnight." With this meagre result she
returned, and the clergyman regretfully decided that
the relation was not suited to his style of pulpit
oratory.

Children have often, unasked, told me long and complicated stories with great fluency. One day I offered
a penny to a very talkative child in the fourth
"Standard" if she would tell me a tale she had read
at school. She was most anxious to earn it, but just
because she had been asked she could only give me a
few hesitating sentences about a cat and a bird which
I declined to rate even at a halfpenny. Spurred by
the disappointment she said—

"I'll tell you about hist'ry instead."

"What is history?"

"It's about the early Brittings. They lived in houses
with no chimleys and no clo'es, and painted theirselves
blue. Everybody *must* ha' laughed!"

At any rate she knew more about history than a
mother who told me—

"I don't mind their learnin' Emma jography; but
hist'ry, I don't call it according to her station."

The elder sister's fiancé holds the same position among
the children of the poor as in other classes. One day
a little girl rushed up to me, and asked—

"Miss, please what does knee—plush—ulster mean?"

With some difficulty I recognised the nine-times-
removed Latin, and gave the required explanation,
adding: "Why did you wish to know?"

"Well, I didn't, miss, not patickly; but I ast Polly's
young man, and he said it wasn't fit for kids to talk
about, so I was sure you'd know! I 'xpect"—with
the sudden recognition of the obvious which is the
natural child's nearest approach to suspicion—"he

don't know hisself. I'll tell him the cake mother has made for tea a-Sunday is *ne plus ultra,* and see if he understands."

The Higher Grade schools produce boys whose questions are occasionally a little embarrassing to some of my less brilliantly educated probationers. " Nurse," demanded one of them, " is your thermometer Fahrenheit or Centigrade ? " She said, " I have brought a Fahrenheit to-day," and changed the subject before he could ask her if she knew " how to turn them into Réaumur." She knew that to acknowledge that she was scarcely on speaking terms with vulgar fractions would hopelessly lower her in his estimation.

At the present day the children of the poor show much greater kindness to animals than formerly. Their treatment may often be ignorant, but a boy wishing to practise deliberate cruelty would have to select his companions rather carefully ; even a chance stone, if intended to do more than " scout " a cat, meets with unfavourable criticism. Not long since, however, I saw a London boy leading a dog by a chain, pulling and dragging the bewildered animal until its neck was half dislocated. A crossing-sweeper remonstrated : " Don't drag 'er like that. It's enough to maike 'er savidge ! "

The little rascal turned on him contemptuously : " I wants to maike 'er savidge. *I* don't care fer yer taime dorgs ! "

I have often heard certain Acts of Parliament intended for the prevention of cruelty called " The Children's Charter," but, necessary as these acts were, it would be a libel on the working classes to say that they have affected the daily lives of more than a minority. To me the children's charter is the compulsory Education Act. It would be no exaggeration to say that it has nearly doubled the years of permitted childhood, and added incalculably to its interests and pleasures.

" Here's John-Henry nine years old, and never earned a farthing yet!" said one north-country mother to me ; but parents as a whole have adapted themselves with wonderful quickness to the fact that children's earnings before the age of thirteen are now almost a negligible quantity.

People speak of children being " shut up in school-rooms instead of playing in the fields," as if that would otherwise be the ordinary or possible employment of the sons and daughters of the urban poor! School is naturally more popular in large cities than anywhere else, but never yet in town or country have I found children welcoming the holidays or sighing over their close.

Again, people protest against the cruelty of making half-starved children study, forgetful of the fact that unless those poor little wastrels had been compulsorily collected in a schoolroom, no one would have known if they were ill-fed or not, and equally forgetful of the fact that fireless rooms, aimless wanderings in cold streets, and entire absence of occupation, would be no allevia-tion of the pangs of hunger.

The Board Schools (Council Schools, one must learn to say !) are constantly accused of drying up all the poetry and mystery of child life, all the romance of the unseen. For many years, whenever I have found a child familiar with an old legend, a fairy tale, or a nursery rhyme, I have asked, "Where did you first hear it?" The answer is invariably, "I read it at school"; or, if the child is younger, "They learned it to my sister, and she learned it to me."

Strangely enough, in *games* the old tradition of hating school is kept up, and little maids who shed real tears when the holidays begin, still wipe away imaginary ones when they sing, "This is the way we go to school."

"Playing school," too, is still carried out on the traditional lines of—

> "Reading, 'riting, 'rithmetic,
> And don't ferget to give the stick."

The only change is that, instead of being confined to mere "make believe," instruction is really given and received, and the younger children in the family, to the generous and unbounded pride of their elders, often start their life at school knowing as much as their seniors acquired there in a year.

"Londoner" is with many people a synonym for sharpness and being well able to take care of oneself. This may be true of the Londoner with a bad home or none at all, but it would be difficult in the most Arcadian village to beat the simplicity of girls I have known who had been born and bred in some of the most crowded districts south of the Thames. I recommended one of them, a girl of twenty, living near the "Elephank an' Cawsel," and who had been in good service since she was fourteen, as housemaid to a friend living in the country. On the first Sunday evening her mistress explained to her where she was to sit, a pew on the north side of the church, and asked her when she returned if she had been able to find it.

"Yes, m'm; but very few sat there, and no one very near except me; not liking it, I suppose, on account of the corpses. But *I* didn't mind, not a bit."

"The *corpses*, Rosina?"

"Yes, m'm; the corpses laid out to be buried."

My friend scarcely knew which to be most astonished at, the girl's nerve in sitting almost alone in a dimly lighted aisle close to "corpses," or the ignorance which thought such a proceeding possible, and failed to recognise that the figures were stone effigies of ancient date.

Struck by some comment of another London girl of seventeen, I asked if she knew what butter is made of. "Fishes' 'eads, miss!" was the confident reply.

A girl of fifteen employed as a nursemaid brought her mistress's little girl to see me one day, and I took them both into the garden. The child asked me to pick her a bunch of apple-blossom growing on a small standard tree. I declined, explaining—

"If I leave the flowers there, by the end of the summer they will turn into apples." The child was incredulous, and on the verge of tears, so I turned to her attendant: "It's quite true, isn't it, Lucy?"

The girl had passed the fifth standard, and had once drawn me a very good map of India from memory, but she blushed and hesitated, and then replied frankly—

" I'm sure I couldn't say, miss ! "

I must acknowledge that the children of the poor, although possessed of many admirable qualities, are as a rule exceedingly disobedient, especially the boys, while they have an irritating habit of scrupulously remembering their parents' wishes when personal advantage is to be gained by doing so. A little boy was invited to tea in a working farmer's kitchen. He was offered cake, bread and butter, bread and jam, biscuits, but refused them all. Finally his indulgent hostess asked him what he wished to have.

" I should like some toast, please ; mother always likes me *to have my food aired !* "

The same little boy heard of a man who made it his boast that he had not washed his feet for forty years. He turned the matter over in his mind for a long time, and then asked—

" How did he manage when he had his baff ? I s'pose he always remembered to hang his feet outside ! "

If I did not correct my impressions by occasionally reading statistics, I should boldly assert that boys are far more numerous in the homes of the poor than girls, and whatever may have been the case formerly, daughters are generally preferred by both parents. " Girls will work *some*times, but boys is all fer marbles," is the common verdict.

I once visited a three-roomed dwelling where there were twelve little boys, all as young as they possibly could be. A widow with five had married a widower with six, and the twelfth son was born within a year.

The youngest but one—I think it belonged to the widower—was allowed to sleep in the parents' room, but visiting the family late at night I found all the remaining ten sleeping peacefully side by side in neat little beds made out of orange boxes.

In hospital wards I remember the children chiefly by their extreme docility and their eagerness to occupy the traditional post of honour, the bed nearest my writing table. I was obliged to let them take it strictly in turns, unless the distinguished illness of a child gave it a special claim, or a crime had been committed so black and so destructive of discipline that the head nurse thought it could only be expiated by banishment to a spot from which only an intermittent view of the extreme corner of the table could be obtained.

"Sister!" one poor little mite would cry eagerly before I was well inside the door, "I was awake *all night*, but I just lay still and didn't disturb *nobody*; and don't you think I'd ought to be nearest to your table to-day? If you'll let me keep your pen-stand on the bed, so's I'll know when you're using the red ink, I won't say a word, not if I'm awake twice as long! And mightn't I keep the ruler too? Jennie said *she* did, but pr'aps you weren't so busy then?"

CHAPTER IV

THE ART OF POLITE CONVERSATION AS PRACTISED AMONG THE POOR

WE were frequently told at school that we should live to regret the intellectual opportunities we had wasted, and certainly in district work I have often had reason to deplore the persistence with which I stopped my ears during the weekly hour devoted to sewing and Sir Theodore Martin's *Life of the Prince Consort*. I squandered the time mentally rehearsing the portion of Racine due the following morning, or an especially thorny chapter of Latin grammar, or strained my eyes over the complications of the crochet or tatting then in vogue. I could hardly say which I have found of least general use as a district nurse, French poetry, Latin prose, or crocheted covers for things that need not exist; and even the author of the once despised book would pity me if he knew how bitterly I have deplored my ignorance of the private lives of the Royal Family, and how I have mourned the occasions when a timely anecdote would have smoothed over a situation bristling with difficulties.

I have not merely repented; I have gradually, and unlaboriously, repaired the gap in my education with tales, on the whole, rather creditable than credible. Nearly all the stories have reached me through my patients, and I flatter myself that there are now few people who can repeat a larger number of apocryphal anecdotes in a manner more fluent and convinced. I have added *one* to the stock, and, whether from its bald veracity or its utter pointlessness, I find the effect so powerful that I only relate it in really desperate cases, such as a battle between 'In Laws.

("Laws! What's laws?—I don't think nothin' o' laws!" said one old woman who had no anarchical leanings.)

I well remember the first time I repeated it. I was nursing an aged and greatly suffering woman, and to distract her attention from a painful dressing, I told her that a few days previously I had been to Windsor, and had been near enough the Queen to hear her say, "Get into the carriage, Louise." She listened entranced: "You heard Her *speak?* You HEARD Her?" Then, with an effort of which I should have thought her incapable, she raised herself in the bed, flung her withered arms round my neck, and, pressing kisses on my face, murmured fervently: "You are worthy, my dear, you are *worthy*."

It is a curious fact among the poor, that while superior education makes a woman less talkative, it makes a man much more so; nowhere are there such incessant talkers to be found as in the upper ranks of artisans and the non-commissioned officers in both services. The latter especially delight in telling interminable strings of tales, of which the following, repeated to me perhaps a dozen times in the course of three weeks, is a fair specimen. "So the third lootenant he says to me, in a sort of little way he had as you couldn't help liking, 'Davis,' he says, 'I've got orders to measure all the water that blessed old tank holds. I've bin puzzlin' half the night over it, but I know now how we'll tackle it. We'll have up a working party and empty it all out in two gallon buckets. All you've got to do is to count the buckets, and keep a look-out that every man has them properly full. Then we'll tot 'em up. I always know my two times table, and we needn't turn the gallons into gills, or any rot of that kind.' 'Beg pardon, sir,' I says, 'but the tank isn't full,—not by a very great deal,' saying this, as you'll understand, just to get at the depths of his iggernance. He looked a bit chopfallen for half a shake, and then he says, 'You can guess how much emptiness there is, and I'll have a shot at it too, and we'll split the diff'rince. That's what they calls the personal equation,' he says. 'Begging your pardon, sir,' I says, and I was that flabbergasted at his owdacious iggernance that I could hardly get my breath,—' Begging your pardon, equations wasn't lower-deck talk in *my* day, but *I have* heard o' cubic contents.' 'Cubic contents?' he says, laughing fit to kill hisself; 'why, that's *carpets!*' Well, I was mortal afraid that him and me would be laughing-stocks to the whole fleet, so I argied the point with him, and I don't say but what there ought to ha' bin a little more Queen's Reggylations in my way o' speaking, but I *will* say he was pleased as Punch when I had calkilated it all out for him. And then, if you'll believe me, after all my trouble to keep him and me from looking like the pair of ninnies that one of us wasn't, if he didn't go up to one of them greasers with a bigger twist for learning than they have for manners, and tell him, ' What a splendid dodge Davis had put him up to,' and that blessed greaser smiled like sin, and asked, ' Was it you as invented that—er— remark'ble abbreviation of 'rithmetical processes, or your father ? ' ' It would have been my father, sir,' I says ; ' but he was never one to brag.' Ha, I had him there, had him on the hop, didn't I just ! "

As a matter of fact, however, I believe it was his father whose complete ignorance of arithmetic amused a whole fleet. He was overheard muttering, " Blest if them paymasters ain't a discontented lot ! First they had ' eighths ' and they wasn't satisfied, and now they've got ' tenths ' and they're still a-grumbling, and you may take your oath that if the Admiralty was to give 'em ' twefths ' they'd still be at it."

Many of the stories told by the older men have for their point the drunkenness of their officers. A favourite one is—

" Some feels it most in their legs, and they're all right as long as they don't have to walk ; some can walk, but you dish them if they have to talk. The doctor, he was one of the first kind. The captain was getting pretty tired of having him always drunk and always in the right, so one night when the doctor came aboard half-seas-over, ' Walk a plank, sir,' says he, ' if you're sober.'

" The sawbones he looked at the plank, and he looked

at his legs, and he looked at the captain, 'Walk it
yourself!' says he. So that was the end of *him* ! "

The following story was related to me with many
prefatory doubts as to whether it was "quite the thing
to tell a lady." A certain officer was strongly suspected
by his messmates of never using his rather conspicuously
placed bath. There were many bets on the subject,
and when the ship was on her way home, one of the
lieutenants, to settle the matter, took a valuable tiger-
skin belonging to him, carefully wrapped it up, and
placed it in the bottom of the bath. Three days passed
quietly, and then there were loud outcries from the
owner, his tiger-skin had been stolen ; never were there
such thieves as blue-jackets, never such blue-jackets as
those he was condemned to sail with. Day after day
at the mess-table it was the established joke for one or
other of the conspirators to ask sympathetically, " Have
you found your skin ? " and the angry tirade that
followed was capped by the relation of similar losses.
When the ship paid off, but not until then, the tiger-
skin was unearthed from its hiding-place.

Practical jokes play a large part in all these yarns.
In another of about the same date, the third lieutenant
of the ship, a handsome black-haired, blue-eyed Irishman, excusably proud of his appearance, had a bad
attack of fever, and was obliged to be closely shaved.
The hair grew slowly and unwillingly, and he went
ashore at St. Helena and ordered a wig, for which he
paid five pounds. Shortly before the ship sailed the
wig arrived, a flaming red. He rushed off to the barber

to protest, but the man (probably it was the only wig he had in stock) declared that he had specially made it to match the customer's own hair. The vehement Irishman dragged wig and barber back to the ship, to overwhelm him with evidence that his hair had been black as a r-raven, and burst in on his messmates, who, to his unspeakable wrath and amazement, mildly but firmly supported the barber's assertion: "What's wrong with it, my dear fellow? A very good match, as far as I'm any judge of colour. Did you wish to try brown or black for a change? Far better stick to the original colour. The skin and eyes always betray it if you make a change of that kind."

And the unlucky young fellow was actually forced to wear it, haunted by a horrible fear that when his hair grew it really *would* be red. For a long time it obstinately refused to grow at all, and it was many months before he could triumphantly push aside the wig and display some thin and babyish but undeniably black curls. The relief was so great that he could well afford to laugh at his tormentors' solemn warnings that hair dye produced softening of the brain.

One favourite "yarn" amused me the first time I heard it. Two powerful blue-jackets had been told off to take a lunatic from Portsmouth to London. They were warned to keep their eyes on him constantly, and carried out their orders so precisely that they did not notice that there was no lamp in the railway carriage. The train dashed into a tunnel, and a fearful struggle immediately began; when daylight was reached, one

strong man, panting but triumphant, pinned the other
to the floor, while the lunatic "smiled superior" from
the improvised hammock formed by the light luggage
rack.

Only three religions are acknowledged by non-
commissioned officers: Church of England, which of
course must be right, because it is generally attended
by colonel and adjutant, captain and first lieutenant;
Roman Catholicism, which must be tolerated, because
without it you could not have Irishmen, an inconceivable
state of affairs; and Wesleyan Methodism, which they
privately prefer. With regard to all others they would
like to repeat the order actually given by a sergeant of
Marines one Sunday morning: "Fancy religions to the
rear!"

Their politics are generally Conservative, and their prejudices strongly aristocratic. A medical officer, formerly
in charge of Yarmouth Hospital for the insane,
described to me a little scene which took place during
his residence. A distinguished man had paid an unexpected visit, and he took him to the bedside of a
veteran of ninety-eight. The old fellow was only mad
north-north-west, and he thought that an interview
would afford mutual pleasure.

"MacTavish," he said," the First Lord of the Admiralty
has come to see you."

The old man sat up and stared at the visitor for a
few moments.

"And what may your name be?"

"William Henry Smith."

" Smeeth ?—Smeeth ? "

" Yes, Smith."

"Then it's juist a dommed lee! If ya'd said Eliot, or Fanshawe, or Beauchamp, or Rice, I might ha' believed ya, but wha ever heard of a *Smeeth ?* "

He dropped back on his pillow, and the slightly disconcerted First Lord and the greatly embarrassed Inspector-General retired in broken order.

The poor are always most unwilling to ask one another the meaning of any strange word, but will readily own their ignorance to any member of the upper classes, even to children. I once listened to a conversation between a servant and a washerwoman with reference to an outbreak of smallpox. The laundress, a very old person, declared that she had no fear of it, as she had been nokkle-ated. " What did she mean, Mary ? " I asked, when she had taken her departure.

" Law, missy, I'dno."

" But you spoke as if you knew quite well ? "

" Oh, I wasn't going to let on to the likes of *her* as I didn't know ! "

Apologies are often, as in all classes, veiled reproofs. I was walking one day with a friend, and rather absorbed in what she was telling me, when I noticed a former patient, a most disreputable old vagabond, taking off his hat to me. Of course I responded to the salutation, and thought that was the end of the matter. The next time I visited his wife, a " chronic," he said—

" I hope you didn't mind me speaking to you in the street the other day, mum ? "

6

"Certainly not," I replied, with perhaps an un-conscious touch of patronage in my voice; "I hope you will always speak to me wherever I am."

"Well'll - ll, mum, it's a long time since I learnt manners, and I can't say as the twopence extry was paid, not *reg'lar*, but I do seem to remember that when people is acquainted it's for the female to move first."

"Move" is the usual word for a bow or a curtsey.

The same man begged me, as a personal favour, not to speak of bell-ringing, but of campanology; and on another occasion he told me that he had not washed his face for forty years, "because alkali is bad for the roots of the hair."

Long words, like other adornments, are more generally delighted in by women than men, and as they are usually acquired by reading, they are often used in strange senses and pronounced in an almost unrecognisable fashion. Speaking of the late Queen, a patient said solemnly: "I always have thought that she lived too much in solution." When a less refined neighbour was compelled to enter a large hospital to undergo an opera-tion, the same woman told me: "I couldn't help saying to her how sorry I felt for her; knowing nothing but the vulgar tongue, she'll feel so out of place like."

There are a few who err on the other side, and prefer the crudest forms of speech. I was told recently of a woman who puzzled the lady Sanitary Inspector who had asked the nature of her illness by replying, "The doctor says I'm awful rose in my lights" (*i.e.* had congestion of the lungs). Certainly she was "worlds away" from a small working farmer's daughter who said to a friend of mine, hearing her remark that Suède gloves wore badly: "Oh, Miss R——, I always call them mangel-wurzel gloves; Swedes are such horrid common things!"

Quotations are sometimes strangely "translated." A patient told me one day: "Miss —— come to see me, and she said, 'Whom the Lord loveth He chaseth'; I said to her, I says, 'Ah, miss, I've had a peck o' trouble. He *have* chased me lately.'"

A few months ago a former patient of ours took her nephew to the Eye Hospital, and was subsequently presented with a bill for £15. She came to me, her face aflame with anger, and poured out a tale so full of sound and fury, that I could understand little of it, but it ended with: "And wasn't it wrote plain on the door for everyone to read, *For the Indignant Poor?*"

"Jack," said an invalid wife, calling her talkative old husband to order, "fetch the hot water for nurse, and the box with all the things in it that she wants."

"I'm only telling nurse a little antidote," was the aggrieved reply. The "antidote" was of a son by a former wife whose occupation was making the parish coffins, and who was constantly worried by being given incorrect or insufficient addresses for their delivery. "One night he went knocking at every door in K—— Street, and asking, 'Does anyone live here what's dead?' And then he left the whole show and went to America."

"It's the spirit of the age," was the wife's somewhat irrelevant comment,—"very selfish. 'I'm aboard, Jack, pull up the ladder!' that's what the spirit of the age is."

" *We* went for nothing, because father worked on the estate," another woman told me; "but every antelope had to pay." After all, it was a person in a very different position in life who said to me gravely, "I think it a duty to decimate good literature," and on another occasion complained that her dog suffered from "stertorian breathing," a compound, I imagine, of stertorous and stentorian. It well described that animal's performances during its very frequent naps.

Words are sometimes used in a sense which, though unusual, cannot fairly be called incorrect. "Herbert looks very thin and delicate, and I saw him smoking this morning," I said to the mother of twelve children, eight of them boys. "Yes, m'm, I know. He's so bigoted, he *will* do it!"

Inquiries for health are as a rule expected to receive an answer, but answers tend to be given in more general terms than formerly, and no doubt are on the way to become as much a pure formality as with the upper classes. "Old Mr. Waters he *do* have such old-fashioned ways: he always ask how you are as if he wanted to know!" said a rather sophisticated village girl.

Conversation among the poor is largely made up of repetition: the most ignorant will repeat themselves commonly five or six times during the same interview, and even those of superior culture will do it in all times of excitement. If the story told is comparatively new, its form varies from day to day, but the favourite version is ultimately adopted, and crystallises into unvarying tradition. I visited one woman constantly for four years, and at least six times a month she told me that the old vicar had once been to see her, and how he had turned the two cats out of the room before he began prayers, saying, "*You're* not communicants, I'm sure."

This deficiency of memory is of an entirely one-sided kind. As a test, I have sometimes knowingly repeated a story told to amuse a patient, but I have never ventured to make it more than a thrice-told tale, although few of my hearers would have uttered any equivalent of "connu!" A little girl did once protest, "You told me that before, nurse," but hastily retrieved her reputation for "knowing manners" by adding, "It was very funny. I should like to hear it again."

The same small joke can, however, be made to do duty scores of times: I rarely have a patient too old or poor or suffering to laugh if I suggest cooking a diminutive egg in the boiler, or propose increasing the number of blankets by taking one out from the bottom and putting it on top, or in fact anything that they call "Irish."

"Good old days" are not a tradition among the poor: all old stories are of hardship. "I married on 6s. a week," said an Essex labourer's wife born about 1818, "and when my husband got a rise of 2s. we thought we was *made!* What did we eat? Well, potatoes was pretty cheap, but dear at any price by the time the year was well turned. We hadn't no potatoes then that would be white as flour when the new ones was ready to eat. We grew a few vegetables, but we hadn't much of a garden, nor time to see to it. The bread was dear, and made o' sharps, same as what pigs gets now. How did I live? I used to scour for the farmers' wives. It was hard work and little money, but they gave me good food, and it kept my health. We'd eleven children, and nine grew up, and all of 'em scholars. Ah, schooling's an easy matter now! My father paid for me, but nothing but reading and sewing was teached. I scraped up ten shillings to learn writing after I was a growed woman. We never took charity but once. It was after my fourth child came. I couldn't get back my strength so as to work, and the longer I bided at home on bad food the worse I got. At last the clergyman come to see me, and he said plainly, not like his us'al way of talking, ' My poor creature, tell me what you want and you shall have it.' I said, ' It's good bread I want, sir. The sharps is killing me.' So he sent me bread and beer every day, and a bit of meat twice a week. I soon got fierce [strong and well] on that, and I never got so low again. Oh, the things I used to buy for a shilling you wouldn't never believe! I never had more than a farthing's worth of thread at a time. I used to wake up early in the morning and plan how I'd patch the children's clo'es. When they was once up, they was all round me like bees, and I couldn't think for the best what to do. Ah, to think of my husband in his first strength getting six shillings a week, and a rent to pay, and me here an old woman getting five shillings and fire and light and houseroom just for doing for the doctor's groom, and keeping the place clean against any of his grandchildren sleeps here."

The same old woman used to relate with touching pride, that when she was a child of six her father, a labourer with a "long" family, firmly refused to allow her to be adopted by a childless couple in a slightly better position: "But I'd always run and hide whenever I see them; I was scared they'd get me for all father's saying no."

The daughter of a small farmer in a neighbouring village, one of fifteen children born between 1830 and 1846, told me that to save the bread they used to have to take it in turns to eat potatoes and milk. One morning they had a hot dispute as to whose turn it was to eat the detested mess. Their father silently left the table, returning a few minutes later with a blackish lump about the size of his fist. It was damp, and stuck to the cloth when he laid it down. "Children," he said, his voice trembling with indignation, "*that* is the breakfast that my horsekeeper and his son carried for two miles in the dark to eat after nearly two hours' hard work. While *that* is all that honest men can get, never dare to complain of the food provided for you."

Scarcely thirty years ago, a labourer in one of the Royal Dockyards was observed to slip behind a screen every day during the dinner-hour. It was in the direction of a ship nearly ready to be launched. Some evil design was suspected, and men were set to watch him and discover how he spent his time. They did so, but their report was received by the foreman with horrified incredulity; it was not, it *could* not, be true. Next day he kept watch with them, and found that the man secreted himself not indeed to eat sawdust, but something which to a Southron's eyes seemed little better, a *handful of raw oatmeal*. The case was inquired into, for it was difficult to understand how even on fifteen shillings a week a steady man could be in such straits, and a pitiable story was unfolded of a large young family, an invalid wife, and the almost hopeless effort to keep out of debt. His name was transferred to the eighteen shillings list, and, like the poor Essex woman, he thought himself "made." There are many old men still living who can remember years when the most highly skilled artisans of the period were thankful to save their families from starvation by working as labourers ten hours a day for twelve shillings a week.

In whatever state you find the poor, they speak nearly always of worse times that they have experienced. "I'm sixty-five," said a poorly clothed man working on the roads in a freezing London fog. "Look older'n that? I know I does. I've nought to complain of now, nought; but I had hardships when I was young. It tells on a man, *that* does." During a bitter winter a little girl told me, doubtless repeating her parents' words: "Father feels another man now he doesn't have to go out *not before five in the morning*."

Open self-praise forms an amusingly large part of the conversation of many of the best members of the working classes. Perhaps they only say what we all

think, but it is difficult to listen with due gravity when
a woman exclaims, "Ah, there's not a many like *me!*
The world would be a different place if there was": or
a hedge gardener assures me, "Colonel and Mrs. ——
would be just lost if I didn't manage to get out there
every week."

Considering the number of houses that district nurses
enter, the poverty and suffering of many of their
patients, the degradation of not a few, it is astonishing
how seldom they hear any bad language. Of late years
I have only once seen reason to complain. I had taken
a young probationer to a house where there were two
invalids. I left her to attend to the chronic sufferer,
an elderly man, and went into the next room to the
acute case. The walls were thin, and such "opprobrious
epitaphs" reached me that I quickly rejoined her. The
old man's daughter offered a half apology: "You see,
Sooper, we're used to 'im. We don't think nothin'
of it."

"I do not intend my probationer to become used to
it," I said severely. "I will give you three days to
make your father understand this, and during that time
no nurse will be sent to him."

Nevertheless, in spite of his blasphemy, in spite of
his far more unpardonable coarseness, the poor old
fellow's condition weighed on me, and I was greatly
relieved when at evening report the probationer told me
shamefacedly: "I went to see Tompkins again. I
thought you would *rather* I did."

Men placed under the unusual discipline of having

"to pick and choose their words" adopt a strangely childish form of diction. "Why did you leave the army so soon?" I asked a patient's husband. A wonderfully innocent pair of blue eyes in a very battered face were turned on me, and he drawled gently, "They ast me to go, ma'am."

Mr. Atkins at home always refers to us as "Lady Nurses," but occasionally his voice floats in at my open windows, and the more picturesque expression used then is "them Jubilee Tramps."

Even uncouth phrases are rarely used in our presence. Visiting a patient one day while his wife was out charing, I showed him how to bandage his own shin. At my next visit his wife was there, but he proceeded to display his accomplishment, and when she ventured to prompt him at the point where a "reverse spiral" should be taken, he roared impatiently: "Howd thy rag! Ah've bin *teached!*" In the same house the usual order to close the door was, "Put the boord oover tha hole;" and, happening one day to glance at a boy of three while he was eating his dinner, he said threateningly, "Ah'll bat yer ear-holes ef ya look at my pudden." He was a perfect little savage, taught by his grandfather to watch like a cat outside a mousehole, and catch the mouse with his fingers. I have often seen him crawling on all-fours with the tail of his victim between his little white teeth, shaking its scarcely dead body with a terrier-like action of his head. His only soft spot was his love for his sister, an unusually plain child about a year his senior. "Angie too!" was the peremptory order when cake or sweets were given him. The grandfather told me proudly: "If I went to kick anyone, Tom 'ud do his best to help, unless 'twer Agnes, and then he'd kick *me!*"

Nothing but "straight English" is considered the correct form in which to address us, but an invalid policeman, who had noticed that nurses do not long remain in the same district, amused one of my probationers by saying earnestly: "I hope, miss, you'll stop on my beat till I get well."

Policemen, by the way, have always been rare among my patients. In hospital life they are chiefly connected in my mind with what used to seem to me a foolish waste of public money. When a case of attempted suicide was brought in to us, a policeman sat night and day by the patient's side until he could be removed. Each policeman remained on duty eight hours at a stretch, and even then one case of the kind meant the entire work of three constables in twenty-four hours. As a rule, the patients had not the smallest desire to complete the interrupted act, and in a large number of cases they were literally incapable of doing so. When it was absolutely impossible for the bandaged and helpless sufferer to do himself any further injury, I used not to think that I was distracting the men from their duty by asking them to roll up bandages if a few hundreds had just come back from the laundry. They accepted the work gratefully as a relief to the tedium of "settin' and starin' at a person that couldn't move if he wanted to, and that *don't* want to," and it was a real assistance to nurses. This may explain to the general public what is meant in annual reports by, " Constables employed on other duties " !

Once we had a policeman as a patient under slightly ludicrous circumstances. A great ceremonial was taking place in London, the crowds were enormous, and a long roll of victims was expected, especially in our immediate neighbourhood. A large room was arranged to receive them, and all the zealous students hung about the place expecting a field-day, compared with which the excitement of seeing " The Captains and the Kings depart " sank into childish insignificance.

About ten o'clock we sent out an ambulance, and precisely ten minutes after the men returned, bringing a partly unconscious policeman, but throughout the day not a single other person needed their assistance.

Early the next morning the policeman came to take leave of me, thanked me solemnly, and presented me with half a crown " for the use of the patients." I naturally hesitated to take the money, thinking that the accident had happened so suddenly that he had not had time to grasp the details, but my scruples were needless. I found he was perfectly well aware that the zealous ambulance, before picking him up, *had knocked him down.*

Sharp, definite statements are generally avoided. I heard one man say to another, in reply to the question, " Did you go and speak to him about it ? "—" Well, I kinder went over there, and I sorter remarked, as you might say "—

Formerly it was difficult for members of the educated
classes to keep up any conversation with the poor, but
now they have a much greater variety of topics, and
a greater similarity of interests and ambitions. Take
their children, for instance; they have a thousand things
to tell you of them beyond the fact of their being well
or ill, do-syle or bigoted. A child's "standard" has
become of exactly the same concern to the poorest mother
as the public schoolboy's "form"; drawings and maps
are exhibited to me, and the children are constantly
called on to "say that lovely po'try what you learned
last week." Recitation is not a strong point in Board
Schools, and I fear that they have often passed from
Eliza Cook to Shakespeare, and from Shakespeare to their
prayers, without my being able to discern where one
began and the other left off. But it was none the less
a gratifying spectacle, and I think the parents' innocent
pride would soothe even that copious letter-writer,
"Indignant Ratepayer."

What used to be called Devonshire compliments are
still very common. A friend of mine was recently
offered a present of a fowl by a lad of eighteen in the
following terms: "Mother's going to send you a fowl,
if you'd like to have it. We've only got two, and it
isn't worth worrying after them, and father says they
do scrat up the garden shameful, and this one's always
stealing the pig's food, and we can't none of us abear
their meat, and its back is humpty, so's it wouldn't
never do for market, and mother 'ud be glad to be shut
of it; and shall I bring it a-Wednesday?"

Except from semi-professional beggars, one rarely receives any flattering remarks among the poor. In four years' work in one town, the nearest approach to a compliment that I ever received was: "Eh, you've an oogly moog, but ah laike to look at it." During the same period I had a very two-edged one from a nurse, but, gruesome as it may sound, it was uttered in all innocence. She had been one of my probationers, and had remained in the hospital after I left it. Three years later I chanced to meet her; she gave cheering accounts of the progress of the institution, but added: "Oh, Sister, the doctors *do* miss you! Mr. —— said only last week, 'It isn't the same place since Sister Agnes left; I never get any post-mortems now!'"

Curious metaphors are sometimes heard. "And how are you to-day, Mrs. Shewry?" asked one old lady of another. "Oh, I'm like flowers in spring, I ebbs and I flows, I ebbs and I flows."

There is often a difference in the use of words which may well cause misunderstanding.

"Amos used to be a great flirt," said his sister-in-law, "but he's quite give it up now."

"But," I objected, "you told me six weeks ago that he had bought a ring for Kate, then that he was 'walking out' with Anna, and now that he wishes to marry Gladys. What is that but being a flirt?"

"That isn't flirting, m'm; not when you only has one at a time. Flirting's going out with three or four at a time *all unbeknownst*."

The standard of truth is always rather low, but still

less is expected of great conversationalists. I was told of one man with admiration: " Why there, I do believe that he might talk to you a whole evening and you'd never catch him out in a lie ! "

The workhouse in all refined circles is called the Infirmary, and it seems to be a point of honour with most of the elderly inmates to speak of it as a well-managed place to which they have voluntarily retired. " I have a day nurse and a night nurse," said an old man solemnly, although he knew that I knew that he was not in the Infirmary at all, " and every comfort as the doctor orders. Whatever he says I'm to have is purvided without stint. Yes, it's a blessing there *is* such places, ma'am."

I should like people who think that the masses are equal among themselves to hear the patronage with which the man who did not enter the Union until he was seventy-five will speak of the weakling who drifted in at sixty-eight, and the contempt they both have for the man or woman inmate who is merely middle-aged. Those who " come in for the winter " are hardly con-sidered worthy to speak to the regular residents, while tramps are the lowest pariahs, whose habits are observed with lofty curiosity and commented on with disdain.

Few things are more pathetic than the effort to keep from yielding to the burden of the growing weight of years. Two old almshouse women, one much feebler than the other, were taking a walk together. Presently the elder expressed a wish to turn back. "No, no," said the other, firmly, " we must go on to our destynation." Curious to know what this might be, we followed them ; they reached a certain lamp-post, solemnly walked round it, and returned to their well-earned " coop o' tay."

It is a mistake to imagine that the poor, as a rule, can recognise a lady when they see one. Women with every claim to the title have " gone the rounds " with me, but their position has never been detected by any patient. They always pass for " persons as is thinking of taking up the trade," and a distracted husband with an invalid wife offered to engage one of the most distinguished among them " by the day or the 'alf day as might be convenient." I had been attending a most respectable old person for nearly three years, when one day she greeted me with intense excitement, and reproachfully exclaimed, " Nurse, you never told me you was a lady, but I've *found you out !* "

" It was extremely clever of you. How did you do it ? "

" The doctor's missus was here, and she told me. There *was* people as said the nurse that come afore was a lady, but I never believed it, not with her hair so rough and curly."

It may be true that in certain country districts there is a more practised perception, but in what a patient called the " ganglions of poppylation," myriads live and die without ever having known a lady.

" I'm sure I dunno what we'd do without 'em now, but there *wasn't* no ladies when I was young," said one old woman.

" Oh, I suppose you had something else that did quite as well ? "

" No, there wasn't nothing," she declared comprehensively.

I will not say in what county it was I heard the statement, " She used to be a lady, but she has lost nearly all her money now," but such ideas as the poor have of gentility are almost solely made of idleness and extravagance. The first definition of a lady that I ever received was a characteristic one: " *Your* aunt ain't no lady !" said a contemptuous maid-servant.

" Why not ? " I asked, feebly defensive of the family claims.

" Ladies is people who lies on the sofa all day and reads novels."

Since then, when I have heard my patients using the word, I have often tried to induce them to explain it. One woman got unusually near the mark when she said : " Ladies wouldn't play mean shabby tricks on you, not like common people does."

Asking how a girl was getting on in her new place, I was told : " First class, m'm. You see, her mistress isn't a lady."

" But what difference can that make ? "

" Oh, ladies is people that must have things *just so.* Rhoda's missis isn't one, so she just suits her."

A pitiful little version of the ordinary views of ladyhood was given to me by the daughter of a once prosperous baker, a girl who had been educated at a

7

"select seminary." After she had been a few weeks in service, she said to me : " I would have taken a place long ago, instead of starving over fine needle-work, if only I had known what ladies were like. I suppose it was very silly of me, and I don't understand how I could have been such a goose, but I thought ladies were so haughty they'd never speak a word to you. I didn't like to go where there were other servants, because they might be rough, and yet, always having had mother and Kate with me, I dreaded going where no one would ever talk to me."

It has often been remarked that even the most prudent among the poor are entirely lost as to the spending powers of any sum beyond £5, and if one doubled the amount it might truly be affirmed of nineteen-twentieths of my patients. Towards the close of the South African War a rather intelligent woman said to me—

"People will have it that it's the war as has drove prices up, but how can that be?" I tried to explain a few of the many ways in which such a prolonged contest raised prices, and I flatter myself I made some impression on her mind, for at the end of my dissertation she heaved a sigh, and said solemnly—

"Yes, I dare say if it's rightly counted this war will have cost several hundreds of pounds!"

It is this inability to calculate the spending power of money that makes a legacy, in most cases, such a deadly misfortune to the poor. In a small provincial town an old grocer asked me : " Did you notice a new tailor's shop open three doors off? It's that idiot Simpson who was Mr. Crossby's cutter. Twenty years he's been there, and two pounds a week paid him every Saturday as reg'lar as the clock struck. It's very good wages indeed in a place like this, with rent so cheap. If a man'll do a bit of gardening and live a mile out, his rent needn't cost him anything at all."

"I suppose he had saved something considerable? It is only natural for a man of that age to try and get into a more independent position."

"Save! He hadn't saved a farthing; hadn't even decent sticks of furniture. His uncle died and left him £100—on paper. When the prop'ty was sold, his share turned out to be £27, just thirteen and a half weeks' wages; but even when he knew what it 'ud be to a penny he wouldn't take back his notice. Crossby give him the chance, he told me so himself. You see, miss, there isn't work enough of that class for two, and if there were, Simpson wouldn't get it."

"Well, if the worst comes to the worst, I suppose Crossby would take him back?"

"Not he!—Crossby would never have give him the sack, he has a kind of feeling for people when they've worked for him as long as that, but he's got a son of his own apprenticed in N—— who is nearly old enough for the work. He'll just make shift for a few months and put *him* in to it. Simpson's wife ought to have put her foot down. It's surprising how a bit of money turns their heads. She must know what twenty-seven divided by two comes to as well as I do. Before three

months is up Simpson will be tramping the roads
looking for odd jobs."

All of which speedily came to pass.

But I once found a labourer whose good sense had
borne up against a legacy of £800. Some years after
receiving it he said to me, with good-natured scorn—

"People keeps on asking why me and my wife and
daughter don't "live right up" now I've got all that
money. Why, look here, miss, with three hundred of it
I bought a machine, and by loaning that machine, and
working of it, I s'pose I've earned forty shilling a week,
taking all the year through, ever since, and I've took
such care on it that a man as is a good judge told me
it's worth *now* pretty well what I gave for it. On the
rest of the money I only get two and a half in the
hundred, but you can't make none of them understand."

To "live up" is to subsist, as this man did, partly on
earnings and partly on the interest of capital. In order
to "live right up" he would have had to exist on the
"two and a half in the hundred."

The conversation of the middle-aged women is as a
rule the quintessence of common sense applied to the
matters of life as they know it, and I like to collect
their opinions and pass them on to younger persons in
the same position. One thing that they are strongly
averse to is married women's competition in the labour
market. They do not, of course, comprehend its most
far-reaching effects, but they see many of the results
clearly enough to dread it. I know one woman who,
notwithstanding the influence of her surroundings,

which were all for "going into business" (*i.e.* serving in
a shop) or learning a trade, and although as a girl she
had worked in a factory herself, insisted on sending
every one of a large family of girls into domestic service.
"A single woman or a widow," she always said to those
who would listen, and to many who would not, "can earn
a better living as a servant than in any trade; and I
don't mean *my* girls to earn their husbands' living for
them, and end by getting their heads punched because
the money won't run to hot meat every day of the week.
I never earned a penny from the day I married until
my youngest child was going on six, except when my
husband was ill, and not often then, for if he was bad
enough to stop at home he was bad enough to want
nursing. I met a man th' other day, one that's always
on for girls learning trades, and wanting married women
to work, and he said to me, 'What, Mrs. Borroughs, Jim
bin bad seven weeks and you've rings on your fingers!
When I'd bin ill half that time, even my wife's wedding
ring went.' I said, 'More shame to you, then! I've had
him ill many a time, and myself too, but I never had
need to part with a thing in the house yet, for all that
you twit me with knowing no trade and never earning
nothing."

"Ah," said a poor woman to me one day, "fifteen
years ago my husband was out of work, could only get
odd jobs. I got sick of the cold and the bad living, and
I went back to my old work of cooking by the day, and
kep' him, kep' him better'n he could keep me. I'll only
regret it once, and that's all my life. Last winter there

was a place where he could ha' done five and a half days reg'lar, but he's no drunkard, even now, and two days' wages pays his beer and tobacco. He looks to me for the rest. Bless you, he ain't the only one in *this* town, and he ain't the worst. Why, there's men as'll only take two days' work, and then makes their wives go and beg for charity, because that's all the work they've got. There's lots of people foolish enough to believe it. I could show you people as goes on all the winter at that trick, and every winter of their lives. Ah, there's only one rule for women who want to have a decent home for their children and themselves : If your husband comes home crying, and says he can't find any work, sit down on the other side of the fire and cry till he *does*."

I well remember the case of one man which gives special point to her views. He was sober, and an excellent artisan, but constantly losing employment owing to his bad temper. He had a wife and three little children. The day after he was out of work she always went charing, or appealed for help to her former mistress. In the course of a few years it became the established rule that the wife worked always, and the husband a few days now and again. This man was neither a brute nor a maniac ; he had a certain amount of affection for his family, and a justifiable pride in his skill at his trade. If his wife had tacitly refused to work for money—a man has already gone some way downhill before he orders her to do it—he would have been compelled to live up to the not very exacting standard of civility demanded by his master, a much-harassed builder and contractor, driven over and over again to re-engage the man "in spite of his tongue," as he ruefully complained.

A friend of mine whose income was about £250 had for her servant a girl, whose father, a superior artisan, earned at least half that amount. When raising her wages to £20, my friend said to her: "I hope now that you will try and save a little money. Remember that £20 a year is more than many of the ladies you see in my house can afford to spend on dress."

The girl looked at her in genuine astonishment: "Why, ma'am, I thought every lady could have a hundred or two whenever she wanted it!"

The title "Queen's Nurse" is taken literally by some of the patients. Nine or ten years ago, an old woman complained bitterly to a superintendent that the nurse had not been to see her on the previous day. Excuses were made as to pressure of work, etc., but she could not accept them.

"'Taint that I wanted her to *do* anything, not to speak of, but if she don't look in reg'lar, *how's the Queen to know how I am?*"

The naïveté even of the shrewdest of the poor is often striking. A friend, at my request, wrote several letters from France to amuse a bedridden man, a great newspaper reader. It happened to be at a moment when the bonds between the two countries were in an unusually frayed condition. On her return he asked her most seriously—

"Miss, d'you think the Pressy-dunt had the first read of them letters you sent me?"

She said she did not think the President had had time, but found this expression of opinion so bitterly disappointing to him, that she hastened to add the comfortingly libellous suggestion: "He may have ordered an official to read them." "Ah, I don't doubt but he did!"

The wife of a Welsh vicar told me that she and her husband had been up at the Coronation, and while fresh from its glories she went to pay a round of parochial visits.

"And did you really see the King, ma'am?" asked one old lady.

"Oh yes, we both saw him several times."

"He *must* ha' been pleased."

The sarcasm was totally unintentional.

Pleasure is said to lie chiefly in anticipation, but the poor know how to make the most of retrospection. People who have worn themselves out at school treats, mothers' outings, days in the country, etc., and have felt disgustedly "The whole thing has been a failure," would have their reward if they could hear the entertainments that seem to them to have fallen so flat eagerly described a year or more afterwards. I could hardly say how many times an old woman of seventy-six, living in a single room by herself from year's end to year's end, has told me every detail of one glorious day when "All us old girls was took to Brighton, and we'd a lunch and a dinner and a tea *and* a supper." Her grief and disappointment this year over a Christmas treat which somehow faded into nothing, was childishly keen. She had plenty to eat at home, and a nice fire; it was the " party " that she longed for.

I remember one poor woman at a mothers' treat whose anticipations of enjoyment were scarcely realised, for, in order to do justice to the dinner, she had starved herself for two days, and then was so ill that she could eat nothing.

Expressions of gratitude are everywhere rare, but for coolness in receiving favours I hardly know whether the palm should be awarded to north-country people or to Londoners. In the Peak district the usual form of words with which any borrowed appliance was returned to my lodgings was, " Tell her ah've done wi' it." It is mere prejudice, but I always found " Ef ya laike "—a chilling substitute for " Yes, please— worse even than the ambiguous " I don't mind if I do."

Some years ago I had a nice little pea-jacket made for a boy of seven. His parents were not really poor, but they were obstinate, and declined to see any connection between his frequent severe colds and his ready-made waistcoat-less suits often drenched through before he reached school. It was made out of an officer's great-coat, only twice worn and then accident- ally burnt in the front widths, and I had been very particular as to the cut, the buttons, etc., and it was a garment that any lady would have been glad to have for her little son. No thanks reached me. Some

weeks later, when wretched weather set in, I said to
his eldest sister, a girl of eighteen—

"I suppose Willy is glad of his coat now?"

"Well, miss, he says the sleeves is too long, but acept
for that he don't complain."

I gave an old cobbler a coat that I had recently seen
worn by a naval lieutenant, whose outfitter (he told me)
"always expects sixty pounds a year out of my pay."
The old man held it out at arm's-length, examined it
closely, and then said judicially, "It'll do nicely to set
and work in."

But neither of them reached the calm level of a
child aged four and a half, who told me that a certain
Miss —— was making a dress for her. I had vague
beliefs that children ought to be taught gratitude, so I
said—

"I wonder why she is doing it for you?" a question
which seemed to me to lead up to the orthodox reply,
"Because she is very kind." The child reflected, sitting
on the floor with the palms of her hands pressed downwards, her wide blue eyes fixed on my face, and finally
drawled out—

"I s'pose she'd dot a piece of eed (rag), and she
fought she'd oose it."

Except when mothers have been in service, or in
some way brought into contact with their social superiors,
it seems to me that they rarely teach their children to
say "Thank you," even for a gift. A really refined girl
of seventeen showed me a present sent to her from
India by a bachelor uncle, then in his sixteenth year of

foreign service. Knowing the habits of the district, and picturing the exile's disappointment, I asked if she had written to thank him. She was frankly surprised; she could write, and write well, but such an idea had never entered her mind.

It may be said that the scraps of conversation I report are merely those between a foreigner and a native. There is some truth in this, for, not being the heroine of a first-person-singular novel, I cannot blamelessly overhear very much. One result of unconscious eavesdropping I respectfully present to all district visitors. One of them had just left the house, when I heard the cautious but not sufficiently modulated inquiry—

"Ja-ane, *what's the young woman left behind her?*"

"Rice pudden."

"Ooof!"

I attended that household for many weeks, but I think that was the only genuine expression of opinion that ever fell on my ears.

I sat once in an isolated cottage waiting until a violent summer storm blew over, and waited so long in the half-dark room that I think my presence had been forgotten. The father, a morose, surly-looking man, came in from his day's work, and sat down in the only easy-chair with a heavy sigh. I knew him well by sight, and had always carefully timed my visits to avoid him, as it seemed hard that the only living room should be turned into a surgery. The youngest child, a boy of ten, went up to him, and, resting a hand on each knee, swung himself to and fro silently, but with evident satisfaction.

"Weer's Sam'el?" asked the father at last.

"I d'knaw."

Another long pause.

"Dost keer?"

The boy shouted with laughter, jumping himself up and down faster than ever, and a smile twitched one corner of the man's mouth. After all, he was a father, and although he did not say so, he liked the pressure of those grimy little hands, and the boy's weight on his tired knees was no burden.

Waiting in a kitchen for the kettle to boil, I heard a young and previously unsatisfactory daughter-in-law who was cleaning out the invalid's room overhead, address the slowly dying patient in these terms—

"Mother, you can't say as I've sauced you, not since you've bin took bad." An interval of vigorous scrubbing, and then, in the comparatively quiet process of using a house flannel, "I don't say but what I didn't use to sauce you before, but I'm doing my duty by you now, and I *will*. It's not long you'll be here, mother."

"Ay, lass, ay," murmured the poor old woman wearily but placably, not in the least resenting the terms on which she was receiving the girl's long-deferred kindness.

Death is constantly referred to without having any apparent ill-effect on the patient's mind or health. I was recently visiting a woman who in all probability would never leave her bed again, but who was by no means in imminent danger. To make conversation, I remarked, "You have a nice piece of ground round your house" (I could not well say "garden," for it was bare as the road, and almost as hard).

"Yes, and we had a nice lot o' flowers in it last summer, but my husband wouldn't plant it this year, because when I drop off he'll have to give up the house and go and live in a room by hisself."

Few things do more to sweeten the lives of the poor than the generally diffused sense of humour. Every misfortune may be laughed at, provided only that it is one's own. I was told of a lady visitor to a hospital who found a patient convulsed with laughter, and asked the reason of his mirth.

"They've give me a track, ma'am !" he gasped.

"Yes ?"

"It's a track against dancing."

"Well ?"

"Both my legs is cut off!" and again he laughed like a schoolboy.

A few weeks since, an old man from the workhouse came to see me. He was getting on for eighty-six, and had supported himself until three years previously. Crossing the threshold, he remarked : "I must remember to take my hat off, else everyone will guess where I come from." And he laughed as gaily as if all his bitter and unavailing struggles were forgotten.

A London artisan who could not afford to look old, told me one day : "I used to give Polly and Tom [his eldest children] a penny a dozen to pull out my grey hairs, and they thought it hardly earned; but, goodness me! I've had to cut the little ones down, they find 'em too easy by half."

A favourite form of humour lies in an extreme moderation of statement. One summer's day I saw a handsome girl of eighteen or nineteen passing a house where some painters were engaged on the upper windows.

"H'm!" said one, "that's a nice sort o' girl, Bill?"

Bill surveyed her critically.

"H'm, yes. Do to go out walkin' with—*week days*."

On another occasion my fox-terrier was inquiring rather fussily into the proceedings of artisans occupied in testing the telephone tubes just outside the house. "Now, why d'you wanter bite me just because I'm here for ten minutes?" asked one of the men in mildly argumentative tones. "Why, if I was to set here half the day I shouldn't never think o' biting *you!*"

One frequently hears such warnings as these addressed to children: "Get off that there wall, you'll break your neck, and your mother mightn't like it; mothers does have queer ways o' lookin' at things sometimes."

Perhaps this form of humour reached its highest point in a man who told me one stifling August day that he "doubted whether the Underground Railway was very well ventilated."

One day a girl of twenty-three brought her future husband to see me, and said they were to be married in a few weeks' time. She had been employed as a ward-maid, and had been obliged to pay into a superannuation fund, and bitterly regretted the loss of the money, something considerably under two pounds.

"Is there no way of recovering it?" I asked.

"There *is*, miss," said the lover, opening his mouth for the first time. "We could wait until she was entitled to it; but Katie," with an admirably assumed air of a reasonable man yielding to an extravagantly unreasonable woman,—"Katie she says she don't want to wait, not till she's sixty-five!"

One day I watched a fine team of horses pulling a waggon up a steep hill. It was a heavy piece of work, but they were in splendid condition, and the driver walked by their side doing nothing worse than crack his whip and remark admonishingly: "Jenny, I sees what you're at. Just you get to work!" An old lady stopped him, saying in reproving accents: "That's a very heavy load for your horses!"

"It is, ma'am," he replied genially; "in fac', if 'tworn't for the ladies pityin' of 'em and givin' em' sponge cakes, I dunno how they ever *would* get up the 'ills."

"My husband saw my father give me a good hiding once," said a patient.

"Why was that?"

"For walking with *he*. My father said he didn't want to have his daughter living on fourpence a day. But I married him all the same."

"And how did you live?"

Quick as lightning came the reply—

"I *didn't* live. I lingered."

Removed from their surroundings, these specimens

of unconscious humour may seem poor, and at all times a jest's prosperity lies with the hearer. I once wrote an article which I believed to be amusing, and when a not unimportant editor accepted it, I thought that at least one person agreed with me. But only for a few days. The cheque in payment arrived, and with it a note referring to my paper as "very touching." To this day I do not know whether he wept over my joyous tales, or whether, as I naturally prefer to believe, the note was really intended for the gratification of some other "Dear madam" who, in her turn, was equally mortified to learn that her pathos had added to his gaiety.

It will be noted that none of my patients or their friends speak any of the exasperating jargon which in a very large class of novels passes for "dialect," and readers are so accustomed to orthographical orgies that they will feel doubts as to the genuineness of these conversations. Nevertheless they have been written down exactly as they were uttered. I have often listened to the poor day after day until the sound of a cultured voice strikes on my ear like the rarest and most exquisite music.

At the present day the language of the poor differs from that of the middle and upper classes only in the following points—

1. *Intonation*, which cannot possibly be reproduced or even indicated.

2. *Pronunciation* and *accentuation*; the differences, although unmistakable, are often too slight to be

represented by any arrangement of the alphabet, however distracting and uncouth. The long missing " h "
is rapidly finding a home all over the country. The
termination *ng* is disappearing, but this is true of all
classes. Twenty years ago an old Oxford don told me :
" You will live to hear *ng* as completely neglected as
the *ent* in the third person plural of French verbs. I
can remember when to clip one's *g*'s was considered a
vulgarism. I have almost lived to hear people say,
What an old fogey ! He puts in all his *ings !* "

Difficult combinations of consonants are avoided : *ct*
is simplified to *k*, *ask* is nearly always *ast*, while few
persons clearly pronounce such a word as toast or posts.
Abbreviations are much more common than among the
educated classes, and three or four or more words are
often run together almost inextricably. I'd'no's'ish'l
—I do not know that I shall do it.

3. *Vocabulary.*—This is more limited, but the difference
in that respect rapidly decreases ; the poor begin to use
freely the language that they see in print, while the
rich carefully avoid any bookish tinge. Not long ago
a gentleman was giving evidence in a police-court with
reference to a charge of cruelty to children. I read one
of his sentences in the shorthand report, " I spoke to
the mother about it, and she told me it was the children's
own doing." An agricultural labourer's daughter, whose
age was seventeen, and who (by an oversight) had been
allowed to leave school at ten, told me : " He said that
he had complained to their mother, and her reply was
that the children were responsible for the condition

8

they were in." There are, of course, different words in use among the poor for the same things, but they are not nearly as numerous as some novelists would have us believe. Quite recently, however, I have heard the words collied, moucher, and scout (used in the sense of to chase away, to frighten), the corrupted French words brussy (broussailles) and faussy (fausse); and in naval and military towns I have heard the almost extinct words ullage and burgoo.

4. *Superabundance of negatives.*—For example, I asked a London girl of eighteen, the daughter of a superior artisan, if she could solve the old puzzle about the stranger who had found the sign-post blown down, and wished to replace it in order to learn his where-abouts. After a few seconds' thought she said: "I shouldn't think no one couldn't guess that, not nohow!"

5. *Other grammatical errors.*—These are nearly all on the lines of simplification. It is correct to say myself, herself, yourself, ourselves. Very well, let us complete the list with hisself and theirselves. Most verbs are regular, why not all? Let us say comed and goed, seed and bringed and teached.

Another general error is in failing to make the verb agree with the subject. A child wrote me a copper-plate letter in which the sentence occurred: "I go to school still, and are in the Sixth Standard." However, I have often heard well-educated people ask such questions as: "What are the price of those hats?"

What is considered a strong preference for dragging in the objective case would perhaps be more fairly described as the unsatisfied craving of the language for disjunctive pronouns. "Me and him, we went to see her," would translate easily into French, and is a form in common use.

The second person singular is still much used in the north, but in other parts of England I have only occasionally heard the affectionate use of it among elderly people, and the still more rare contemptuous use of it among little boys. "I won't play marbles with *thee* again!" cries the unexpected loser.

6. The constant use of "as" for "that" seems a deforming feature, but it is only slightly out of date. It is still used by literary Americans.

These, carried out in detail, exhaust the differences which mark the speech of the poor as I know them.

CHAPTER V

THE POINT OF VIEW

SOME years ago I read a book on ethics, which began with an inquiry as to what virtues were recognised among the ancients, and the relative importance in their eyes of these virtues. If for "ancients" we substitute the poor, a subject opens up of which it is necessary for all workers among them to have some knowledge.

The poor undoubtedly recognise the same virtues as the rich, but they do not range them in the same order. One sees this most plainly in the way in which they bring up their children. With uneducated parents the worst crime of which children can be guilty is "cheek," and the next is breakages, even if purely accidental. Theft is very severely dealt with if the article is stolen from any person not related to the child, but within the boundary of the family it is far too lightly regarded. I have known several cases lately where boys have broken open locked cupboards belonging to their parents and helped themselves to the contents, and scarcely *any* notice has been taken of the offence. Furthermore, although the children may not steal from outsiders in the sense of taking possession of their goods, carelessly or even wilfully damaging other people's property is seldom regarded as a sin, and to be idle during the time that they are paid to work is scarcely ever regarded as wrong. Disobedience is thought little of, provided that it is not *open*. Falsehood comes a very long way down the list, and the sin of tacit deceit is scarcely recognised.

A year ago I knew a mother who had ten sons. The youngest, a boy of nine, was in training for the church choir. Twice a week, however busy the mother was, she "tidied him up" and sent him off to the class, which took place at an hour when he would not otherwise have been allowed to go out of doors. One day the organist called at the house, complaining that for nearly two months he had never seen the child, and asking why the parents had not written a note if they wished to withdraw him. Any mother of the middle or upper classes would have felt heartbroken to find a child of nine capable of such prolonged deceit, and would have had much searching of mind and conscience as to how far her imperfect training had caused it, or her blame-worthy lack of watchfulness had allowed it to continue. But how did this respectable woman view the matter? Out of respect to the organist, the boy was punished by being confined to the house and garden on the next holiday, but I heard the mother positively *laughing* over the occurrence, and I fear that the child also heard her.

Not long after this, the mother of eight sons told me that she strongly suspected one of them, a boy of twelve, of having appropriated a small sum of money given to him for his parents, and of having told her numerous falsehoods with regard to the occurrence. In order to relieve her mind of what one would have imagined to be a torturing suspicion, all she had to do was to walk half a mile and ask a single question, or to waylay an old man who passed her house a dozen times a week; but this was far too much trouble to take, and the child (wrongfully, perhaps) still rests under the suspicion.

The poor are extremely tenacious of the few forms of politeness with which they are acquainted, and often understand its essentials. The way, for example, in which they will restrain their children from touching anything belonging to a visitor at their house, from thrusting themselves into the conversation, or from making any unwelcome advances, would afford a much-needed example to many parents.

People are too apt to think that chivalry is confined to the upper classes. The encrusted forms of it may be, that is all. I saw a man and his wife, a shabby, miserable-looking couple, pushing a cart along a suburban road. They came to a part where it had not yet been "made," heavy waggons had passed over it, and it was rather worse than a ploughed field. "Git out of the dirt!" said the man, and his wife walked on what did duty for a pavement, while he struggled with the cart alone. Could Bayard have done more?

A few weeks ago I walked about a hundred yards behind a tramp and his wife on the high-road; she carried the child, and he a heavy bundle. Presently it began to rain. What did the man do? Carefully re-arranged the thin shawl to shelter the child more effectually, put the wife to leeward, and *lent her his pipe*.

Few have any conception how much poor men are in the habit of waiting on their wives, and not only in times of illness. I have known men who thought nothing of carrying their wife's bundles half way across London to see her off by a midnight excursion, and of being there to meet her at four o'clock in the morning a few days later, although in the one case they had finished a hard day's work, and in the other had it still before them. And this kind of thing is a mere matter of course, only related to me incidentally, interspersed with accounts of how indifferently they had managed during the wife's absence. "Tom's a poor hand at doin' for hisself. I'd left some dahlias in a vawse, and their leaves had all fell; and if you'll believe me, nurse, he'd never even swep' 'em up. There they was laying, and there they might ha' laid for all he'd care. Oh yes, he had to walk all the way there and back. There's no trams at that time in the morning. The train was a hower late coming in, and after we got back he'd only time to snatch a bit of breakfast before he had to be off."

If only one began one's work among the poor merely ignorant, with no prejudices to shake off! How often one hears a woman who would be rich if her social ambition did not soar so far beyond her means, say with a sentimental sigh: "I envy the poor: it must be so delightful not to have to think about appearances. I have so often wished to sit on my own doorstep."

Philosophers of the eighteenth century envied savages
because they were free: it is now generally admitted
that even the King of Spain or the Tsar of all the
Russias is not more rigorously bound by etiquette than
the tatooed savage.   Perhaps some day another Spencer
will arise, who will give us a learned work on
"Ceremonial Institutions among the Poor of Great
Britain and Ireland, with special reference to those
Families whose Aggregate Income is below Twenty-
five Shillings per week"; from these heavy folios the
information will gradually filter down to newspapers
and popular novels, and the fact that the poor of this
country are martyrs to fashion will be among the things
that "every probationer knows," and will make due
allowance for in her daily rounds.

Even the smallest children are half-voluntary slaves
to inexorable laws.   When it is the time for hoops, no
child dares be seen with a skipping-rope; when it is the
moment for tops, marbles disappear.   If you are not
possessed of the correct toy, you can pretend that you
do not want it, but you must use nothing in its place.

In the matter of mourning the strictest forms are
observed.   Black clothing is not merely a sign of
respect, but a distinct element of *sacrifice* can still be
traced in it.   Hearing that a poor woman was about to
buy "new black" for her mother, I said to her daughter,
who was grieving over the expense : "It need not cost
very much. It is so short a time since your little
brother died that she must have plenty of mourning."
The girl stared at me in blank astonishment at my

ignorance, and I learnt for the first time that *new* clothes are indispensable for each death in a family. If you already possess mourning there is no credit in wearing it; even a pair of black kid gloves already bought and "lying by" must not be used.

I should not wish to see the custom of wearing mourning given up among the poor; there is a touch of idealism in the practice that they can little afford to lose; but it has often gone to my heart to see fifteen or twenty children put into complete suits of black for a grandfather who has been allowed to die in the workhouse, and to think that less than half the money spent on it would have spared him the grief and humiliation of the last few months of his life.

The rich—and by the rich in this connection I simply mean those who are in a position to give something away—fail entirely to recognise the numerous grades of social position that there are among the poor. A Nonconformist minister's wife, who lived in a great manufacturing town, told me that she had been trying to get the money to send two factory girls away for change of air; they had had long and dangerous illnesses, their savings were entirely exhausted, and they were by no means fit to begin work. She said: "A day or two after, I found that the money had easily been raised for one of them by sending round 'a penny whip.' The girls had been educated at the same Board School, worked in the same factory, lived in the same street, and I thought that I could not be doing wrong in suggesting that the same expedient should be adopted by the second one. I found that I had made an almost unpardonable slip: it was correct for M. to do such a thing, and roused no unfavourable comment, but for N. it was *infra dig.*, and impossible. If the money could not be raised with strict privacy, she must remain at home, and live or die as it might chance."

The poor are, of course, equally unable to recognise shades of rank among the rich. One day I heard a little boy, the son of a London police-magistrate, say to his nurse, "When I'm a man I shall be a railway engineer." He was very small, and I think he meant an engine-driver, but had somehow picked up the name of a more probable occupation.

"My dear," said the good woman reprovingly, "I don't know what to make of you, you have *such high ideas.*"

The men of the working classes are still less able than the women to recognise their social superiors when they come into chance contact with them. Early one evening I was travelling in a very dirty and ancient third-class carriage on a local line. My fellow-passengers were an elderly gentleman and his wife. They had evidently been paying a round of calls, and he was decidedly out of temper. He had knocked an invisible dent in his silk hat on entering the unusually low door, and it seemed to have been suddenly borne in upon him that life on small means was unendurable. At the next station a beery workman lurched in, and the instant the train started produced a pipe which was already lighted "You don't mind me smokin', missis?"

" Oh no, not at all!" said the old lady hurriedly, prepared to endure anything rather than let her peppery husband be drawn into an altercation. The man smiled affably, and puffed out a mouthful of the poisonous mixture.

" No more don't *my* old woman, neither!"

But the humours of third-class travelling are chiefly connected in my mind with a different branch of the Queen's Poor—retired officers. One of the many unexplained differences between naval and military men is, that the sailor who lives on his pay holds himself freed from the expense of first-class travelling directly his name is off the active list; while the soldier, however ill he can afford it, thinks himself bound to continue the habit, at any rate in all places where he is known. One day a retired vice-admiral ordered up his brother (I cannot say *invited*), a retired major-general, to go on a short excursion with him, and insisted on taking third-class tickets, to the enormous disgust of his junior. They arrived much too early for the train, as sailors always do, whether admirals or second-class boys, but it was already in the station. The soldier wished to seek seclusion in it, but his overbearing brother insisted on their walking up and down the platform.

Presently the major-general exclaimed in an agonised undertone—

" What *shall* we do ?   There's General ——!"

" *Do ?*—What *is* there to do ?" roared the admiral. " If I saw him astride the engine, what should I care ? Isn't it a free country ?"

His brother certainly had not found it so that afternoon, but the wind was tempered to him. The general also was travelling third-class—by a coincidence not entirely unconnected with the loudness of the admiral's voice, for he found it necessary, a few minutes later, to display such a minute portion of his ticket that a suspicious country-born guard took it from his hand and held it up to the light, to the immense amusement of the admiral, who of course "had his weather eye lifting" at that moment.

Are the poor grateful? Any replies to that question will be as contradictory as if asked of the rich. Gratitude depends on character, not on riches or poverty, and there never seems to be any proportion between the benefit bestowed and the thankfulness experienced. Sometimes, in return for a few days' work, we receive, for a period of years, countless small services whenever we are nursing anyone in the same district, while other natures will accept years of devoted attention with apathy.

Three or four years ago we had a boy of fifteen on our books. He was nursed through a severe attack of pneumonia, and, as it happened, entirely by one person. Owing to the extreme poverty of the family (resulting from the father's drunken habits) no donation was made to the Association, but with infinite difficulty the lad saved up five shillings, and walked the streets for hours with it in his pocket, hoping to meet the nurse, but never succeeded in doing so. He knew where we lived, but dared not come to the house,—because in the meantime he had put on the uniform of a very distinguished regiment, and was unaccountably ashamed of it, and convinced that we "should not like to have a soldier come knocking at the door." He never spent the money, and for a long time carried it with him wherever he went. Three years later we were called in to nurse his dying father, and then the long-postponed gift to the Association was made.

Drunkenness before marriage, but more especially if the man is engaged, is generally regarded seriously, and I think the advice that I heard very late one night, bestowed by a young man in the didactic stage of intoxication upon a respectable elder whom he had never seen in his life before, was hardly necessary. "Here I am— lying in dish—like good S'mar'tan. Father—you're old 'nuff to be m' father—if ever you get—son-'n-law like me—you take an'—frow him in the dish."

Occasional drunkenness after marriage is considered on a different plane, but is quite as much disapproved of as it was among the professional classes sixty years ago. In spite of all that teetotallers tell us, many a workman is drunk once or twice in the year, and yet never "fills a drunkard's grave." A month or two since, I asked, with reference to a highly respectable workman, and without the smallest idea that I was touching on delicate ground—

"Is your father going to G—— on the Bank Holiday?"

"He isn't sure, not yet, m'm."

"Cannot his master spare him?"

" Mother isn't sure yet whether *she* can go, and she don't mean to let him go by himself. Last time he went he got drunk. Mother said he was pretty well paid out for it, for he was as ill as could be for three days after, but she don't feel as if she could quite trust him to go alone."

I must add that the husband was fully trusted not to waste what the wife called " the children's money," and the children called " mother's money "; the poor woman's fear was of the hospitality of a relative " in the trade." Many people dread giving small tips to men, because they think that they are at once spent at the public-house on liquor that may be " doctored," and prefer giving a little of their own whisky and water, or some good beer. In my experience, a small unexpected money present to a married workman, and most of them are married, commonly reaches the home in the shape of fruit or toys or sweets for the " kids," while the " glass of something that won't hurt them " often rouses an unexpected thirst for more, and the ordinary taste and quality of that " more " can be gathered from the following story.

One night, a few winters ago, some acquaintances of mine, an old gentleman and his wife, living in a London suburb, engaged a cabman to drive them home from a quiet dinner-party. It was bitterly cold, deep snow on the ground, and when they reached the house the old gentleman asked his wife to get some whisky for the man, while he fetched a little water. The cabman drank the mixture thankfully and drove off. He had scarcely done so when the old lady exclaimed, with horror: " John, I gave him *furniture polish !* " The unwitting crime weighed heavily on their minds; they searched the newspapers for days after, they were afraid to look at a cabman and yet fascinated by the sight of one. Some weeks after they again hailed a cab at about the same hour, and, to their joy, it was driven by their victim, to all appearances in the best of health, and—more surprising still—showing no sign of resentment, although he evidently recognised them. Arrived at their door, the old lady asked him what he would like to drink.

" Same as you give me last time, mum, please. That warmed me for a week after, that did ! "

The poor, even many of the most superior among them, have a great horror of inspectors, foremen, etc., and never can be got to see that their work is necessary, and this feeling leads to a determined protection of all subordinates, that makes it easy for great abuses to creep into every institution. We had a ludicrous instance of this a few weeks ago. The wife of a retired sailor was ill. It was an easy case, and was usually attended by a probationer ; but one day, when she had more work than she could manage, I sent a staff-nurse to take her place. She happened to be a tall and imposing-looking woman, who wore her uniform " with a difference." The old man opened the door and looked at her disapprovingly : " And who may you be ? A leading man come to see after our nurse's work ? "

" Oh no, I am only an ordinary nurse come to help your wife."

His face was as full of suspicion as only a simple-minded man's can be—

"I know the superintendent, and the young woman she has sent does her work very well, and my wife can't abide new faces. Good-night, m'm."

He shut the door gently, bolted it, and went joyfully to tell his Joan how the enemy who had "come a-spying into the work of the young woman" had been routed.

The poor have, it must be acknowledged, what is commonly called a "love of horrors," but it might be more fairly described as "a love of distinction at any cost." When one considers the monotony of their lives, can one wonder at it, even if it takes forms which at first sight seem to alienate one's sympathy? A girl friend, long since dead, was once telling me that her father's servant, always a delicate young fellow, had died while on a long voyage with him, and that, acting on her father's instructions, she had been to see the relatives, and assured them that he had had excellent nursing, and had died painlessly after a very brief illness.

"I hoped it would comfort them to know that he did not suffer, but it did not seem to do so in the least."

A young naval officer had been listening impatiently to the tale, and broke in—

"My dear Norah, how *could* you say such a thing? How could you *expect* them to like it? I always write the funeral letters wherever I am. I've done it for years. I'm an awful dab at it."

She turned her beautiful eager face on him with a feminine desire for instruction.

" What do you say in them ? "

" Why, I always say their sufferings were atrocious, and they bore them with heroic fortitude."

" And then ? "

" Then they're awfully pleased, and write and say they're glad he died a Christian, and when can they have his clo'es."

It was a caricature, but founded on truth, and nothing delights and flatters my patients and their friends so much as when they can report to me : " The doctor say he never heard of a case like it before."

Generally speaking, if the doctor ever said so, he must, to put the matter politely, have been " directing his intention " to their description of the case, and not to his own observation of it.

Suspiciousness is an inconveniently common quality among even the most respectable of the poor. If they were invariably suspicious, one might say that it conduced to their safety, but a tendency to misplaced confidence is equally marked. Patients will question the doctor closely as to the knowledge of the trained nurse, and press the latter to give them her opinion of the doctor, but instantly accept the most brazen quack at his own valuation. The clergyman " makes *something*, you may be pretty sure," out of the Coal Club ; and his wife, " well, it don't stand to reason she does it for *nothing* " when she first laboriously collects their pence for the Provident Club, and then with still more

9

trouble collects from her friends the bonuses which are to be the bribes for taking the first difficult steps in acquiring thrift and foresight. But the fraudulent traveller they have never seen before, and who will take good care that they never see him again, the bogus agent of every description, all find an easy prey, and would find a still easier one if they were not mercifully under the delusion that to succeed they must be, like genuine commercial travellers, "of gentlemanly appearance and address." The more closely they appeared to resemble the classes they were trying to rob, the more readily they would obtain credence from them.

I fear that if the rich knew the estimation in which they are held by the poor, they would hardly have the moral courage to go among them. It is easy to say, "They think badly because they are bad themselves"; but this by no means solves the problem: men and women who are capable of the greatest devotion, generosity, and disinterestedness, appear unable to conceive that any person whose income is apparently above about £200 a year can possibly show them any kindness except from purely selfish motives.

Generations of education will be required before this suspiciousness can be swept away, but every one who will be his own almoner, who will remember that "the gift without the giver is bare," and devote his spare time and thought to a few families with whom he is personally acquainted, can do much to reduce its power for evil. As long as it remains in its present force, it

detracts enormously from the value of every agency
for improving the condition of the poor.

This is a trifling instance of the apparently un-
conquerable suspiciousness that one meets with. A
small present of grouse was sent to the hospital where
I was working, and was cooked instead of chicken for
a few of the women patients who were almost well.
It was accepted by all of them without comment, and
the probationer who cleared away the plates did not
notice that one of them was missing. The next day
the committee walked through all the wards to receive
any complaints or requests that might be made. A
patient drew a plate out of some secret fastness with
the untouched portion of grouse on it.

"Please to look at what they've been and give me
for my dinner,—*bad chicking*."

That woman had been nursed by us for many weeks,
and was making an excellent recovery from a dangerous
illness, and yet she was perfectly ready to believe, first,
that we had given her bad food; secondly, that it was
not an accident that she could afford to look over in
consideration of our general good conduct; and thirdly,
that it would be useless to apply to me, whom she saw
many times a day, to the matron, whom she saw at
least twice, or to any of the doctors. Her "rights"
could only be obtained by appealing to outsiders. The
man to whom she addressed her protest had shot the
birds himself, so his opinion of them, as grouse, was not
unbiassed, but he was conscientiously able to assure her
that they had never been "chicking," and could not be

expected to look like them. It is more than probable that many of those who submissively ate their portion held the same opinion with regard to it, and only differed from her in their lack of courage.

A poor person's excuse generally sounds feeble. For example, servants will offer the most childishly weak excuses for giving up this or that situation, or for not accepting it, and educated listeners rashly conclude that they are illogical and absurd. The absurdity lies as a rule with the person who accepts the offered excuse as the real reason. A lady finds, perhaps, what seems to her an excellent situation for a girl who is certainly not needed at home. The mother objects that it is too far off, or that the girl is too young to leave her, or that the work would be too hard. A week or two later the lady hears that she has been sent to a very rough place, three times as far off, and for considerably less wages than her friend would have given. It is not until months or perhaps years after that she learns that the mother was well acquainted with the real character of the " excellent old servant " under whom it was to be " such an advantage " for her daughter to be trained, and had, after carefully considering the matter, deliberately preferred placing the girl where, although the work might be harder and the pay smaller, she would be constantly under the eye of a respectable working mistress.

One day I received a message from a deaconess asking me to send a nurse to a certain house where there was a bedridden woman left almost entirely alone. If

possible, the first visit to a new case is always paid by
the superintendent, so I went myself. The old lady
received me politely, but to every suggestion of nursing
attendance that I made she declared either that it had
been done for her that morning, or would be done for
her that night, or that her married daughter "came
round" and did it for her three times a day.

I changed the subject to matters in general, and sat
talking to her for a long time. When I at last rose to
go, she said, with a sudden burst of confidence: "If you'll
come a-Monday, I'll have some hot water ready."
Nothing but the lack of hot water and the unwillingness
to own to a perfect stranger that she had none, and no
immediate means of getting it, had been at the bottom
of her refusals of attendance that she obviously needed.

Often it is only by a frank expression of personal
opinion that one can arrive at what the respectable
poor really think. A sensible young woman, the eldest
of a "long" family, said to me with apparent admiration
of the act—

"Mr. B. [a dairyman] is very good to the Lukyn
children. He'll often tell poor little Winnie to bring a
jug, and fill it right up for her."

"I call it anything but kind of him," I replied; "for
he knows as well as I do that Lukyn's wages are nearly
half as much again as your father's, that they each have
the same rent to pay and the same number of children
dependent on them, and yet the Lukyns are perfect
mudlarks, while your mother's little ones would be a
credit to any nursery. Mr. B. gives the milk to Winnie

because he cannot bear to see her pinched and grimy face, and does not think that it only means another threepence for Mrs. Lukyn to spend on drink. The only real kindness that anyone can show those poor children is to frighten their mother into feeding them, and their father into seeing that he has not 'done his duty by them' simply because he hands her over the greater part of his wages."

"That's just what mother says. She often feeds the Lukyns because she can't abear to see 'em go hungry, but she knows she hadn't ought to do it. It isn't even fair by *our* children. But Mr. B. isn't the only one who gives Winnie and the others another push in the mud when he thinks he's helping them. You know, I told you about the Clothing Club mother joined, and what a pinch she'd found it sometimes to keep up the subscriptions, but how she'd done it, and what a lot of nice things she'd got ? Well, Mrs. Lukyn joined too, but she only went on for a short time, and when Christmas come she was weeks and months behind. Mrs. K., one of the ladies as got it up, went to her house to speak to her about it, and saw everything looking so poor and wretched, and she told her a lot of lies about her husband, throwing the blame on his drinking—which he don't get drunk three times in the year—and then Mrs. K. went and paid it all up for her, and she got her things just the same as the others. And what was the good of that ? The money that she'd have *had* to spend on clothes for the children because the Cruelty man had told her he had his eye on her, all went in drink. Lady

P. was dreadful cross with Mrs. K. about it, but the
money had been give, and it couldn't be took away.
Lady P. said it was such a bad example. Of course she
knew people like *mother* don't need to be bribed to keep
their children decent, and people like Mrs. Lukyn won't
do it for anyone short of the p'lice; but she said Mrs. K.
had ought at least to ha' thought how many of the half-
and-half sort there is, and how a push like that'll sometimes send 'em the wrong way."

Through what secret intelligence office Lady P.'s most
justifiable reproaches to Mrs. K. had reached her I did
not inquire.

CHAPTER VI

STATE-SPREAD TABLES

THE causes of the insufficient or unsuitable feeding of many children in the poorest classes are numerous and complex, therefore no panacea is possible. Moreover, it is a serious mistake to imagine that all ill-nourished, badly developed children are suffering from lack of food, or even from food of low nutritive power. Their low vitality commonly results from other factors, the most frequent being bad ventilation at night. I know numberless children, in the country as well as in towns, who are carefully fed, washed, clothed, and tended, and then have to sleep in rooms in which they are slowly poisoned. Again, not a few of the feeblest specimens at Board Schools, so far from being proofs of their parents' ignorance, apathy, selfishness, or poverty, are the results of unremitting attention bestowed upon offspring delicate from birth. Formerly, boys and girls of this type, fed on milk, tonics, and cod-liver oil, clothed from head to foot in flannel or chamois leather, were only to be found among the middle and upper classes; if born among the poor, they perished at a very early moment in their existence. " Want of food " is the verdict if a workman's child looks thin or pale. Let the people so hasty in passing it count up the puny sons and daughters of their well-to-do and even wealthy acquaintances, let them imagine those little creatures dressed in the ordinary garments of Council School boys and girls, instead of in clothes carefully designed to minimise any personal defect, and enhance any fragile childish prettiness they may possess, and they will be forced to own that these children would infallibly be among those picked out by the benevolent as objects of charity. " Poor little dear, she do look pale. I s'pose she's come to you for change of air?" was the remark made to me by a kind-hearted woman with reference to a child— decidedly dirty at the moment—whose parents were well enough off to keep four servants, and whose home was in one of the healthiest parts of England.

Most of these children will die before reaching maturity; it can only be hoped that as time goes on fewer of them will be born. People talk of infant mortality as if it were *entirely* a loss to the country. I say nothing of illegitimate children, the waste of healthy lives among them is incontestable; but in ordinary family life among the poor nearly every child in arms that I have seen die has died because no amount of care would keep it alive.

Some years ago I was working in a large provincial hospital, and a most starved and wretched-looking little boy was brought into the children's ward. The doctor in attendance on him in his own home strongly suspected the parents of deliberately starving him, but did not feel justified in openly accusing them of it, and wished to have him kept under close observation for some weeks. Day and night we tended him, and he was fed with everything that the knowledge or imagination of the combined staff could suggest. The little mouth eagerly swallowed everything put into it, but the only result was the rehabilitation of the parents' character. At the end of fourteen weeks the child was discharged, not an ounce heavier, not a shade less wretched in appearance.

Where underfeeding exists, the causes of it, as far as I have detected them, are—

1. Ignorance and apathy of one or both parents.

2. Laziness of either parent, more especially if on the part of the mother.

3. Meals extravagant in amount and cost eaten two or three times a week.

4. The disgracefully bad cooking stoves commonly provided in workmen's homes. (I have measured kitchen ovens 10 inches wide and 12 in depth, the rest of the range being in strict proportion.)

5. The vanity which prefers fine clothes to good food.

6. Gross selfishness, drunkenness, or deliberate cruelty of the parents.

7. The fastidiousness and indulged whims of the children.

8. Mistaken ideals of duty, which turn the mother into a second wages-earner.

9. Temporary poverty owing to want of work, or to ill-health of either wage-earner or wage-expender.

10. Permanent poverty.

I may as well say at once that of those working-men who are permanently unable to provide the necessaries of life for their children, I know nothing. I do not dispute their existence; I only say that if they exist as a class it is doubtful whether they should be allowed, and certain that they should not be encouraged, to call large families into the world. If their children are to be fed gratuitously, or under cost price, the father's wages will sink proportionately, or even disproportionately. In addition, the expense of supporting a rapidly increasing semi-pauper population must inevitably fall to an appreciable extent upon the very last persons whom we should wish to injure,—those who, owing to their industry and thrift, have just a little more than is needful for decency and health.

The remedies that I should suggest for improving the food of school children and of the poor generally, would be—

1. All girls to be taught cottage cooking throughout their *last* year at school. For departmental reasons, such instruction as is given is often received at the age of eleven, a period of life when the ordinary managing mother would not allow a child to wash her own face for fear she should waste the soap, and the lessons are nearly forgotten before they can be put into practice. I once saw a girl of that age cook a dinner of meat pies and boiled potatoes for her father and the younger children, and make beef-tea and a custard pudding for her sick mother, but such precocious handiness and intelligence is—happily—exceptional.

2. All girls between fourteen and eighteen, not engaged in domestic service, should be compelled to attend a certain number of classes in cooking, nursing, and the feeding and general care of young children.

3. Cooking classes for married women should frequently be held. Thousands of them would thankfully attend an afternoon lesson between three and four, paying an entrance fee of a penny, and buying a printed copy of the recipes. The lessons must be strictly practical, and with a keen eye to cost. Full details were given to me a year ago of a cottage cookery class paid for by a County Council. After the introductory lecture, the audience were expected to say what they wished to learn, and the teacher brought the ingredients the following week. The squire's cook attended, and she was the only woman who opened her mouth — until afterwards. Consequently puff paste, lemon curd, pancakes thin as wafers, sweet and savoury omelettes, and afternoon tea-cakes made with eggs and butter, filled up most of the teacher's time. It is true that instruction was given in the making of Irish stew, but as it contained a piece of rump steak that cost 1s. 3d., and as the husbands of the women present were earning from 15s. to 18s. per week, and most of them had large families, even this dish was scarcely adapted to their means.

In the very same schoolroom, and to almost exactly the same audience, a thoroughly practical set of lectures on nursing was delivered. Special stress was laid upon infectious diseases. Since then scarlet fever has twice broken out, and diphtheria once; but, chiefly owing to the precautions impressed on the mothers at these classes, the illness has never spread beyond the original cases. In addition, nearly every child with a cut or burnt finger goes to school with its hand neatly bandaged, and many of the cheap pamphlets sold by the nurse have been carefully studied.

4. At all mothers' meetings the usual mawkish story-book which covers the undercurrent of petty gossip, should be displaced by a twenty minutes' lecture on hygiene (with especial reference to the prevention of disease), the feeding of infants under two years of age, and the moral training of children. The last being given, if possible, by women who have not only brought up families, but have done it on narrow means and in crowded homes. Unfortunately, poor parents are too little in the habit of regarding a child of six or seven as a reasonable being: they do not think it necessary to speak the truth to him, still less do they demand truth from him; they do not look for obedience except under compulsion and in their presence; they do not even insist that he shall keep his hands from picking and stealing. And nevertheless, at twelve or thirteen they expect the same child to be more than half "grown-up."

5. Mothers often seek anxiously for the simplest information, and cannot obtain it. "Doctor," said one woman, "my baby is sick after everything it eats. What shall I do for it?" "Put the little squeaker's head in a bucket of cold water," replied the doctor cheerfully, and raced

down the long flight of stairs. I doubt if he had ever seen a baby since he was a medical student, and he had never been in any way responsible for the feeding of one.

The space usually filled in parish magazines, picture almanacs, and all similar literature, by calculations of how many cows' tails it would take to reach the moon, or anecdotes of His Transparency the late Duke of Kahlkopf-Leerendorf, should be occupied by brief paragraphs rightly coming under the heading of Health and Home. All existing agencies for spreading knowledge should be used to the uttermost before fresh ones are called into action.

6. Leaflets on all matters directly and indirectly concerned with health should be drawn up by the practical and distributed by the charitable. Surely these subjects are capable of the same sprightly and narrative treatment which makes my patients pore delightedly over the advertisements of quack medicines, even when they have no money to buy them ?

7. Illustrated books on hygiene, nursing, etc., should be in every Sunday school and parish library, and should be pressed upon the attention of all women and girls borrowing books. District nurses should attend daily at elementary schools, and all children apparently ill-nourished should be carefully examined to ascertain whether lack of food or generally unfavourable conditions are responsible for their state of health. If they are proved to be under-fed, the cause must be inquired into, and if the semi-starvation arises from the persistent

cruelty or habitual drunkenness of the parents, steps should at once be taken to remove the children from their guardianship, and to compel them to pay the full cost of maintenance as borne by respectable fathers in that class of life. I say the full cost, because I have known parents condemned to pay one shilling per week, and they have boasted to me how much they were allowed to leave that shilling in arrears. Small wonder that one of them, looking at an ordinarily tiresome little boy of seven or eight, said in tones of cheerful anticipation: " He'll be took too, along of his brother, if he don't look out."

On strict and close inquiry, it would be found that many of the worst nourished children had parents with ample means to feed them properly. I recently worked in a house where five grimy children of school age slept in one bed under one blanket, or crouched apathetically on the filthy floor, watching a handful of fire. They were obviously suffering from prolonged insufficiency of food. Who or what was to blame ? The wildest tariff reformer could not have fixed it on Cobden. The father was in regular employment, and had been so for the previous twenty-three years. His wages were not high, but all the neighbours on a smaller and far less certain income had not only well-fed and well-clothed children, but completely furnished and carefully decorated houses.

Last winter, in a village school with over a hundred children on the register, the only ragged, dirty, and half-starved ones were the four belonging to a man whose wages were *double* that of the ordinary agricultural labourers whose children formed about sixty per cent. of the whole. The three boys had not even a shirt, the girl's rags of underclothing were held together with pins and twine. In spite of everything, they were pretty children, but all their little school-fellows of corresponding age were fully three inches taller. No words would describe the horrible state of dirt they were in : when the girl in a sudden impulse of affection threw her arms round my neck, I could scarcely force myself to return her caress.

Now, suppose these unhappy children had been at a large town school with 4000 on the register ; even at the same low rate they would have numbered 160. Nearly 200 starving children in one school ! Let us curse Cobden, let us batter at the relieving officer's door, let us try and upset " the wretched constitution of society " !

What was done in the village ? The parents were prosecuted. The children are now, without having been removed from their guardianship, amply fed and decently clothed. I cannot say that they are positively clean, but they no longer excite repulsion, and they are rapidly catching up lost time in their general development.

What was done in the village should be done in the town ; whatever the cost of making inquiries might be, it would be the cheapest plan in the end.

A farmer's daughter lodging by the seaside for her health, told me that in the same house there were two miserably fed children. Every morning they sawed themselves a slice of bread from the loaf, which they ate with cold water, unless one of the lodgers took pity on them and gave them a cup of tea. They then went off to the nearest Board School. About ten o'clock the parents got up, and about eleven had a good breakfast of eggs and bacon or fried steak. When the children returned to "dinner," they were lucky if they could rub their bread round the greasy frying-pan and unwashed dishes. The parents had a second substantial meal while the children were at afternoon school, and their share when they returned was any cold vegetables that might be left. If there were none, the meal was again bread, and perhaps a little butter or jam. Are parents of this type worth subsidising?

There is one reason why the upper classes are too ready to listen to the plea, "such a lot of little ones to support." Professional and business men, generally speaking, earn a much larger yearly income between forty and sixty, in many cases one might say between forty-five and sixty-five, than they do between twenty-five and forty; and if they marry even moderately early, the hardest part of their lives, from a financial point of view, comes when they have three or four children in the nursery and one or two more already needing expensive education. They do not sufficiently realise that this is *not* the case with the ordinary wage-earner. If a workman marries at the usual age, he has the "large family of young children totally dependent on him" precisely at the time when he is earning most. Feeding his children gratuitously is not a question of tiding over a difficult point in his career, but of pauperising him when his earnings are at their highest.

10

If he cannot support a family then, he can *never* do it.

If the bad feeding is due to any of the first five causes that I have named, the parents should be warned, preferably by an inspector of the R.S.P.C.C., that if they do not speedily alter their ways their children will be condemned to dine at the school for two, four, or six months, making them clearly understand that this is neither a right nor a privilege, but a disgrace,—and an expense.

It is nonsense to speak of providing a wholesome dinner for a penny; it cannot be done. The average cost of feeding each child suitably and sufficiently in its own home is about fourpence a day; of this at least twopence or twopence-halfpenny ought to be spent on the dinner, and it would only be just to penalise negligent parents to the extent of another halfpenny to pay for firing and labour.

With regard to the dinner coupons issued to this limited class for limited periods, a precaution not mentioned by any of the advocates of State-spread tables would be necessary. Each child has (I presume) a number on the school register, and this number would have to be stamped on each of its coupons. Otherwise, such ill-trained children would sell them for a halfpenny or even a farthing, and grasping men and women would buy them for their own belongings, or make a profit by retailing them. Disobedience and prolonged deceit is so common in homes of that low type, that this course of conduct might go on for days and weeks undiscovered and unpunished.

The fastidiousness and fancifulness of many poor children plays a large part in their ill nourishment. It is caused partly by the feeble appetite itself resulting from various unfavourable conditions, and partly from whims indulged to an extent incredible to those firmly convinced that " a word and a blow, and the blow first," is the ordinary system of child-rearing among the poor. In the middle and upper classes the rule " eat what is given you " still prevails, and is commonly maintained until reasonably good habits are formed: even the melancholy choice, " Go without, then ! " is denied in the majority of nurseries and schoolrooms. This wholesome discipline is little known among the poor : if the children do not like what is set before them, they ask for something else, and they end by getting it. I have seen four children eating their dinner in an artisan's kitchen, hot meat and potatoes, to be followed by a milk pudding. One of them had asked for tea, one for cocoa, the third had coffee, and the fourth some teetotal mixture largely composed of citric acid.

Mothers who have knowledge and energy to provide wholesome soup, or potatoes and gravy and suet pudding, are often the very ones who lack the strength of mind to refuse when the children turn away from the carefully prepared meal, demanding bread and jam. A woman said to me one day, pointing to a puffy, unhealthy boy of five, youngest but one of a large family : " Three separate things, one after the other, if you'll believe me, ma'am, he fancied he could eat for his breakfast this morning, and when I got them, not one would he touch." Imagine such a scene taking place in any household where the work was done by paid servants!

When mothers apply their one idea of discipline, the remedy is perhaps worse than the disease. "Lillian looks pale this morning," I said inquiringly, glancing at a downcast, heavy-eyed little girl, an only child.

"Yes, nurse," said the mother, radiating self-satisfaction, "That's because of the beating she had yes'day. You told me she wanted more nourishin' food, so I cooked her a chop and some pertaters, and she wouldn't eat it, and she didn't neither; but I took a stick to her, and I beat her well, that I did!"

Children of this delicate and obstinately fastidious type would abound at every State-spread table, and when the first novelty of the diet had worn off, the Board Schoolmaster's arm would ache to an unwonted degree before the plates of "wholesome food" were cleared. If no compulsion were used, enormous waste would result. If the waste were utilised, it would be devoured by an unlicensed mob of boys whose parents should rather be prosecuted for cruelty, neglect, and drunkenness, or for not having them under proper control.

There is a general complaint now of the early age at which town children are emancipated from all domestic control, and I can see for myself how hard it is for poor parents to keep their children in check. They have ceased, to a great extent, to be their educators, and if they ceased to be the immediate providers of food, there are thousands of young boys, and not a few girls, who would never enter their homes except to sleep, and not always then. How would middle-class parents like to try and manage healthy boys between eight and fourteen if they had not the certainty to fall back on : "Oh, he'll come home when he's hungry"?

All the more refined children would be disgusted by the publicity, noise, smell, and bad serving of the State-aided meals, while, if the same order were maintained as while they were learning the rivers of India or where to place the decimal point, I doubt if Irish stew eaten under such strict discipline would be as nourishing as bread and scrape interspersed with laughter.

In providing meals, it would have to be remembered that habits of order and refinement have spread among the decent poor to an extraordinary extent during the last twenty-five years. A few weeks ago, I saw the five younger children of a labourer at tea, their ages ranging from three to thirteen. Although I knew them to be gentle and well-brought-up, I was secretly astonished to see the manner in which they held themselves, and what old-fashioned governesses would have called "the propriety of their deportment." I mentioned it afterwards to their elder sister, a girl of seventeen, who replied—

"Oh, if they didn't eat their food tidily, father would send them out of the kitchen at once. He can't stand any messing. If mother gives them so and so, or so and so," naming dishes that it would puzzle the greatest authority on etiquette to eat elegantly, "father can't go so far as to say they shan't have it, because it's cheap and they enjoy it, and mother likes to please them when she can, but he takes himself out into the garden, and there he'll stop till they're done eating."

This man is a totally illiterate labourer earning fifteen shillings a week, and the mother, but only since the youngest child could walk, gets a little by half-days' washing and charing for her neighbours; and of the two daughters in service, one is still partly dependent on her parents. Yet I can no more imagine those children clearing a tin plate at a penny dinner, surrounded by all the neglected wastrels of the neighbourhood, than I can picture the little daughters of the largest ratepayer in the district doing it.

Old friends of mine, who from their earliest girlhood have arranged school treats, mothers' teas, choir suppers, and so forth. in a parish adjoining a large town, told me a few months ago—

"Formerly we used only to ask ourselves, Is there enough to eat? now our constant thought is, Will they eat it? There are people here who persist in giving the same plain plum-cake and sweetened tea meals that were the greatest possible treat fifty years ago, and very thankfully received within the last thirty, and the waste after one of their 'entertainments' is simply awful. It is carried away in buckets."

A country surgeon, who was workhouse doctor for three parishes, told me that the cheese he most frequently sees on his poorest patients' tables is Gorgonzola. One day he pointed to it, and asked a woman of ninety:

"Is that what you had when you were young?" She gave a satisfied chuckle, and said it was the only cheese she could "fancy."

Any woman in my position could bring forward thousands of similar facts, and in the face of them it is folly to speak as if all that was necessary to reform the diet of even the very poorest children would be to put three-halfpenny-worth of food on a tin plate and sell it for a halfpenny.

If the State undertook to provide dinners for school children, ignorant mothers would be left in the same or an increasing state of ignorance; lazy mothers would become yet more idle; the extravagance of Saturday and Sunday meals would be increased, and yet more money would be spent on tawdry finery; the righteous discontent of those mothers at present hindered from cooking by their wretched stoves would die away; worse than all, industrious mothers set free from cooking for their children, would seek paid employment in increasing numbers. This would lower the wages of spinsters and widows, and ultimately lower the wages of men, while the immediate results would be disastrous to their necessarily neglected family.

"*Grub?* Children wants more than grub!" said a well-trained father contemptuously; and then he proceeded to tell me perhaps a hundredth part of what his home-keeping wife did daily for their four young children.

And why stop short at dinner? Most poor children require—and get—four meals a day. Why stop short

at school children? Boys and girls leaving school
at thirteen or fourteen are unable to earn their
entire living for several years after; they are forced
to exert themselves far more; they are often growing
at a rapid rate, bread and jam has lost its satiating
powers, and the mother truthfully exclaims: "I'd
rather feed three of the little ones than that great boy
or girl."

"Send the girls to service" is a favourite reply. I
know one county where country mothers are generally
anxious that their growing boys should "live in." The
result of this competition is that recently the only offers
made to a woman for her sturdy, well-knit son of fifteen
and a half were board and lodging without washing
or wages; a taller boy a year older received in addition
sixpence a week; a third lad of seventeen had what
was called, and I believe correctly, "not quite enough
for his boots." If girls were as willing to go to service
as they are now averse from doing so, wages
would rapidly fall, and the general treatment would
deteriorate.

If the children's unsatisfactory condition really arises
from the parents' poverty, in any decent home are the
little ones the first to suffer? Long before the traces
of deprivation could be marked in them, the father
would be pinched and haggard, the mother nearly
starved. In such cases dinners for the children alone
would be a pitiful half-measure, and the public provision of them a needless humiliation. Food should be
supplied to the whole family by charitable individuals,

or, under due restrictions, temporary outdoor relief should be given.

What grounds have the promoters of these schemes for saying that, while charity weakens parental obligation, State aid would strengthen it? We know more of private charity than we do of State aid, and that is the chief reason why we can say more against it. The only system at all resembling what is proposed, was that of the allowances made under the unreformed Poor Law to fathers of families. We all know what its results were.

Charitable assistance has many weak points, but if well organised and used strictly for tiding over temporary difficulties, I think it may fairly be said—

A. That it can be applied quicker than State aid;

B. With more discrimination;

C. That, as it is not a "right," people whose conduct sinks below the average level will not hope to receive it;

D. That even the most ignorant persons know that charity is limited in amount, that it ebbs and flows and often runs dry, and they never learn to place absolute dependence on it, and give up all personal effort in the way that they would do if they received State aid.

But strict organisation is needed. Not long ago, a benevolent old gentleman came to me and asked breathlessly: "Will you give me the names of forty people in real want of a dinner?" When I told him that I did not know of *one*, he simply thought that he had come across a stony-hearted official where he had hoped to find a Christian woman, and went away convinced, in spite of all that I could say, not only that such people could easily be found among the stationary population of the town, but, which would have been still more difficult to prove, that they would have been benefited by his plan. If I had known forty, or even four, I should have picked out the two most deserving and given them twenty dinners each. Twenty dinners might restore a convalescent's strength, or tide over "hard times," but what would one meal do except teach the recipient to look for more?

Furthermore, it would be far better to give them the money, two or three days' supply at a time. Not only would it be more economically spent, but with far greater satisfaction to the recipients. The rich do not like the cooking of the poor, nor their choice of viands: do they imagine that the poor enjoy *theirs?* I have known one instance in which food from a rich man's kitchen was appreciated. It was a meat pie sent weekly to an old woman living on outdoor relief, and she liked it because she had been allowed to explain to the cook precisely how she wished it made, and the cook good-naturedly smothered her own prejudices and made it in that way and no other. I must own that until the excellencies of these pies had been pointed out to me by the consumer, I attributed them to the sulkiness of the kitchen-maid.

To speak of a "living wage" has always seemed to me an absurdity. It is not so much a question of what a man earns, as of what his wife can do with the money. I know houses, even in large towns, where every necessary and decency of life, and many of its comforts, pleasures, and refinements, are provided for a family of the average size on an income of £1 a week. I know others, not tainted by drunkenness or profligacy, where expenditure of the same sum results in bread and tea, American cheese, an occasional rasher of coarse bacon, patent medicine, thin, dingy clothes and bedding, and a " bit o' fire." I have known yet others where twice, thrice, and even four times the wages have been spent in such filthy and miserable surroundings, by such desolate and ragged persons, that it was impossible for me to keep charitable people at bay,—half-crowns simply flew into these dens of idleness and housewifely incapacity.

To arrive at the real income of any one household is a slow and difficult matter. On close examination, incomes are generally found to be composite, though not quite so much so as the retired sailor implied when he told his former captain, who had been pitying him for the smallness of his wages: "Oh, thanky sir, with what I has, and what I earns, and what I begs, and what I steals, we does pretty well!"

Not long ago my attention was drawn to a family in the country, consisting of father, mother, five children of school age, one in service at £6 a year, and one at £12. I was told that the father's wages were 16s. a week, that the rent was £10 a year, that the younger daughter in service cost her parents at least £2 a year, and brought her washing home to be done. All this

was perfectly true, but as I found the children well
fed and well clothed, I knew that, as miracles do not
happen, there must be other sources of income.

On closer inquiry, I discovered that the father's over-
time money averaged 1s. 6d. a week ; that the mother's
earnings were 3s. 6d. ; that the eldest child of school
age earned 1s. every Saturday, and the second child had
3d. from a neighbour for running errands ; and that
the two elder children between them earned 4d. a week
regular attendance money at school. (The third child
was delicate, or the sum would have been 6d.) This
raised the money income of the family from 16s. to
22s. 7d.

I then proceeded to discover and estimate the income
in kind. There was a large garden, which produced
the year's supply of vegetables and fruit, and the mother
bought sugar and made all the jam and pickles. The
supply of apples was used freely until Christmas, about
which time (as they were not "good keepers") the
remainder was sold at 1d. per pound. Even at this
low rate they produced on an average 15s., or nearly
three-fourths of the price of the young pig that was
bought and fattened every year on garden waste and
a modicum of meal. Salt was bought to cure it, and,
with the exception of "compliments" to non-pigkeepers
who had contributed to its support, the family kept
the whole of the bacon for their own use. A farmer's
wife, for some reason that I have forgotten, gave them
a pint of new milk every day, and if there was illness
among the children it was increased to a quart. The

eldest girl was a careful manager, and her money presents to her mother more than balanced what had to be spent on the second sister. In addition, the children had all the things that she had grown out of, or that were considered too shabby to wear in service. The girl's mistress made frequent presents of her own children's half-worn clothing, and one of the three persons who employed the mother for charing did the same. The real income of the family therefore, instead of being 16s., amounted to at least 30s. Some months later I discovered two other sources of income: the father "planted gardens" for idle or infirm neighbours, and helped other men kill and cut up their pigs at a charge of 2s. 6d. per head.

Let us take another instance. Husband's nominal wages 22s. 6d. Rent and taxes 8s. a week. There were no children, but I needed no one to tell me that a well-dressed man and his wife did not live, pay club subscriptions, and spend about £8 a year on holidays, out of 14s. 6d. per week. Two rooms in their house they let regularly for 5s. a week, and a third (a mere cupboard in size) for 1s. 6d. The husband earned on an average 1s. 9d. over-time money, and he was given every week five teas and one supper, the value of which could not have been less than 1s. 3d. The wife earned 1s. 3d. by 3½ hours' washing for a near neighbour. The garden, though badly looked after, yielded quite 2s. worth of fruit and vegetables. Therefore the real income was about 28s., and the real rent and taxes 1s. 6d.

I came across a third instance which puzzled me far

more. Husband's nominal wages 12s. ; wife's earnings nil; four young children; rent 3s. 6d.; only garden visible very small, and devoted to flowers. That is to say, 8s. 6d. a week to feed and clothe a man, his wife, and children of three, five, nine, and ten. As they neither begged nor stole, as the house was well furnished and the whole party were well fed and well clothed (I remember noticing that the children were never sent on an errand *in the summer* until their mother had buttoned their gloves), I knew they must have some other source of income, but although I visited them four times a day for five weeks I did not then succeed in discovering it. Some months after, I learnt that, although the man's guaranteed wages were only 12s., his average earnings were nearly 21s., and much later than that I happened to see in the house a bunch of unwashed carrots, and then for the first time was told that the 3s. 6d. rent included a large garden on the other side of the road. From its size, and the way in which it was kept, I should say that it was worth at least 4s. a week to the cultivators, not counting the surplus vegetables which they were in the habit of exchanging for eggs.

I could multiply these instances indefinitely. At the present moment I have patients all of whose sources of income I do not know, but whose ostensible income would not provide two-thirds of the comforts they enjoy, and, I firmly believe, earn unaided either by charity or dishonesty.

In all the cases mentioned above, it must be noted that it was the excellence of the result on such an apparently insufficient income that roused inquiry. If the people had looked miserable enough to match the alleged income, even an experienced person might have accepted the first statements made as being complete.

If it takes me and countless district nurses many weeks' intimate knowledge of a family before being able to state their real means with accuracy, how is it that totally inexperienced newspaper philanthropists can polish off a streetful of such families between breakfast and luncheon? Two examples of the way in which work of the kind is done by "benevolent committees" were related to me by a very intelligent woman of the well-to-do artisan class.

A woman of about fifty was asked her weekly earnings, she replied 10s. 6d.; her rent, she said it was 6s. She was an untidy, haggard-looking person, her furniture was shabby, the general appearance of her rooms squalid, and she was at once presented with charitable assistance from the special "Fund." Her replies were true as far as they went; she simply omitted to mention that her two grown-up sons lived with her, that *they* paid the rent, and paid her in addition for washing and "doing" for them. Her income, rent and tax free, instead of being 4s. 6d., was nearly 15s.

Not half a mile off, and during the same winter, philanthropists were "thoroughly investigating" cases at the rate of about twenty an hour. They entered two little houses next door to one another; in both there was real (though temporary) distress, but in one dwelling the poverty was accentuated by dirt, rags, and disorder, and in the other it was hidden from superficial observers by cleanliness, well-dusted furniture, a few strips of carefully preserved carpet, and a general determination to put the best side foremost. In one house a liberal donation was given, and from the other the distributing members quickly walked out, saying patronisingly: "We are glad to see that you need no help. A pleasure to see a house look so nice after the sad scenes of poverty we have witnessed among your neighbours."

Another point with regard to what constitutes a "living wage" must not be lost sight of: are the wages entirely earned by the husband and the children over thirteen, or does the wife earn an appreciable portion of them? A guinea a week earned by the father, plus the entire time, strength, and attention of an intelligent woman, is worth far more than a money wage of 30s. earned by the combined labour of husband and wife. A heavy reduction must always be made from the value of married women's earnings, even if but part of their time is occupied. I knew a very clever manager, who, when she had five children just at their worst in the way of eating and wearing out their boots (between four and fourteen), worked as a charwoman one whole day and two half-days every week, but as soon as the eldest child had work that made it practically self-supporting, the mother gave up charing and remained at home, because, as she explained to me: "While I am wearing myself out earning half a crown, the children are wasting eighteen-pence, let alone there being no one to cook for them, and their running wild half the time with the worst little ragamuffins in the place. What can you expect if you go out and leave 'em? They are but children, and though Lizzie does her best, they won't mind her same as they does me."

Although I rarely enter a house where there is not one or more sick persons, in all my experience I can only recall three families which seemed in real want of food. The first case was that of an ex-soldier with a large young family. He walked about looking for work until his feet bled, and ultimately he found it. If State-aid had been given to his children, I doubt if he would have persevered in the weary trudge from employer to employer, and if a berth had been found for him immediately without any trouble on his part, I am tolerably certain that he would have thrown it up in a few weeks.

In the second case the sufferers were half-starved old parents, who had long been partly dependent upon the allotment papers of their only son, an unmarried seaman-gunner. Unhappily he had entangled himself with a woman in South America, and had deserted from his ship. Their fortunes were at the lowest ebb, for when I asked for a piece of bread to make a poultice I found I had been given the last scrap in the house. I remembered the "forty dinners" longingly, but that night help arrived, and from the only right quarter. The deserter returned, having come to his senses and worked his way home on a merchantman. When he

11

found the deplorable state to which his parents had been reduced, he emptied his pockets and gave himself up to the authorities. Imprisonment of course followed, but the prospect of the allotment papers was sufficient to restore the old people's credit. If the man had found them charitably supplied with every comfort, they would now be paupers, and he would be, at best, a casual labourer living under constant fear of arrest.

The third case was in London: the foodless and fireless condition of the house so weighed upon my mind, that I paid a second visit in the afternoon to ascertain whether it might not be wise to break my hitherto unbroken rule. I found the family eating a hearty meal of eggs and bacon cooked by a large fire.

No! the chief reason why many children go practically breakfastless to school—a slice of bread and a drink from the tap—is precisely the reason why at church and chapel schools they would arrive at a quarter to ten instead of nine o'clock, "Their parents objecks to religious instruction? *Them* poor little wretches? Why, ma'am, their fathers don't know whether they gets it or not, and their mothers objecks to leaving their beds," an indignant old woman told me in Cornwall; and persons equally shrewd, if unlettered, have told me the same in Hampshire, Essex, and Derby.

It must always be remembered that men are "out of work" for various reasons, but often for ones well within their own control: they lose their billet by neglecting their duties, by remaining away without leave, or returning drunk and quarrelsome. Once assured that the "kids" would not suffer, the happy-go-lucky men who now return to work on Monday, late and reluctantly, but who *do* return, would absent themselves until the middle of the week. "The missus and me, we'll manage all right. 'Sides, now the kids gets fed, what's she got to do except fill up her own nosebag? Let her work, same as me!"

One advocate of State-spread tables urges the measure because the mothers are "so frequently laid by." My experience in town and country is very large, and I can safely assert that it is rare for a woman with a young family to be incapacitated at any time except during her confinements, a period which would be well covered by one fortnight in eighteen months. With regard to nine days of this fortnight, no superior midwife will attend any mother who has not arranged with a neighbour to cook for husband and children. I have seen this plan rigorously carried out in some of the poorest districts in London, but no mother was too poor to comply with these and other equally necessary conditions.

Paris an example for us? How many of the people who admire its government have ever lived there, ever talked intimately with any of its working-class inhabitants? I have done both, and to me Paris is first and foremost a city of the half-fed. My *femme de ménage* was the wife of an artisan, and had but one child. She was frugality itself, and during a six months' acquaintance with her I never heard a word against the husband,

and yet that woman was thankful to work for thirty-five centimes an hour, and to work for a single hour without charging for the time spent in going from one house to another. Until the child was old enough to attend school, she begged permission to bring it with her. The little thing used to arrive blue with cold at nine on bitter winter's mornings, and I am convinced that mine was always the first fire that she had seen that day. "Un peu de froid? Oh, cela fait du bien d'avoir un peu de froid, mademoiselle," the mite said bravely when I rubbed her stiffened hands in mine.

"How many children has Marie?" I asked one day, naming a woman who sometimes worked for me, and who was being mentioned in tones of the deepest pity. "She has two, mademoiselle,—*two*. It is a great struggle for her, as you can well guess. Oh, la vie est bien dure à Paris!"

Marie also had a husband, a man in regular work. A friend on the other side of the city told me: "Our *femme de ménage* has four children. She tells me frequently, 'Madame, it is terrible, just conceive it, four children, *four*, for me and my husband to support. Whenever I have time to think, I cry.'"

"When are you going to be married, Florentine?" I asked a strong, capable, handsome girl of twenty-two, who told me almost daily how hard she found it to make an honest living. "Mademoiselle, think of the children! I ask you, how could I support them, and perhaps my husband too, when I find it so difficult to support myself?"

Oh, the hungry graspingness of the Parisian poor, of men and women whom one cannot accuse of a day's voluntary idleness, of an hour's self-indulgence! We should, indeed, observe what is done in that city of suffering, and let it be a lighthouse to warn us off the perilous rocks of State-aid.

CHAPTER VII

A DAY WITH A DISTRICT NURSE

IT was striking half-past eight as Nurse J. came down the garden path. There was a slight fog and a drizzling rain, and she seemed faintly surprised at my having kept the appointment that I had made with her.

"There are one or two temperature cases that must be taken first, and then— What do you say, little man?" as an untidy urchin stops her with some shrill but indistinct request. "Mrs. Naylor ill, and wants to see me? What is the matter with her?"

"Her wants yer to put a mustard poultice on her."

"Very well. Run off, and say that I am coming at once. We had better take this case first. They often send for me, and I have never found much the matter with them, but they are both over eighty, and naturally they might have a serious illness at any moment. In addition, they are not specially kind to one another, and they have no relatives and no friends."

We stopped at a house, in the front room of which, on the ground floor, the Naylors lived. The place was fairly well furnished, and a large fire was burning, but there was a general air of dirt and disorder.

"Good-morning, Mr. Naylor; who is the invalid

to-day, you or your wife? You know, you promised me that you would only take it in turns to be ill!"

"It's my wife, mahm," speaking in gasps, and in a tone of deep personal injury. "She says her chess is mortal bad. All night she've bin a-worretin'. Not a hower's sleep have I had."

"And she is in bed, I suppose?" drawing aside the wispy cretonne curtain.

"No, mahm. There worn't no mustard in the house, and she's gone to fetch it. She won't be above half a hower, if you'll set down."

Nurse realised that it was one more cry of Wolf! and said apologetically: "I am afraid I cannot wait now. This is a very busy morning. Will you tell your wife that I am sorry to have missed her, but that I hope to come in this evening and see the plaster safely on after she is in bed."

"How do they live?" I asked, as we walked quickly away,—"the place looked miserable."

"Oh, they are quite rich. They have six shillings a week from their club and the same from the parish, but they are an unhappy old couple. They married rather late in life, and had both been married before. Among the poor these second and third marriages, even when there are no children to complicate matters, always lead to comparisons and recriminations. I have one bed-ridden old woman who lies gazing at the photograph of her 'first' and sighing, 'Well, he was a *pilla*', and to think I have changed him for *this!*' 'This' seems to me a bland and blameless old man with a really remark-

able gift for making custard puddings that never
'split,' and keeping up a bright little fire on next to
nothing."

"And the pillar?"

"Well, the neighbours tell me that he used to beat
and starve and overwork her, and that her suffering old
age is entirely due to him, for she belongs to a sober
and healthy family. I have one patient who has lost
four wives. I am sorry to say that I have nursed two
of them myself. There is an only child by the first
marriage, and she is convinced that he means to marry
again. I beg her not to interfere. She may 'break him
away' from this person or that, but she can never defeat
every woman willing to accept the post. After all, she
may be as lucky as the not very brilliant son of a north-
country mayor, who was asked how he liked his father's
fifth wife, and replied, 'First rate. Better than any
mother I ever had!' Not long ago, a little girl about
ten years old told me that she had lost her mother a
year previously. I said, 'How very sad! What did you
do, poor little woman?' She looked at me with un-
disguised contempt for my ignorance, 'Got another.'
Here is my temperature case,—an only child of ten,
and I fear the worst. Last night he seemed to me to be
slowly sinking."

A pale-faced woman, with reddened, sleepless eyes,
came to the door, and, in answer to the question that did
not pass the nurse's lips, said, with a dull composure
more distressing than tears—

"Yes, ma'am, he left us last night, not two hours

after you was here. Me and his father was both with
him. He went so quiet that we couldn't tell when he
left off holding our hands, and 'twas only us a-holding
his. We don't know how to thank you for all you done
for him, ma'am. It's early to talk of comfort, and him
our only child, but if there is a comfort it's to think that
he had you and Dr. —— so constant. It seems to me,
if there was anything that hadn't a-been done for
him, and if, as you might say, God was willing to ha'
left him here if we'd done it, then it seems to me that
I couldn't ha' bore it, nor my husband neither. But
both on us feel sure that unless it had been God's will
and meaning to ha' took him, you and Dr. —— could
ha' kept him here, and him so patient, too."

"Indeed he was, Mrs. Waters. Dear little fellow,
something happened yesterday that touched me very
much, and that I am sure you will always like to
remember. I was attending to him, and you know how
at the last even the lightest touch hurt him. He did
not utter a sound, he was always so brave, but the tears
ran down his poor little face. Suddenly he heard your
step on the stairs, and he caught hold of the towel, and
said, 'Wipe my tears away, nurse, quick! It hurts
mother to see me cry.' Ill or well, he always thought
more of you than of himself. More than once, when I
have been passing the school soon after four, I have
heard him refuse to join a game, and say, 'No, I've
something to do at home,' and run off as if it were the
greatest treat in the world to help in the garden or to
go on an errand for you."

" Will you come upstairs and see him, ma'am,—and the lady too, perhaps ? "

I bowed silently, and followed her up the little canvas-covered staircase.   A fair, delicate-featured boy, painfully emaciated, lay on the small iron bed, a few flowers in his thin white hands.

" He looks very sweet," said nurse gently,—" so calm and free from all trouble and pain."

" You'll come in again, won't you, ma'am ?   Me and his father will always be glad to see you, and talk about him."

" How strange people are," said nurse as we walked down the street.   " If I had lost my child, I should never care to set eyes on the doctor or the nurse who had failed to cure him."

" Were there never any more children ? "

" No ; the husband drank and treated her so brutally that she left him a year after the marriage, and supported herself and the boy until a few months ago.   Then the husband was induced to take the pledge, found out where she was living, and begged forgiveness.   He had saved a little money—you must have noticed how new all the furniture looked ?—and they have been living together since then, and thought it was the beginning of a long and happy married life."

" Do you think drunkards often reform ? "

" I know two other men—one took the pledge fifteen years ago, one seventeen.   Of course, they may relapse even now, but in the meantime their wives live in peace and comfort.   One of them had ' sold up the home ' twice, the other three times, but I do not think they had ever personally ill-treated wife or child."

"And have you known any woman reformed?"

"No; but then I have known very few who *needed* reformation. When a woman takes to drink, it is generally from ill-health or from great unhappiness, and how can one change these circumstances? I am inclined to think that the men who drink, and later on reform, were simply led into it by the love of pleasure. When they drink for the same reasons as a woman, I doubt if they ever give it up. My next patient also is dying, a beautiful woman of thirty-four. Six years ago she received a violent blow on the jaw, and has never been able to open her mouth since. She has to be fed with a tube. She has a devoted mother, who nurses her day and night. I think you had better not come in. The place is clean, but intensely poor, and as they have known better days they are sensitive. I went five times myself before I gained admittance, and after that it was nearly a fortnight before I was allowed to touch the patient."

It had left off raining, and I walked slowly up and down the shining wet pavement.

"Is the nurse in there?" asked a little voice.

"Yes; do you want her?"

"You tell her she's got to go t'wunst to Mrs. Mann's little gal. She's pretty nigh cut her thumb off. Now, don't you forget, and then say you wasn't told nothin' about it, because Mrs. Mann ain't going to give me the penny, not till the nurse have been."

I promised meekly, but resisted the suggestion that I also should pay a penny because he " had given us the job." I delivered the message as soon as the nurse re-appeared, and she paused an instant to consider the nearest way, striking off into a newly-built part of the town.

"Good-morning, Mrs. Mann. I hear that one of the little ones is in trouble. What, *Annie?*"

"Yes, nurse ; got her little thumb nearly pulled off in the wheel of the boys' go-cart yesterday. Their father said she never *was* to ride in it, but she cried, and they can't none of them bear to cross her. I had to tell her dada she done it with the wind blowin' to the door when she was playin' in the yard by herself while the others was at school. He's wonderful set on her, her dada is. It wasn't never the same with none of the others, and it do seem strange ! "

Glancing with a puzzled air from Annie with her hemp-coloured hair, bulgy forehead, twinkling grey eyes, incidental nose and portentous upper lip, to the new baby with its primrose curls, blue eyes, and placid mouth, and then at the brilliant little Gertie with her vivid, responsive face, and at a handsome, sulky-looking boy who keeps well in the background.

" I suppose she amuses him. She is clever, and utterly fearless."

" She do get on wonderful with her talking. Her dada will have it that's it's all along of your having been here so much just when she was learning herself. He says she brings out her words just like what you do."

Nurse accepted this with due gravity, though privately convinced that Annie was the most unlovable child in the district.

"Now, ducky, let nurse look at your little thumb. Don't you remember how you took nurse's umbrella and broke it, and how mammy was going to smack you well for being such a naughty girl to touch other people's things, and how nurse wouldn't let mammy do it?"

Supported by this exciting reminiscence, and murmuring, "Norse—berelly—dain," Annie allowed the tiny hand to be unmuffled without a whimper, but much cajolery was needed before the work could be finished.

"I have done all I can for her, Mrs. Mann, but I think your husband had better carry her down to Dr. Thompson. The joint may be injured, and if we let her thumb stiffen she will never be able to work properly when she grows up."

"I'll tell him what you say, nurse; and seeing it's for Annie, I don't suppose he'll make no objection."

"How well all the others are looking. I always think Gertie looks the happiest child in the town."

The mother pinched her lips in judicially.

"She's stubborn sometimes. I have to take the rod to her. But as to Charles,—well, I often says to him, 'Charles, y'ant fit to be grouped wi' the donkeys.'"

"I suppose," said nurse, as we walked away from the house,—"I suppose you are a little scandalised that my sweet woman, my favourite patient, if I have one, should tell her husband a circumstantial lie, and that I should make no protest? If I found fault, she would say that she knows as well as I do that it is wrong, but that *I* do not understand what it is to have to deal between young children and a man who does not know the weight of his own hand. The father is a steady, respectable man, but except when he has had a little too much to drink he is surly and unapproachable. The poor woman cannot help enjoying these occasions, and I think no one but herself would guess that the amiability resulted from drink,—it seems just like the ordinary good humour of a man returning to a comfortable home after a successful day's work. She is a most wonderful mother, almost the only woman I know who teaches her children to do all kinds of housework, and always does it so pleasantly."

" But surely none of the children are old enough to be of much use ? "

" Oh, there are *five* older than the ones you saw. Two are already in service in good families. They were not obliged, as many girls are, to go to a 'working mistress' first, just to take off the edge of their ignorance and clumsiness on that unlucky person. Most poor people show no discretion at all in the way they train their children to do housework. Either they think that a child of seven ought to be able to scrub a floor, polish a grate, and clean her father's boots, or else girls of thirteen are running about for hours with a hoop or a skipping-rope, and are thought incapable of washing up the tea-things and peeling the potatoes.

"Another reason I have for respecting her is the extreme kindness that she shows to her old father. He has lived with her ever since he lost his wife. Special dishes are cooked for him, he is always helped first, and at tea-time a separate table is laid for him, with a plate of thin bread and butter, and some little dainty to tempt his appetite. Even on washing days I have never known him forgotten. In the winter his chair is always by the fire with a screen round it, and in the summer he sits nearest the door. He has only a tiny pension, so there is no self-interest in it. He is a gentle old man, and a better model for the children than their saturnine father.

"The case we are coming to now is an especially sad one: a boy of three-and-twenty with a terrible cancer in his face. Just a lad like thousands of others, neither better nor worse, and this awful tragedy to come into his life! He cannot resign himself: over and over again he asks, ' *Why* should it be me? 'Taint as if I'd been worse'n other chaps.' It is most pitiable. I shall be a long time with him. Suppose you go and rest in the church at the top of the street?"

About an hour after, Nurse rejoined me, looking pale and sad.

"He cannot live much longer, Death is too merciful to wait. He has asked to see the vicar, and perhaps he may be able to give him some consolation. Poor boy," a smile breaking over her face, "one thing that he said amused me. He asked if I had been to see the Hills, the 'awful examples' of this—comparatively —respectable neighbourhood. When I told him that I had been there every day lately, he said, 'Ah, they wants the likes o' you to *knock 'em about and show 'em what's right.*'

"There are two more visits that I must pay, and that will finish my morning round. In a little house down that muddy lane lives a brave old woman. She is over seventy, and not only earns her own living by cleaning out offices, but supports a consumptive niece. The girl, formerly a servant, is now quite helpless, probably within a few weeks of death, but the aunt has not yet given up hope.

"Ah, Mary, how are you to-day? Your aunt left you everything all comfortable as usual? What a wonderful old lady she is!"

Nurse felt the girl's pulse, and without more questions prepared a cup of arrowroot and a strip of toast. Then, after bathing her face and hands, and combing out her long yellow hair, she re-arranged the bed and said good-bye, promising to come again in the evening. "And then we must sponge you all over, and re-make the bed, and perhaps you will get a good night's rest."

"I wouldn't care for myself, nurse, if only I could keep from coughing. I do break the night up dreadful for aunt. You see, office cleaning isn't like ordinary charing; it's got to be done so early and so late, and aunt is always so busy over me that she'll never take a sleep in the middle of the day, though she's need of it, with me such a burden."

"Burden! If the dear old lady were to hear anyone breathe a whisper of such a thing! She says you are what you always have been, the greatest blessing of her life, and if she could only see you strong again "—

" Oh, nurse, she sees me every day, and she *can't* see. It had ought to be broke to her, for it might come sudden. I haven't known it myself about a week or so."

" Our last visit," said nurse a few minutes later, " is to a poor woman who has brought on paralysis by worry and over-work, taking in lodgers when her husband and children were enough for one pair of hands. Dropsy has set in now, and she cannot be here long; she has already been tapped three times. I think you might come upstairs; the days are long and sad, and the children are with her so little. When my advice is asked as to whether a cottage invalid should be upstairs or down, I feel that it depends entirely on character. A selfish, exacting person is better upstairs, but one likely to be neglected or overlooked should never be out of sight and hearing. The old mother takes the sick woman's place wonderfully well with the husband and children, but seems to have no conception of nursing. She cooks and cleans and scrubs, but the idea of washing her daughter now that she is helpless never enters her mind. And the poor thing is so refined that to lie there unwashed is a torment to her."

We spoke to the mother, a tall, upright old woman, with clear-cut aristocratic features and remarkably beautiful hands, and then went to the invalid, whose soft dark eyes brightened when she saw nurse.

" I was so afraid you wouldn't be here to-day, ma'am ;

12

and the vicar's coming this afternoon, and I didn't know *how* I should get washed. Mother's set the room straight, but it didn't seem as if she could bring herself to touch *me*. She was always a bit like that with anybody sick, even when we was quite small, but she's wonderful with my husband and the children, and she'll be everything to them when I'm gone. If he's kept comfortable, I doubt if he'll marry again, and that would be safest for the children. They're too big for another woman to take to them, and not big enough to mind themselves, and they never had pretty ways, not like some. It's only me or her as would have patience."

"This finishes my morning round," said nurse as we came out. "I start again at half-past four, but as my first visits will be to people you have already seen, suppose you meet me at a quarter to six outside the old church?"

I agreed, not sorry for the prospect of a longer rest. It was about twenty minutes after the appointed time when the nurse joined me.

"I was delayed by a new case," she explained,—"a man down with pneumonia. One of the few instances when nurses can do anything more than alleviate pain. It is hardly too much to say that if these patients are well nursed they generally live, and if not they die."

"Have you many men patients?"

"Not nearly so many as women. In the first place, they have better health; and, in the second place, when they are ill they are generally fit cases for an hospital, and no one would wish to nurse a man in his own house if there were any satisfactory alternative. Years ago I used to wonder why people said that women patients were so much easier to manage than men, for in hospital life both seemed to me equally good, quiet, and unexacting,—in fact, the only troublesome inmates we ever had were healthy boy babies of about eighteen months old, who had come in for some slight operation,—but see the ordinary man being nursed in his own home, and one understands the character that they bear as invalids!

"We must stop at that corner house to see twin babies, the youngest of seven, although the mother is only twenty-eight. She has never been able to nurse her children, and I taught her the orthodox way of bringing them up by hand. I only hope I shall not find them each gnawing crusts, and with tea-stains on their pinafores, and be told that they cry half the night and most of the day!

"Well, Mrs. Barton, I am quite a stranger now, but I have looked in to see how you and the babies are getting on."

"They're just off to sleep, ma'am," leading the way to a long basket cradle at either end of which lay a girl baby, fair little creatures with softly rounded cheeks and rose-leaf complexions.

"I need hardly ask how they are," said nurse, laying a practised hand on the firm, cool cheeks.

"They're nicely, thank you, ma'am."

"I am sure they are a credit to you. You keep strictly to the diet sheet I wrote out for you?"

" Yes, nurse, except as to adding the cream; I couldn't manage *that*, not without skimming Johnny's, and he's none so big and strong himself yet, though he gets on a sight better since you said we mustn't expect him to eat precisely what the others did, not at two years old."

" And is your husband very proud of them ? "

" That he is, ma'am; and does a lot for 'em, too. He boils their bottles every night reg'lar like what you told him, and he never said a word when the first two lots went smash. I didn't take no notice, and he just slipped out and bought some more. In fact, if 'tweren't for all he does, and all he's willing to go without, I couldn't hardly manage, though Katie's a real good child, and Frank's coming on a bit now. I can trust him with most of the errands. Four things he can bring without having it wrote down. Katie could bring six or seven when she was no bigger than him, but you can't have 'em all alike. Yes, my husband says they're as pretty as roses. He purtends he can't tell Dorothy Beatrice from Beatrice Dorothy, but even my little Willy knows 'em apart now. He says, ' Their faces look alike most part of the time, but they don't laugh alike, and I 'xpect they won't fight alike.' I told him little girls wouldn't never fight same as him and Franky, but he has his doubts ! My husband never had much to say to the others, not till they'd found their feet and could call ' Daddy.' It's true they cried a good bit, specially of nights, me being ignorant of their feeding."

" Ah, well," said nurse tolerantly, " one must not expect a hard-working man to like being kept awake

at night.   Good-evening, Mrs. Barton.   I am so glad to
see the babies looking well."

"Good-evening, ma'am; and thank you kindly for
looking in.   My husband will be pleased to hear that
you're satisfied with their looks.   He was a-saying only
yesterday how long it was since you'd been in.   I was
telling him, just to tease him, that the babies smelt more
of tobacco than you'd like."

"Now we must look at matrimony under another
aspect," said nurse, as we turned away from the delicate
but proud and happy mother.

"I must say that the husbands of your patients do
not seem to be shining lights as a rule."

"Ah, this is a backward neighbourhood, and naturally
I see more of the worst homes than of any other.   Even
in the poorest streets, the élite get on very well without
us.   After all, the men seldom go beyond strong language,
and just consider what threats and abuse many of the
women pour out on the children, and how little they
mean it!   Possibly the labourer's wife who is called a
blank fool may not feel much more insulted than the
professional man's wife when she is told that she does
not understand politics, or has no sense of humour.
And it might well be argued that the persistently selfish
husband is worse to live with than the one who is
occasionally violent.

"But it is really a miserable family where we are
going, and they live in a miserable hovel.   I have been
told that it belongs to the Duke of ——.   If so, I should
like to see photographs of it hung beside those of his

better-known residences. There is a single room downstairs, and a kind of lean-to open at one side. I have
never been upstairs, but from the slope of the walls—
the house is shaped more like a tea-cosy than anything
else—the one room there must be smaller as well as
lower. In the last drunken quarrel the man kicked his
wife in the leg, and the doctor fears that caries of the
bone is setting in. She ought to have complete rest, but
she limps out every day to work at a laundry. The
husband, to do him justice, does not insist on it, but
unless she went she would have no money for drink."

" Have they any children ? "

" They have had more than I can count, but there are
only two here now, lads of seventeen and nineteen.
There is one girl in service ; some lady took pity on her
when she was about thirteen, and she gets on well.
The elder son is very good to his mother, but between
drink and ill-treatment she has become such a craven
creature that she simply despises him for his forbearance.
She told me one day, ' When Davy says to me, " Han't
you nowt but bread and butter for my tea, mother ? "
and I say, " No, lad, that's aw," he joost eats it. Now,
his feyther, he'd oop wi' his fist, and he'd coom wi' a
roosh ! And Tom'll be like him when he's a bit older.'
I said, ' Davy does not seem much like his brother. I
suppose he takes after his grandfather ? ' ' His *gran'-
feyther !* ' she shrieked,—' why, his gran'feyther kicked
his wife to death right where you're standing. They
joost lifted her oop on to tha settle, and '— I had
better spare you the rest. My nerves are hardened, but

it was in the evening, getting dusk, and the woman's wild look and gestures more than half terrified me."

"Have you known her long?"

"I attended her once a year ago, but it was a comparatively trifling injury then. At first she would not let me in, said she had no money to waste, but when she heard it was what she called "a thank-you job," she yielded, and later on she was most anxious to make me 'a apern.' One day I found her poring over a book of the sentimentally evangelical type so popular about fifty years ago. She told me she had often 'cried by the hour' to think of 'them poor London children.' I do not think I have ever seen anyone worse housed or more pitiable than herself. In spite of her degradation, she shows traces of positive refinement, as well as good feeling. Although the cottage is excessively grimy, she is personally far cleaner than many of my patients who live in a seven-roomed house with a fixed bath and a continuous water supply."

We reached the hovel, and a tall, thin woman, with a battered, disfigured face, asked us to come in. The door was left open, as the small, dirty window did not admit enough light for the "mester" to have his supper. He growled out something that I took to be "good-evening."

"Sithee doon, yoong woman," said his wife, and I hastily took the chair nearest the door.

"And where might you coom fro', missus?" she continued.

"From London."

"And a mucky place you live in, from all I've heard. But you look clean, considerin'."

She began collecting a few things that the nurse needed, limping painfully in a pair of unlaced men's boots. I looked furtively at the husband. There were no special signs of brutality in his high-featured, strongly marked face. He was evidently quite un-ashamed of the cause of his wife's sufferings, and began talking to me with greater affability than distinctness about the superhuman "sharpness" of his blind grand-mother, a former tenant of the cottage, while I rolled up the bandage destined for the discoloured leg when nurse had finished dressing the wound. In the middle of the conversation he startled me by suddenly rising and lifting the heavy earthenware basin that she had used.

"I'll empty it for ya, missus."

Nurse was evidently beyond being surprised, and thanked him without being overborne by his condescen-sion, but I felt my jaw drop with astonishment. If the landlord had walked down from the castle to wait on her, it would have seemed to me, in comparison, a mere matter of course. It was a painful twenty minutes, and I was thankful to be safe outside.

"I have only two more visits to pay, and they are both outside the town. Perhaps we shall be able to catch the omnibus."

We were fortunate enough to do so, and it set us down not far from a pretty cottage in the middle of a large and well-kept garden.

"That is where my patient lives. How many of her complaints are real, and how many imaginary, I cannot say. The doctor calls it hysteria. Her husband died suddenly about four years ago, and she has never recovered the shock.

A refined-looking woman of about fifty gave us an eager welcome.

"I've got some of the new embrocation, so perhaps you'll rub it on for me."

Nurse began, trying as she did so to distract the woman's mind from the countless symptoms and exactly detailed sufferings of which her bright eyes, smooth face, and plump neck and arms afforded no confirmation. Forgetting herself for a moment, she said, with a humorous twinkle—

"I've got a message for you, nurse, although I did say I wouldn't give it. I said Mrs. Brown could give it herself when she see you."

"Well, what is the message? I am going there to-night."

"That's just it, nurse. It was to ask you kindly not to go, as they don't see you can do Minnie any good. It's my belief they've got that quack from Overbury for her, and finely he'll bleed them!"

"At any rate I must go and see her. It is quite true that I cannot make the child well,—all the doctors and nurses in the kingdom could not cure her,—but it will be easy enough to do her harm, and she must not be left to the quack's tender mercies if I can help it."

Then Mrs. West's own ailments came to the front

again, and their recital lasted until she reluctantly parted from us.

"What a discontented woman she seems," I said hastily, "and living in such a comfortable house. The greater part of her complaints must be imaginary. She said her throat was so bad that she could not speak, and the pain in her ankle prevented her from walking, and yet she talked incessantly and stepped about nimbly."

Nurse sighed.

"She never mentions her *real* trouble. Her only son, although not more than six-and-twenty, is an habitual drunkard. Now, will you wait at the gate while I interview Mrs. Brown, and either drive off the quack or get my own dismissal."

In a few minutes she returned.

"The quack holds the field. Poor things, one cannot wonder at it. They are too ignorant to understand that cure is impossible, and the man makes alluring promises. One point irritates me : it is eighteen months since they paid the doctor a farthing, and yet the quack will manage to screw two or three pounds out of them within a fortnight. There, we have lost the last omnibus. We must walk."

"Is this your last visit? How about the mustard plaster?"

"Mrs. Naylor has changed her mind. Just after I left you I met her crossing the market-place to fetch herself a quartern of gin, she said she 'felt' it would do her more good! All I have to do now is to call and see the wife of a tradesman who lives near my lodgings. The husband has nursed her himself for four years. I am not admitted as a nurse, but only as a temporary substitute for Dr. Halling, who is away on a fortnight's leave. He hopes to find everything revolutionised when he returns, but I have scarcely been permitted to touch her yet. It is beautiful to see the husband's devotion, but I could make the poor woman so much more comfortable if he would only let me. They have a fairly good servant, but except to clean the grate and sweep the carpet, she is never allowed to cross the doorway."

" Do you get many patients among fairly well-to-do people ? "

" Oh no ; we have to stand out against it, except for operation cases. However, some people who might well be patients are a little too conscientious on the point. A few weeks ago a clerk came to me to ask me to recommend a night nurse, whom, of course, he was prepared to pay. I asked him if I should come and see his wife the next day. He said promptly that he should be thankful if I could, as he was compelled to leave her from half-past eight to half-past six five days out of seven, but added, ' I am afraid we are too well off to be allowed to have you. I only came for advice, as we are in great trouble.' When I found that there were five children under eleven, and that they kept no servant of any kind, and had no relatives in the town, I put the wife on the books at once. It was a case in which doctors could do very little ; she only wanted rest and constant small attentions. The children were very good, and I taught the eldest one all the necessary cooking. When the doctor found me in attendance, he cut down his visits to about one a week. He said I could send for him when he was needed, but he did not wish to run them up a bill for nothing."

" I suppose the doctors are all glad to have your help ? "

The nurse smiled over recollections which she proceeded to share.

" Not long ago a patient told me that a certain doctor had said of me, ' I'd like to burn her and her bag!' Doctors are generally cautious in their remarks, and I might have thought that the tale had been invented for the chastening of my south-country conceit, but the woman unconsciously mimicked his accent so exactly, that he must have said it, and said it more than once. There is another doctor here who evidently had it on his conscience that he had been saying something of the same kind. I had been through several operation cases with him, each of which gave me an enormous amount of work before and after, besides the strain of being the only person to wait on him and a very young and nervous anæsthetist, and then one day, *à propos* of nothing but his own thoughts, he said hurriedly, ' I don't mean nurses like you. *You don't do any harm.*' I said I tried not to."

" But seriously ? "

" Oh, I think most of them are glad to have us when they once understand the lines which we follow. It is true that we sometimes do work that they might otherwise have done, but they would not have been paid for doing it, and as a rule we are occupied with things that they cannot do and are thankful to have done. It is a terrible burden on a kind-hearted man's mind to know that, as far as nursing goes, his patients are neglected or ignorantly treated. Doctors often get very fierce and impatient with feckless relatives, but they cannot *teach* them, and their scolding leads to nothing but an unjust reputation for bad temper and 'goin' on somethin' awful.'

"In addition, we manage to extort the patient's history for the day, and write it down. One country doctor told me that most of his time, and far more than all his patience, is exhausted in conversations of this type—

"'Well, Mrs. Brown, what kind of an appetite has your husband?'

"'Oh, so to say, sir.'

"'How much dinner did he eat to-day?'

"'Oh, he eat some, sir.'

"'What do you call *some?*'

"'Oh, a fairish lot.'

"'I want to know *how much.* Come, was it a bucket-ful, or a tablespoonful, or what?'

"'Law, sir, why, of course I give it him on a plate, same like what you see on the dresser behind you.'

"'And he ate a plateful?'

"'He ate some, sir.'

"He was doctor for three parishes, and had no one to take even the smallest responsibility. Once when he was well over sixty he had to keep his boots on for seventy-two hours. He suffered most of all from being called out needlessly, especially at night. On one occasion he rode five miles in the middle of a November night to see a woman who had sent an urgent message for him. When he reached the house the woman opened the door herself, and said she had an earwig in her ear! He said, 'If an earwig could be such an idiot, why on earth didn't you drown it with a little oil?' and rode off. Nurses can often save doctors from that kind of thing."

"If she had been a rich patient, he would probably have been a little more ceremonious."

"In his case, at any rate, I doubt it. His most 'paying' patient called at his house one day, and said—

"'Doctor, the medicine you sent me was no use. I told the groom to bury it.'

"'Then you had better tell the groom to dig it up again, for there is nothing else that you can have.' She changed the subject to her son, who had just failed to pass what she called a '*vice versâ*' examination."

"The patients themselves seem grateful. Whatever the trials of the life may be, you have at least the consolation of knowing that you are doing a good work, and are followed by blessings wherever you go."

"And flattery. Yes, I am getting quite accustomed to be told that I am a ministering angel, and in general society I shall miss the constant reference to my lovely hands and my 'superior' voice. Whether history repeats itself or not, jokes certainly do. The other day a petty officer, whose wife I had nursed during his absence abroad, said to me fervently, 'You're just a fallen angel, mum; that's what you are!' Good-night; I hope you will not feel tired after our long round."

CHAPTER VIII

THE TRIALS OF A DISTRICT NURSE

WILL it seem an ingratitude to the patient women who have cleaned my muddy boots and dried my drenched cloak twice and three times in a day, cut the thinnest of bread and butter for my visitors, and made me bigger fires than I should have dreamed of making for myself, and never complained (well, not often!) if the supper I ordered at eight was eaten at ten-thirty, and the dinner prepared at one was not eaten at all; will it seem an ingratitude to them if I say that the greatest trial of the district nurse is her landlady? I am not speaking so much of my personal sufferings at her hands, as of the average experience of a large class of women workers.

How many people really like their landlady, even when her "ways" are simply the one drop of bitterness in a summer holiday? How many would be able to tolerate even the idea of living with her, or some one closely resembling her, from year's end to year's end? The strongest-minded, longest-pursed woman is at a disadvantage in struggling against the tyranny of a landlady; but how essentially weak the district nurse's position is compared with that of an ordinary lodger! She knows that she "gives trouble," she knows that she cannot afford to pay a high rent, she knows that, counting all the "nursing requisites," she is heavily weighted with luggage. She is forced to own that she cannot stand comparison with "the dinin'-room and 'is wife," who, being elderly, leisurely people, never go out when the weather is wet, nor stay in when it is fine, come to their meals by clockwork, and yet do not seem impatient if they are kept waiting; still less can she equal the virtues and charm of "top floor front," who absents himself for thirteen hours daily and never requires a meal, and who cleans his boots in the area every morning whistling the chorus of the latest popular song, finishing up with a double-shuffle which is more encouraged by the maids' discreet giggles than checked by the landlady's motherly-severe, "Now, get *along* with you, Mr. Jiffens, and me with more breakfasses to see to than there is howers in the day!" She cannot aspire to the dignity of the drornin'-room and 'er maid," nor ingratiate herself, like the gentle little milliner's apprentice who coughs half the night away in the tiny room over the passage, by taking her meals in the kitchen, and describing with much gesture and feeling "Mrs. Colonel Golightly's new bonnet, which it was *years* too young for her." Above all, the fear of her bringing "things" into the house hangs about her like a cloud.

If, instead of being one of several lodgers, the nurse happens to be the only one, in some respects she is likely to be more comfortable; but, on the other hand, there is a probability that her landlady is painfully ignorant of cooking, and of all the requirements of refined life. Important virtues can be sadly obscured by a habit of providing pork in some form or other five days a week, and mutton chops the other two; by entirely abjuring the use of dishes and extra knives and forks, and by stuffing up the chimneys, and complaining bitterly, if a window be left open, of the incalculable damage done to the furniture and the intolerable "rawrness" of the air. She is not haunted by her more educated sister's fear of infection, but her dread of fire takes the most harassing forms, and 10 p.m. is considered late hours.

How is the isolated nurse to be delivered from the unchecked sway of her landlady? I have invented a new profession for women, but they are not crowding into it. Some time ago I was speaking to a friend of the life led by "single-handed" district nurses, the discomforts of many lodgings, the dreariness of nearly all; the lonely, ill-served meals, the silent evenings, the dull, blank Sundays, the amount of work that must be done that is never entered on any time sheet, and the amount that must be left undone because it is sheerly impossible for any one woman to cope with it. "Every district nurse should have a Dark Star," she replied. Instantly range upon range of lovely possibilities stretched themselves out before me, delightful for the nurse, the patients, even for the Dark Star herself.

Dark Stars would be drawn from the very large class of well-educated unmarried women who have independent means. Often the income is too small to admit

13

of house-keeping on their own account, often they are still so young and vigorous when set free from all family ties, that they think it wrong to settle down to the comfortable, quietly happy life of maiden ladies. They feel called on to do some good in the world if they can compass it, and yet they do not feel drawn to a life of complete self-sacrifice; they do not even wish to work as hard and incessantly as if struggling for their daily bread, and they prefer to maintain some independence of action. Or perhaps their health will not stand a long and hurried working day, or they shrink from responsibility, or they have not been regularly trained for any profession, and feel that it is too late in the day to begin at the beginning, and yet know that they are capable of following the right lines if friendly direction were always at hand.

The Dark Star would live with the district nurse, and her duties towards her would be to see that her meals were well cooked, neatly and punctually served, and promptly cleared away,—the latter a most essential point in lodgings where one sitting-room must serve for many purposes. She would do the catering, and take care that the food was sufficiently varied and nourishing, and, wherever practicable, she would induce the landlady to let her enter the kitchen two or three times a week to make soup, puddings, pastry, and cakes. She would also keep a strictly private duster, and supplement the maid's feeble daily efforts and ferocious Saturday onslaught. If a real friend, she would not be above doing a little sewing for the nurse. Oh, the luxury to a tired woman of finding every button and string miraculously in place !

After receiving the necessary instruction from the nurse, the Dark Star would take charge of the medicine cupboard and the district cupboard, and do a large share of the work necessary to keep up the supplies in the latter. She would cut dressings, etc., for the patients, and have the nurse's bag ready for her morning and evening, and disinfect and re-stock it for her at the end of the week.

If any books, periodicals, and newspapers had been sent for the patients, she would tie them up, and leave them at the houses indicated by the nurse, whose bag is often more than sufficiently heavy without any other burden. If there is much correspondence, she would assist the nurse with it, copying letters when necessary, and give some help with the books every evening.

The Dark Star must, above all, be an intellectual as well as a sympathetic and practically helpful companion. She must study the daily papers, and remind the nurse "there's livers out of Britain"; look through the magazines and reviews, and point out the articles that she "really must read," and see that her friend is always provided with a good novel, an interesting biography, or the latest book of travels or reminiscences.

In periods of great stress, and after a few months' experience, the Dark Star would be able to undertake all the slight chronic cases; and by attending some of the severe chronic cases with the nurse would be able to greatly reduce the amount of time spent in each house.

The district nurse always knows of chronic patients whose lives would be cheered by the regular visits of someone who would read to them, play or sing to them, talk, or simply listen, and she finds it exceedingly hard to get anyone to undertake the office. There is one excuse for the constant refusals and evasions that she meets with when she asks persons of leisure to visit these invalids, and for the very short period during which the calls are paid if they consent, and that excuse is the rapacity of the patients' relatives, and their ceaseless attempts to extort money as the price of admission to their houses. It must be understood in the district from the very first that the Dark Star is like her friend, a very useful person but with no money to spare, and that she is guided in all her work by the light of her friend's experience. Coleridge compared experience to the *stern* lights of a vessel, but as the Dark Star follows in the nurse's wake the track is sufficiently illuminated for her to pass over it in safety.

It is not suggested that the Dark Star should be paid, but her presence should so far be recognised by the local committee that a comfortable bedroom should be provided for her, especially if she is in one of those awkward districts where there is too much work for one nurse, and not money enough for two. By making the nurse's domestic life thoroughly comfortable, by providing her with cheerful companionship, by saving her about two hours' work daily, and by enabling her to undertake duties which she must otherwise distress herself by refusing, the Dark Star could make even the most difficult district manageable.

There are thousands of women in the world living in narrow and leisured loneliness who might well be Dark Stars. Will none of them give the work a trial? They are not forbidden to be rich, but they need only have an income of from £30 to £50. They will not be prevented from working hard, but they need only work from three to five hours a day. No special training is required: all women who are by nature home-lovers and home-makers would find their "appointed patch," and be welcomed.

Perhaps the next greatest trial is the weather, especially winter weather; and here complaint may seem idle, for, as an old patient told me recently, "Maybe it'll come fine, but ef it don't, we'll hev to hev it as 'tis, and look pleasant"; but the nurse is not utterly helpless in the matter. In the first place, she can to a considerable extent defeat the weather by adapting her clothing to suit local conditions; and, in the second place, she should never accept an appointment in any county with a climate markedly different from that in which she was born and bred. The Yorkshire woman who tries district nursing in Hampshire, the Devonshire woman who tries it in Norfolk, are heaping up their own daily vexations. The breeze which to one is balmy and life-giving, to the other is steamy and enervating; a degree of cold or wind that to one seems exhilarating, to the other is numbing, stupefying, positively dangerous.

And small as our country is, there are differences not only of climate but of manners and customs, and most of us like best to be surrounded by accents and habits that were familiar to us in our childhood: we feel an indescribable tenderness towards the patient who uses some word or turn of speech that we had scarcely heard since we were in the nursery, or in the days when we plagued the gardener for seeds to sow at impossible seasons. The north country is apt to think the south smooth spoken and deceitful, and the south country to find the north rough and ungracious; the west shrinks from the hard revengefulness of the east, and the east scorns the quickly changing loves and hatreds of the west. A patient in the Peak district will tell a favourite nurse that she "can do wi' her better than she can wi' some," while a Devonshire woman would say, "I'm as happy as a bee, now I can set an' look at your lovely face." A Lancashire man returning some appliance lent to a member of his family, will simply say to the servant who answers the door, "Tell hur ah've done wi' it," while a Hampshire man would stand three minutes on the doorstep impressing on her careless attention the message, "Be sure and say as I returned it with grateful thanks from me an' my wife."

The experienced may know—with their intellect— that one phrase means as much, or as little, as the other, but in their heart they prefer whichever is most familiar, whichever is nearest themselves. A very little girl once asked me—

" Is my hair 'ight ? "

" No-o, not very light," I replied doubtfully, never having considered the matter.

" Well," she said, with the funniest assumption of self-satisfied dignity, " if it isn't as 'ight as it *tould* be, it's as 'ight as I *'ant* it to be ! "

We unconsciously judge everything closely connected with us or our feelings in precisely the same spirit. I heard a west-country man complaining because it rained in London.

" It has *begun* to rain," said a citizen, " and presently it will leave off. I've never caught it doing either in your corner of the world."

" *Devonshire* rain, that's quite another thing ! "

Does a nurse ever return from her evening round, especially on a cold, raw winter's night, without saying to herself as she mounts the stairs to her room : " I hope no one has called for me, I hope I shall not have to go out again ? " Tired as she is, would she hesitate or complain if she knew that she were really wanted ? But that is the question. If there is a note lying on her table, it will probably contain not a word beyond, " Kindly go to such and such an address," and the rule is that all new cases arriving before 10 p.m. must be attended to that night. Often the nurse toils out in darkness and rain to find that the patient has been removed to hospital or to the workhouse infirmary, or that it is an infectious fever that she cannot undertake, or that it is a slight chronic case, or that the people of the house are already in bed. I have myself been called out at midnight to attend on a man with a broken leg, and learnt—rather too late—that the accident had occurred three weeks previously, and the patient had received all the usual attention.

This regulation causes some of the most real hardships and unnecessary fatigues of the district nurse's life, and might so easily and safely be modified. The rule should be that no new case sent in after the nurse has started on her second round can be visited until the next morning, unless the note is marked "urgent" by a competent and responsible person. For many and obvious reasons, it is desirable that the first visit should be paid by daylight.

The large amount of Sunday work, often lasting for months without a break, prevents the nurse from devoting any considerable part of the day either to rest, social intercourse, or religious duties. "But people cannot give up being ill just because it is Sunday!" cries the indignant humanitarian. Unfortunately they cannot, but there are strong reasons why on that day they are less in need of outside assistance, and why the visit of a nurse should be almost an intrusion.

No woman can work seven days a week, eleven months in the year, without a strain severe enough to injure herself, and to react upon her patients in the most unfavourable manner. Every committee should set its face against being a society for trying to make ill people well by succeeding in making well people ill. The rule should be, "None but severe cases attended on Sunday," and by "severe" should be understood dangerous acute illnesses and chronic cases imperatively needing skilled attendance.

So indifferent have many committees shown themselves in this matter, that I have known a nurse compelled to walk a considerable distance on Sunday, simply to wash the face and hands of a patient, brush her hair, and tidy the room ; the patient having in the house with her, besides her husband and sons, a daughter of fifteen, and an active, cleanly, vigorous mother of sixty. As the woman was perfectly capable of performing her own toilet if the appliances were brought to her bedside, the youngest child in the house could have waited on her satisfactorily.

This is by no means an extreme instance of the conduct shown by some charitable committees to their paid assistants. I have seen a reply to a nurse's application for an appointment, in which she was asked : " Can you work night and day consecutively ? " I tried to believe that this was merely a slip of the pen for " alternately," or " indifferently," but the context proved conclusively that the word used was the word meant.

To drop from needless Sunday labour to the district cat may seem a sudden descent, but I can honestly say that this animal causes me more annoyance than any other incident in the work. I was always one of those who " cannot abide . . . the harmless necessary cat." My infancy (as a district nurse) was fed upon a tale of a probationer who had lost her most useful finger owing to a cat bite ; and although, after years of obser- vation of its devotion to chronic patients and its

invariable gentleness with children, I am forced to
rank it morally and intellectually much more highly
than I used to, my personal aversion to the animal
steadily increases. I can tolerate her in broad daylight, or when she openly takes possession of my cloak,
or sits at the foot of the patient's bed, blinking and
smiling, a family Sphinx; but the cat when she lurks
on dark staircases or crouches in tomb-like entries,
purposely leaving the tip of her tail, or a favourite
paw, as a trap for the unwary, fills me with horror.
Cat-lovers, otherwise reasonable people, assure me that
district cats have not that faith in human nature which
would lead them to sleep in a thoroughfare, that they
are not in the least likely to let me tread on them, and
that the chances are ten million to one against their
making an unprovoked assault. "Ten million to one"
is a good round comforting phrase; the weak point is
at "not in the least likely." I have known so many
things happen that came under that heading, that I
walk warily, and make liberal use of five-minute candles
or miniature carriage lamps.

One of the very real trials of district nurses are the
people who "take so *much* interest in the work," but
who seem to think that because a nurse has been
"trained," her whole nature has changed, and that
she has miraculously become "used to" everything
that might otherwise torture her nerves, overstrain
her health, or depress her spirits. A nurse might well
adapt Shylock's defence of his nation to herself, and
ask, "Hath not a nurse eyes? Hath not a nurse hands,

organs, dimensions, senses, affections, passions? Fed
with the same food, hurt with the same weapons,
subject to the same diseases, healed by the same means,
warmed and cooled by the same summer and winter
as others are!" Cannot those who affect so much zeal
to aid the poor and suffering remember that a woman
who belongs by birth and education to the sheltered
middle classes, or to the rigidly exclusive respectable
poor, who in seven cases out of ten is still young, and
sometimes very young; who did not leave her home
until three years ago, and then only to exchange it for
a strictly conducted hospital; who had never been on a
journey by herself without some anxious elder carefully
marking her route; who until quite lately had scarcely
ever walked alone in a large town even in broad daylight: is it too much for these benevolent persons to
try and recollect that such a person cannot be "used
to" going out in all weathers and at all hours, cannot
be "used to" hearing foul language and seeing drunken
men while she picks her way through ill-lighted, disreputable streets and lanes; cannot be—and Heaven
forbid that she ever should be—"used to" the sights
and sounds of suffering, sin, and ignorance that fill a
large part of every working day.

Would not a sympathetic acknowledgment of her
difficulties do something to lighten them, and an hour's
pleasant social intercourse relieve the daily strain? But
how seldom is the district nurse allowed anything even
faintly resembling ordinary social intercourse! No one
seems to realise that all her heart and soul and mind

cannot be given to purely professional matters, and
that if they are she is in a "parlous state"—for her
patients as well as herself—from which it is the duty
of every kind-hearted person to try and rouse her!

As I have more than once drawn attention to the fact
that the district nurse is separated to an unfortunate
degree from the society of her equals, it may seem
unreasonable to place callers upon the list of her
trials; but that is the category to which nineteen-
twentieths of them belong.

The caller rarely speaks of public events, of books,
music, art, or the theatre; she never mentions her
nine uncles and aunts who are perfectly well, nor the
ninety-nine cousins and friends who are, if possible,
still better. No; the conversation is strictly limited
to the aunt who died young, to the brother-in-law who
is threatened with gout, to the nephew who broke his
leg cycling three years ago, and the niece who *may*
break hers if she continues to coast down slippery hills.
How often, as they maundered on, "Of course, all this
interests *you*, nurse," I have thought with envy of the
range of topics suggested by the walrus to his guests.
They might chatter

> "Of shoes, and ships, and sealing-wax,
>   Of cabbages and kings,
>   And why the sea is boiling hot,
>   And whether pigs have wings."

That is to say, of commerce, travel and adventure, of
politics, agriculture, "sport et high-life," experimental
science and metaphysics. But the district nurse,

whether old or young, widow or spinster, is expected to confine herself strictly to the conjugation of the verb " to be ill " in all its moods and tenses, but not all its persons. If she says, " I am ill," it is imagination, whilst " I have been ill " is sheer egotism, and " I may also be ill " seriously undermines faith in the soundness of her training.

Impulsive and credulous persons are another great trial. They have a real desire to help their fellow-creatures, but they are in such haste to do good that they never stay even to verify an address, much less the truth of a pitiful tale. Late one autumn evening a lady rushed up to me in the street, and told me that a certain boy, a flower-seller, whom I knew by sight and had seen walking with a slight limp a few hours previously, had a gangrened leg, thrust an address into my hand, and would I go at once and see him? The neighbourhood was new to me, the streets were dark and nearly empty, and the few passengers not in a responsible condition. After more than an hour's search, I was obliged to give up and return to my lodgings. Early next morning, with daylight and errand boys, always trustworthy guides, to assist me, I soon found 17 Bryant's Lane. The woman who answered my knock stared at me with some severity, " No one in *her* house wanted a nuss," and indeed it looked a comfortable little place. Slightly appeased by my apologies for disturbing her, she added, " Maybe it's the house joined on to our back; it had ought to ha' bin pulled down long ago, by rights."

Having reached this damp and gloomy region, I knocked at a door that might have led to a cowshed, and was admitted by a boy of eighteen or nineteen, hastily fastening his clothes, having evidently just got out of bed. He told me civilly enough that his mother had gone to work, that his brother was not yet dressed, and I could see him if I went upstairs. The house consisted of a grimy, filthy kitchen, from which a rickety staircase, pierced with rat holes (one of which was being watched with feverish intentness by a ragged yellow cat), led to a kind of loft lighted by one fixed pane of glass. There were two stump bedsteads covered with exceedingly dirty mattresses, and sheets grey from long use. On one of the beds sat my patient. He wore a nearly clean flannel shirt, his hair had evidently been cut and washed within the last ten days, and something indescribable in his manner betrayed that, so far from being a neglected outcast about to receive kindness for the first time in his life, he was a confirmed " hospital bird."

I unfastened the bandage he was wearing, and disclosed a leg slightly harder and stiffer than it should have been, and bearing the narrow white seams of a remarkably successful operation, but perfectly free from a sore of any description. The only practical result of my visit was a fresh appeal to the sanitary authorities to have the house pulled down.

If direct intercourse with the impulsive lady is trying, the indirect result of her conduct is still more so. She begs to be allowed to visit among the poor; she does it with enthusiasm for a week, and then disappears, leaving behind her a crop of extravagant expectations which the nurse has to meet and still as best she can.

It may be considered wrong to count young curates among our trials, but oh, how many complaints we receive of their manner to the poor, especially of their want of respect to the old! If these youths could only remember that there is but *one* code of good manners whether you are dealing with rich or poor, how much heart-burning and friction and waste effort would be spared.

What can be the state of mind which permits a young man of four or five-and-twenty, theoretically a gentleman, to walk straight into a house (sometimes without removing his hat, and seldom waiting for an invitation), and then, after a muttered, perfunctory greeting, "talk relidgin" to a respectable old woman who might have been his grandmother? She may "keep her thoughts to herself" while he is there, for *she* "knows manners," but as soon as he is gone her wrath boils over. "As if I didn't know it when his ma was in her cradle! As if I'd ha' bin let wait seventy-four years for the like of *him* to come and teach me!"

If the same curate had arrived with a bow and a courteous "Good-afternoon, Mrs. Appleby, are visitors admitted to-day?" if he had followed this up by shaking hands, by an inquiry for her health, and a platitude about the weather; if he had shown a discriminating interest in her grandchildren, related an anecdote of his former landlady, given an impossible version of his mother's recipe for toast and water, listened with due gravity to her husband's views as to the racial characteristics of Rush-ons, and at parting had expressed a hope that he should see them at church some day soon, she would have been happier for a week after.

" And is *that* the kind of visit to be paid by a minister of the Gospel ? " I am asked reprovingly. I can only reply that it is a tolerably exact account of what he would have done if he had called on the doctor's well-to-do aunt, or the lawyer's mother, and they, sweet old ladies, would be the last persons on earth to imagine that Mrs. Appleby was farther from the kingdom of Heaven than they, or more in need of a boy's instruction. Well, there are nurses too who go out to teach and come home taught !

CHAPTER IX

A CRITIC FROM WITHIN

HE was far on in his eighty-fifth year, and he had walked a mile and a half from the workhouse one hot July afternoon to see me. We had been through the usual programme,—interchange of inquiries after health, firm declarations that we had never felt better, biscuits, fruit, *very* weak whiskey and water, a turn round the garden, scathing condemnation of the methods of my "stout lad," and counsels as to what "he had *ought* to do." The peas had been admired, and ruin prophesied for the broad beans, and he had become youthfully vehement in his advice to "root up" some trees more picturesque than profitable. I then suggested picking flowers for him to take back to the House.

"If you'll excuse me, mahm,—no! You see, it's this way: if I was to take them flowers—and very pretty they are—d'rectly I was inside the gates that there nurse would say, 'Lewis!' she'd say [raising his voice several notes higher, and speaking with great rapidity] —'Lewis, have you brought them flowers for me?' and off she'd whip 'em."

"And don't you wish to take her any?"

14

"No, I *don't*, mahm. Not a leaf. I'll give her nothing but civility; I don't grudge her that. Leastways, I wouldn't, not if she'd be civil to *me*. On'y the other day she tried to get me into a scrape. It was afore I give up being doorkeeper. I s'pose you know I've gone back to my trade, mahm? When I went into the House eleven months ago, and the master gives me the job, I says to him, I says, 'This is a lazy man's job. Let me get to my trade as soon as there's room, and that's what I'm doing now. Well, one night when I was doorkeeper, two o' them nurses"—

"But how many have you?"

"There's three, and a wardwoman and the matern. The first one's all right. It's the second I bin speaking of. She's a great big *oncultivated* person: that's the best I can say o' her."

"And the third?"

"What do a *young woman of seventeen* know o' nursing?"

"Is there much sickness in the House just now?"

"Well, no; not much. There's bin a few accidents in the hayfield. A gentleman brought in yesterday had his arm hurt very bad. The master told me to pick him out a pair o' shoes to fit him, so I did, and took them to him in the bathroom, and I see he had a difficulty in gettin' off his—um—*weskit*, so I give him a hand. No; there ain't what *I* should call much for them nurses to do. Why, at Q., which is four times the poppylation, they only has one!"

This did not seem to me to add charms to a residence

at Q., but I murmured some meaningless reply, and he proceeded with his tale.

"The gas was lighted, so I couldn't see plain through the lodge window, but I saw two people going out, and I says to myself, 'That's two o' them nurses,' and I shuts to the gate. Of course, they'd oughter looked in and said, 'Two nurses going out'; no more wasn't *necessary*, not if they didn't choose. I kep' a look out for 'em, and when they knocked I wasn't in too much hurry to let 'em in, and when I did, I says, 'I'd be much obliged if you two ladies would look in at the lodge and give me your names as you pass out.' They walked on mutterin' somethin', and I says, 'What can be your reason *not* to? It strikes me very forcibly you're too proud, and that's what it is.' Well, the nex' day the master comes down to give an order, an' he says to me, 'Lewis, I hear that you was very rude to two o' the nurses last night.' 'Indeed, sir,' I says, 'and where might you have heard it? The boot's on the other foot. Mr. Gittens here, the porter, heard every word as I said.' And then I told him what had passed, and I never heard no more of it, though it's a paltry place, that it is! One week my tobacco was stopped, but I spoke to the master,—'A paltry three-quarters of a ounce!' I says, and I said it several times over, and the master give me threepence out of his own pocket, because he didn't want to hear no more of it. I earns my own keep, and two or three people's besides, but whatever you does there's only the ounce—as *they* calls it—o' tobacco. But them nurses, that's where the

money goes! Now, how much an-ny-mal food d'you
s'pose they has *each* a week? Six pounds! Beef,
mutton, and sausages, which o' course is meat, but
mannyfactured different. Some o' the men, the men in
the tramp ward and a few more that does hard work,
has meat every day, and what d'you s'pose they gets?
Six ounces a day. Six times seven's forty-two, that's a
matter of three and a half pounds. And the tea and
the sugar them nurses has, you wouldn't believe! *Our*
tea don't spoil our digestion, and the cawfy ain't
calkilated to knock us down! And that second nurse
asked to have her wages rose from £20 to £25, and
three weeks' leave all on end,—and she got it too! But
the master don't never let them into his garden. 'No,
no,' he says; 'things 'ud soon get finger blight if I did."

" But how do you know all these little secrets?"

He laughed, with childlike enjoyment of his own
cunning.

"Ah, Mr. Gittens he gets talking. He tells me
lots o' things. And then there's fish. We have a fish
dinner once a week. At least, it's *there*, but a many of
us never goes in to it. Boiled fish with flour an' water
for gravy! The box comes o' Thursday nights, and
if there's a bit of flat fish such as I *could* eat, them
nurses gets it. Fish, indeed! Why, last Thursday
evenin' we was sittin' out on a bench, me and some
others, and there was a fisherman there,—he's as old as
me, all but two weeks,—and he was farthest from the
box, which was close up agin the master's door, and
which he hadn't never seen it, and all of a sudden he

give a sigh, and he sings out, ' Ah, I smells Lowestoft.'
Yes, mahm, that he did, true as you're here."

"But it is a comfort to know that the nurses are
there when you want them?"

"*Me* want 'em! Nor their med'cines neither. Last
winter, just afore Christmas, the master he says to me,
'Lewis, you don't look as you'd oughter,' he says;
'you'd better come over the way a few days and see
if them nurses can't set you to rights a little.' I didn't
want to, but there, he talked to me as pitiful as if he'd
been my own father, and not for to disobligate him,
and against my better judgment, as I may say, I goes
over. Well, one of 'em brings me my med'cine. 'What
might this be?' I says to her, just as plain as I
speak now. 'D'you call this *med'cine?* If there was
half as much water and twice as much o' the stuff, then
it *might* be,' I says. And the next day I come out."

"But I suppose the doctor ordered the medicine?"

"Well, I won't say as he mightn't have had the
naming of it, but in my belief it's them nurses as
does all the mixing. And they've a pretty free hand
with water at the best o' times. Why, the water that's
wasted up at our place would supply the whole village!
Last spring I told the doctor, one day as he was passing
in, how queer I felt in my legs, and he told me as
he'd tell the nurses to have something ready for me
always the las' thing as I went to bed. Sometimes
it 'ud be eight, sometimes as late as half after nine,
and I used to have to go right up the front steps to
fetch it, and my legs feeling all nohow, same as it 'ud

be if a wasp stung you, paralysed like. Poor stuff it was, too! It didn't seem to do me no good; and to see them nurses, sometimes it 'ud be one and sometimes the other, measurin' it out like as if they lived on the drops they saved! And then the cook, leastways she's a milliner by trade, and she tells her friends she's the matern's assistant,—well, any way she made a good lot o' pills, and she sent some on 'em down to Mr. Gittens, and he asked if I'd like to try 'em, so I took six that night, and they done me a heap o' good. The next night, when that there nurse was annoyin' me countin' out her drops of water bewitched, I up and tells her so. 'What!' says she, 'you bin taking something besides what the doctor ordered you?' 'Yes,' I says; 'I wasn't brought up to take my med'cine by the half-teaspoonful, nor other things neither.' And that's the truth. Fourteen of us there was, and all strict Baptists."

"But I hear that the children are extremely fond of her?"

"*Children!* Who ever heard tell of children wantin' more med'cine than they was give? She hugs 'em and kisses 'em, and what do they care what's for their *good?* Salts an' senna *we* always had, an' if you weren't man enough to take it at a swallow you had to take it by the gulp, and something to help you if it didn't go quick enough! A thing children don't get enough of nowadays, exceptin' them poor little creatures as gets too much. One of them's bin sleeping in my room for a week, while the gurdeens is deciding what best to do for him. Fifty-eight miles, if you'll believe me, mahm, that boy ran away from his father and his wife—which, begging your pardon, she *ain't*—and not ten years old; and the bruises on him as big as your hand, and you could no more count 'em than what you could the stones in Kit Coty's house. If she made a bit of a fuss over *him*, I wouldn't complain. It's bin due to him many a day. And such a prepossessing little lad, as I may say, no pulling and snatching, but always 'Thanky, sir,' and 'Thanky, mahm,' just accordin'. Talk o' manners, you should see some o' my lot! Last Thursday we was bein' shaved, those as like it. I never *did* hold with moustaches, myself! The barber says he never come across anyone with a skin as fine as mine, it's that delicate. He says the Chairman's is the only one as approaches to it. Barbers do get noticin' in their business, but they don't, as you may say, get very *deep* into things, unless it's in the way of cuts; but he's pretty careful, I will say. Friday's our day, I must tell you, but we was going to a tea-party,—and a very discreet and decent one it was, everything, as I may say, becoming. Well, the master comes in and says to one o' the men, 'George, here's a letter for you,' and he fair snatched it out o' the master's hand, with never a word. 'Ah,' I says, leastways I didn't say it then, but I said it at the tea-party when it comes into my mind, 'there's an old saying, Where ignorance is bliss, 'tis folly to be wise.' 'Right you are, Lewis,' he says,—'right you *are*.' He's a very knowledgeable man, the master. I don't suppose anyone in the House could beat him and me at spelling,—not but what Mr. Gittens is good in a *ordinary* way, but he isn't never above asking me when it comes to *names*. The man that's at the gate now, they only lets him write down things on a slate, not with ink and all in the proper columns same as I used to. Why, how d'you suppose he spelt breakfist the other day? You'd never guess. *Brockfick!* One o' the guardeens sees it wrote down, and he laughed fit to kill hisself, and said, ' I know who done that. There's only one man as *could.*' Yes; they're an ignorant lot for the most part, and I have my doubts about them nurses' spelling, although they has a pianny. ' What's that? ' one man asked th'other night when they was working away at it. ' It's something being misused most shockin'! Is there any pigs here? ' Ah, there's some cursin' and swearin' over that pianny! They begins at it every night at eight, just as we goes to bed. That there big nurse has a voice that rises up above the chimleys, and then drops into her boots. Good size boots they are, too! Big as she can get 'em for the money. She leads the singing in church, but I've only been there twice. Too high for me. If you'll believe me, mahm, Mr. Vicar he preached a sermon last week about heaven and th'other place, and he said there *worn't* no other place!"

" Were the congregation pleased ? "

" Well, it heartened them up *some!* Yes, times is changed, med'cine *and* sermons."

" I suppose some of the changes are for the better ? "

" Well, there's a lot more in the new way o' playing dominoes than there was in the old, I will say that. But there, nothing'll please 'em but to stick to their footy old way. They say they don't know no other. 'There's them as can teach you,' says I, but they take no heed. Real childish, I calls it. Why, if you believe me, mahm, I sometimes talks to the tramps, and gets more sense out of 'em than what I do from the men on *our* side; but of course they're not *respectable*. I don't say as I'd like to live with them more than with a pig. It's conversation, I mean,—their way o' putting things.

"If you could just see some of them tramps wood-chopping! There's an old man on our side, he's pretty near as old as me, and not half as strong. The master wants him to give up work—you know, no one ain't *made* work after seventy — because he says, 'I'm responsible for you, Joey. It's me that'll be blamed if you kill yourself bending two double, not you.' But Joe, he can't stand an idle life, so he binds for the tramps when they chop. With all his good will he's not over and above quick in his movements, as you can guess, but four of them chopping can't ever keep up with him. He'll often stand there waiting till he's got enough to put in a bundle. Joe, he always makes my bed for me. I have to give him a pipe o' tobacco Sundays and another Thursdays; but it's worth it, it's worth it. I never *was* one for housework.

"Tobacco's just the same as money, you know, mahm. Everyone wants it, and there's nothing they wouldn't do to get a bit, but it's only give on *our* side. And a good thing too. It's nothing but the want of it as'll ever drive some men to work. I've never been asked by none of them for a bit of food, though I often have some I could give 'em; but for tobacco, they just beg and pray as if it was to save their souls.

"Ah, there's a many of the tramps as has small excuse for bein' what they are. Why, we had a painter five months in the House last winter, a young man, not thirty. The last four weeks I *will* say he worked, he painted the whole place up quite nice, and when he left one Monday morning he had a sov'rin in his pocket, and the pocket was in a decent suit o' clothes. Well, Friday he was back again, without a blush on his face, not a penny left, and as dirty as you please, and trying to get the porter to let him into the tramp ward on the quiet. He wouldn't put him *there;* he give him a ticket for the outside lodgings the guardeens keeps for when there's an overflow. But he'd better not let the master see him just yet a bit.

"Only last week there was a tramp as swore till all was blue that he was just a traveller [a man genuinely seeking for employment], and couldn't get work no-where. 'Looking for work!' he says; 'I've looked for it until I'm nearly blind.' I'd *ought* to be old enough not to be took in, but I must say I felt for him. I've known what it is to walk a hundred miles to a town, and then not earn enough in it to pay for my shoe leather. Well, he come out on a Tuesday, and there was an extry big cattle market on, and several of the dealers was put to it to find enough drovers. One farmer offered him four shillings to drive two beasts thirteen miles in a d'rection where he might as well ha'

gone as any other. D'you s'pose he did it? Not he!
Then another man was most pressing for him to take
some cattle a matter of fourteen miles, and offered him
five shillings. Not he! Then a drover came along and
offered him sixpence to drive four sheep a mile and a
half. That he took. He got another man to help him,
and then they both went into the village beerhouse and
drunk what they could get for it. Two minutes after, I
s'pose he began begging again, pitiful enough to wring
your heart out!

"D'you know a man, mahm, who's often on this road,
—a thinnish man with his nose a bit on one side? Well,
I'm glad you don't. Us old gentlemen heard him a-drop
a kind of a threat to one of his own sort that he was
coming to call on you, but I s'pose he did it just for to
annoy me. He must have overheard me speak of you
to Mr. ——, which I do talk about you sometimes to
him, but I hope you don't think I'd mention a lady's
name to *anyone!* This man I'm talking of he's always
in rags. Last month a gentleman gave him quite a nice
suit, even to the necktie, so's he'd have a better chance
of getting a job. I saw him two days after, and it was
ripped to pieces. I passed a remark on the way it had
wore, and he said, just as if he was a poor cripple, or an
ole woman who couldn't put one foot without stopping
to think where the other was, ' 'Oo'll give me anything
if I goes about dressed like a torff?' There's another
tramp who comes every month. If he came a day too
soon the master would be down on him, and make
things a little hotter for him. Without exception he's

the strongest man I ever see. He'd ought to be *made* go for a soldier. He gets through his stint of stone-breaking while the others is looking at it, and then sits down and talks. I don't say there's anything bad in him. He's just born lazy, and it ought to be took out of him somehow.

"I don't know but what I hadn't better be starting back, mahm. Not as the master 'ud say anything to *me* if I was a bit late. No one ever saw *me* in a public begging for a drink! 'Go and enjoy yourself,' he says, and he looked me out the best suit he could find, mine being a bit shabby, seeing as I do more work than most ; but I'm not what you'd call an *ordinary* figure, and this was the best he could do for me, so I hope you'll excuse it."

"And you won't soften your heart and take the nurses some flowers ? "

"It's *her* heart as wants softenin'! She ain't got none except for herself. No, mahm ; I wouldn't take her not a leaf! But I'd take matern some. She's a diff'rent class o' person, *she* is ! "

He started off with the best in the garden and green-house, more set, I am afraid, upon the mortification of the " oncultivated " than the gratification of the lady who had won his approval.

CHAPTER X

" Dolf "

It was the termination of a successful case, and, after much interchange of complimentary speech, I was making arrangements for the return of some expensive appliances lent to the invalid and no longer needed.

" Dolf shall carry them back for you to-morrow afternoon, miss. He gen'ly looks in every day to see father don't want nothin'," said the second daughter. She spoke with an air of easy proprietorship, and I had previously understood that her fiancé's name was All-but; but these engagements often last so long, and then come to nothing so suddenly, that I should have made no comment even if she had not added the explanation: " He's Gina's young man. She won't even spend the money to come and see father, so of course she won't to see *him*; but she likes him to come here pretty often, so's she'll know where he *is*, and what he's *at*."

" He must be a very obliging young man," I said drily.

" He is that, miss, and no mistake. I don't deny he's worth two of All-but when there's any fetching and carrying to be done, but how him and Gina'll hit it off is more than I can say. She's that close with her money as never was."

Gina's "closeness" was an old grievance, and I slipped away from it as quickly as possible, thinking that a failing so rare among Londoners might perhaps have its useful side.

I was starting on my second round the next day, when I met Dolf on the doorstep. He was a short but strongly built young fellow of about twenty, with a fluffy moustache and very clear blue eyes. The parcels were heavy, and I asked him to carry them into my office. He lingered awkwardly, and I half thought—unusual as such a thing was—that, not being even In-lawed to the family, he expected payment.

"I suppose, m'm," he said at last, "you wouldn't attend not all kinds of complaints?"

I was too busy for circumlocution, so I came to the point at once.

"Is there anyone that you would like me to go and see?"

He seemed more relieved by my perspicacity than astonished at it.

"It's my little sister, m'm,—her arm is burnt."

"How did it happen?"

"Well, I couldn't rightly say, m'm."

The vagueness of the reply would not have attracted my attention, a grown-up brother was not likely to know much about a child's doings, but the burning wave of colour that passed over his smooth young face could hardly escape notice.

"Is her arm painful?"

"It seems to worry her a good bit, and I'm not sure

if I've done rightly by it.   I'd be very grateful if you
could come in this evening."

"I will certainly do so if I can, but there is much
sickness about, and I may be rather late."

"About what time would it be, m'm?"

I was rather surprised at this unbrotherly persistence,
and said—

"Not later than nine.   Do not keep the child up.   I
can dress her arm just as well after she is in bed, and
she will soon fall asleep again."

District work often suddenly accumulates or diminishes
in equally unexpected fashion.   One of my patients,
strictly against the doctor's orders, had gone for a walk
of indefinite length; a second had called in a quack;
a third produced a note from his medical attendant
ordering the discontinuance of certain elaborate treatment, and it was scarcely seven when I reached my new
patient's door.   I heard a sound of vigorous splashing,
and a joyous little voice : "Adain, Doffie,—do it adain!"
I knocked; there was a moment's silence, a hasty
scramble, and then Dolf's order : "Let the lady in, Janey;
and mind what I told you."

A child of about ten opened the door silently, and
stood aside to let me pass.   A bath-tub was in front of
the fire, and Dolf was on his knees, hastily dragging
down the night-shirt of a sturdy boy of three, the slow-
ness of the operation being caused partly by its narrow-
ness, but chiefly by insufficient use of the towel.

"I'd have bathed the boys earlier if I'd known you'd
been able to come so soon, m'm," he said apologetically,

rising to his feet, and wrapping the boy cocoon fashion in a blanket that had been hung on the back of a chair. "That's Kitty," pointing to a child who sat in an easy-chair with her legs at right angles to her body; "she'll be a good girl and not cry. I'll take Tommy up to bed, and stop with him a while. Janey, mind you fetch the lady all she wants."

With the child's assistance, I found the few things that were necessary, and prepared to unfasten the bandage on Kitty's arm.

"How long is it since your mother died?"

The children looked at me vacantly.

"Tommy is the baby, I suppose?"

No answer. I examined the little arm, and was glad to find that the burn, although painful, was not severe, and had been treated with more skill than Dolf had led me to expect. I applied a fresh dressing, and was bandaging the arm, when Kitty's tongue was suddenly loosed.

"Baby's five munfs old."

"Where *is* baby?"

"Out long o' mother."

"Oh, it's Saturday. I suppose mother is doing the shopping?"

"Mother don't do it. Farver doos it, 'relse Dolf."

The child had revealed more than enough, and to get off such dangerous ground I asked Janey how Kitty had slept the previous night.

"She cried, and couldn't sleep at all, and at last Dolf carried her down here so's she shouldn't disturb us all,

and lighted the fire to keep her warm, and tied her arm
up, and made her bread and sop, and then she fell asleep.
He never knew she was hurt until he heard her crying
in the night.   Mother *did* go on at Dolf when she came
down in the morning and found all the coal he'd burnt;
but father said he didn't see what she had to grumble
at, and he'd have thought more of her if she'd got up
and seen to Kitty herself, specially as it was her as
done it."

" But isn't that what Dolf told you not to tell me ? "

Janey looked mutinous.   " I does mostly do what Dolf
tells me, but I don't see why I should tell lies to hide up
what mother does."

Kitty stretched out her disengaged arm and aimed a
vigorous blow at her sister, which fortunately missed
her by about a yard.

" Dolf *don't* tell lies !   He says it's wicked."

Janey's retort was checked by the sound of a
stumbling step on the pavement.

" That'll be mother," she said, and went with nervous
haste to open the door.   A tall, thin woman staggered
in, and almost dropped the baby into Janey's arms.   She
turned to me with a foolish smile on her face, but a
shade of suspicion in her manner.

" I'm sure it's very kind of you, miss.   Children do
throw theirselves about somethin' shockin'.   How might
you have heard of Kitty's assydent ? "

I caught a warning look on the elder girl's face, and
explained indifferently : " I have been nursing a case
near here, and heard of the accident indirectly through

15

that. I will come in for the next few days and dress the wound, and then I think there will be no more trouble."

She seemed appeased, but irritation rose at the sight of the bath-tub.

"How that boy do keep slopping about with the water! I wonder he don't drown 'em all, and have done with it."

Dolf came quietly in, emptied the bath and cleared up all signs of his labours, while the mother continued to rail at him, and Janey's face grew black with anger. Kitty was inclined to be feverish, and to get her out of this stormy atmosphere I suggested putting her to bed before I left. Dolf carried her up on one arm, lighting my way as he went. The two girls shared a tiny room with no fireplace, Dolf and his two little brothers slept in one not much larger, but better ventilated, while the baby had the doubtful privilege of being with its parents.

As the lad put his sister down on the bed, I heard an anxious whisper, "You won't go out again, not to-night, will you?" and the reassuring reply—

"No, nor not to-morrow, unless it's over to Gina's father to see if he wants anything, and I'll take you 'long with me, if you like."

"Mother says Gina loves money a lot more'n she loves Dolf," said Kitty, when her brother had gone downstairs. Mother's testimony was not of much value, but, happening to coincide with the opinion of Gina's own family, it gave me a foreboding chill.

" Have you no big brothers except Dolf ? "

" No; it's the scarlack fever that done it."

" Did what ? "

" *Everythin'*," said the child, solemnly enjoying herself. " When Doff was little, mother used to baff him *three times a-week*, and she used to do the shopping herself then; and when Doff was about as big as Janey, he took scarlack fever, and mother said as they *got* to have it they'd better have it and be done with it; and the doctor went on at mother somefin' *awful*, and he said it 'ud serve her jolly well bloomin' right if half the kids hooked it. And then Alice and Ernie and Frank and Lizzie all died,—only Doff lived. And then me and Janey and Tommy and Will and the baby come in their steads, but mother didn't never like it a bit the same. You couldn't 'xpect her to, could you ? How'd *I* like it if Doff and Janey was took away, and I just had two squealy kicky babies ? "

" Assy-dents " were frequent in that house, though happily not severe, and as Dolf seemed to think that my visits at uncertain hours were some check on the mother during the long daily absence of the two bread-winners and protectors, I went as frequently as I could. About six months later I found the two little girls full of unselfish triumph and excitement. " Dolf's got a holiday ! His master said it was a shame he shouldn't have one, so he's give him a week, *and* his wages, *and* a sov'rin, and Dolf'll have to go right away somewhere, won't he, else it would be all the same as stealing, wouldn't it ? "

"Quite as bad," I said emphatically. It was Saturday afternoon, and Dolf was in the back kitchen, methodically blacking a long row of little boots, and I hoped that he would hear what I said. He worked in a factory which the children had often pointed out to me; I could not understand from their account what was made there, but the smell was poisonous, and I rejoiced that the lad was to have a few days' freedom and fresh air.

Ten days after, I met Janey taking the baby for an airing, and asked about Dolf's holiday. Storm-signals flew at once over the eager face.

"What d'you s'pose that silly Dolf's bin and done?"

"Not given up his holiday, I hope?"

"No, he couldn't do that, not after taking the sov'rin; he's gone away right enough, but he's gone with Gina's father. He's been ill again, and the doctor said he'd ought to go away for a month, and they've got good club money, so they didn't mind; but there wasn't enough for Gina's mother to go too, and he's very weak still, so Gina said Dolf had got to go and look after him for the first week, and he's as cross as two sticks all the time, and the doctor says it's a good sign, and if 'twas yer own father I daresay you'd be glad, but come to other people's fathers,"—she paused to readjust the baby, not without skill, but with a shade more vigour than was necessary.

"All-but had ought to have gone if it was to be any-one, 'cos he gets a fortnight every year, and half his work is out of doors, and then out walkin' with Fanny every evenin'; but Gina said she wasn't goin' to have *her* father trusted 'long of All-but, and Dolf had got to

go.   But that's on'y talk; they couldn't ha' got All-but
to go, not one of them.   He's as selfish as they make 'em.
I wish it was him to marry Gina, and then Fanny could
take Dolf."

This re-arrangement did not occur to the principals,
and, four years later, Dolf, very proud and with the same
fluffy boyish moustache, brought Gina and their baby
daughter to see me.   I am not well up in "Infants'
Outdoor Clothing," as my poor little friends generally
receive me in their night-dresses and a shawl, but I had
an impression that the baby, although clean and neat,
did not look exactly as one would expect of the only
child of a steady, hard-working man when taken out to
pay a state call.

The next day I met Fanny, and told her that I had
seen the baby, and how pretty I thought it.   She waved
that part of the matter away impatiently.

" What did it have on, miss; did you notice ? "

" Well, not particularly; it seemed very clean "—

" *Clean !*   Was it wearing a white satin bonnet and a
cashmere robe embroidered with silk, and lace rooshings
all down the front ? "

I was able to state confidently that it was *not*.   " Well,
that's what mother'n father give it to go visiting; for
they said it was a shame to expect Dolf to go out with
it looking such a mean little fright, it was enough to
turn him against the child, if anything *could*.   But
Gina's that close she won't even let the child wear it
when it's bin give to her.   It's always going to rain,
or suthin'crother.   Mother'n father 'ull be just mad

when they hear the child was took to see you in *that* style."

"But why tell them, Fanny? There is no need to do it."

Sensations are scarce, especially among such respectable people, and to conceal an annoyance of that kind would be regarded as mental greed; the "in*sult*" that had been put upon me and the grandparents formed the subject of many enjoyably animated conversations.

The next time I heard the child's name mentioned she must have been nearly three. Fanny had married All-but, and was bringing him into better training than could have been anticipated, considering the unpromising nature of the material. I had been called in to admire her baby, a healthy boy of ten months old, who made serious attempts at walking, and I inquired for Dolf and Gina and little Rosemarie.

"You remember all that fuss over the baby's clothes, miss? Well, it's been like that all through, and the way that poor child is fed is just a burning shame,— Gina won't buy *nothin'* for her."

"I suppose Gina thinks she is old enough to eat ordinary food now?"

"Ordinary food! It isn't what the child *has* that I complain of so much; most of the childern about here eats whatever's going before they're half her age. It's what she *don't* have! The child never sees anything *to* eat, except Sat'days and Sundays when Dolf's at home, and she's that thin it's something pitiful. Gina just eats a crust of dry bread and a rind of cheese for

her dinner, and there's water porridge for breakfast. It
may be good for some, but it ain't suited to that child's
stummick, and she'll just pine away."

" Have you spoken to Gina about it ? "

" I've said all I can, and so's mother, and so's *his*
mother, too. Whatever her faults is, it was trouble as
drove her to it, and she was never one to starve her
childern, though ragged and dirty they *might* be, and
with more bruises than she thought it manners for you
to ast after. Gina says it's no use buying things, the
child won't eat 'em. She'd eat 'em fast enough, poor
little dear, if she could get 'em. Why, las' spring, when
Gina was house-cleaning, I had her over here, and she'd
eat an egg for her dinner, and a good helping of rice
pudding, and at tea-time I'd pretty well fill up her cup
with milk afore I put any tea in it, and as long as the
butter was spread pretty thick she'd eat as much bread
as you liked, and then she'd be ready for a bit of supper
when her uncle come back from work. She'd sit on his
knee and take it like a little bird. In the four days I
do believe she put on five pounds in weight. It's a sin
and a shame ! All-but dropped a word to Dolf about it,
for he took wonderful to the child while she was here.
Everyone does, and I don't say as Gina isn't fond of her,
but it was always money first with her, and the rest had
to come in where there was room ! "

I resolved to go and see the child, but she lived three
miles outside my district, and there was a heavy
pressure of work. I inquired for her several times, and
received more reassuring replies, and she slipped from my

thoughts—until I met Janey one day, in a crape hat and a blue dress, and eyes disfigured by much crying.

"It's Dolf's little Rosemarie," she explained,—"only ill a week, and died two days ago. Dolf was with her day and night, though Gina went on at him awful for not going to work. It's a mercy Rosemarie didn't last only the week, for what with seeing her in such pain, and what with Gina's going on, he was almost off his head. I minded Fanny's boy for her, and she was there most of the time. All-but did for hisself, and was more good-natured than you'd think for; but I will say he's changed from what he was when Fanny married him, and he thinks a heap of Dolf. Dolf's at home now; his master said he could stay till after the funeral."

I bought a handful of white lilies and some ferns, and got into the tram, blaming myself for having forgotten the child so long.

Dolf's face looked pinched and grey, but he received me with quiet self-control, and thanked me warmly for the flowers: "Won't you come in and give them to her yourself, m'm?"

"Where is Gina?" I asked.

There was the unmistakable creak of a mangle, and Dolf's old blush rose painfully. To me it seemed natural that the mother should turn to washing and mangling as a relief, but I knew that it was so entirely against local custom to do any hard work until after the funeral, that he would scarcely have felt more humiliated if I had found his wife lying drunk on the floor.

We knelt for a few moments by the little bed, and

then we talked about the child, and how even All-
but had loved her. Suddenly Gina burst in—

"Dolf! I've bin thinkin',"—it was a plan for
reducing the funeral expenses.

No more children have been born to Dolf, and Gina
has not greatly changed, but one alleviation has come
into his home-life. With not much more wrangling
than it had often cost him to get a cup of milk for
Rosemarie, he has been allowed to buy a piano. Several
old people delight in coming in to listen to his music,
and Gina, who has a tenderness for age that she has
never yet felt for childhood, welcomes them hospitably,
and has even been known to press a cup of tea upon
the oldest and poorest. I remember now that, closely
as she stuck to her wages, the phrase always ran,
"Gina's father," "Gina's grandmother," while it was
"Fanny's little brothers and sisters."

CHAPTER XI

THE INCONVENIENCE OF BEING POOR

" THE missis " was seventy-three when I first knew her, and she told me (with some slight tinge of scorn for his inferiority) that " Th'auld mon " was " a good two 'ear older."

The husband was scarcely five feet in height, the wife a little less; except for their childishly small feet, always neatly shod, and the pure human goodness and the touch of spirituality in their faces, they resembled nothing so much as 17th-century paintings of Dutch peasants in winter landscapes. Th'auld mon worked about five days a week for a market gardener, earning nine or ten shillings. At the best of times I do not think he had ever earned more than fourteen. He suffered cruelly from sciatica and rheumatism, which often made work impossible; but he belonged to a club, which, when he was entirely laid by, paid him seven shillings a week, and he generally managed to crawl back to the gardens before the dreaded reduction to the five shilling scale.

They were both ardent Dissenters, but the only touch of intolerance I ever saw in them was in always speaking of the vicar as " Mister Paa-son," and I was never

quite sure that this was not intended for respect.   Twice
every Sunday they walked up the hill to a tiny chapel
in continual danger of being bought and closed.   It was
too poor to afford a regular minister, but was visited
several times a month by itinerant preachers.   I used to
ask sometimes when I met them, " Was there a good
congregation ? "   The cautious reply was invariable :
" Yes, yes, ma'am, *considerin'*."

They lived in a cottage dumped down in the middle
of a cabbage field, a few yards of which they were
allowed to regard as their own.   The house nominally
had four rooms, and they were paying the same rent
as when these had all been habitable, but one of the
upstair rooms could not safely be entered, and the " wash-
'us " had literally fallen down.   The chief difference
that it seemed to make to them was that they had to
board up the hole that was left in the kitchen wall, and
dish-water was henceforth flung out of the front door
instead of the back (drains had never existed), and
when the weather was not too inclement the week's
wash was done on a bench out of doors.

One October night there was a fearful storm : the
slates were stripped from my house like dry leaves, and
several times I heard the crashing thud of falling trees.
I thought of my old friends alone in their crazy cottage,
and soon after daylight I went to inquire for them.
I could see from the road that the chimney had fallen,
and the roof was nothing but a few tiles hanging here
and there on a rotten framework of wood.   I hurried
up the sodden path, and knocked loudly at the door.

There was not a sound to be heard within. I shook the door violently, and, getting more alarmed, flung myself against it, but the rusty hinges held firm. I walked round to the other side of the house to find out if it would be possible to force an entrance through the ruined back kitchen, when a cheerful old voice saluted me—

"Mornin', marm! Bee-you-tiful after the starm, ain't it?" and I turned to see th'auld mon bending over a ragged clump of marigolds.

"I have been so anxious all night about you and your wife, Mr. Kelter."

"You didn't know we'd moved, marm? Two days ago. Jus' as well we did," looking with calm interest at the litter of tiles, bricks, and rotten wood; "we'd a-had a rough night if we'd been here. No, the missis an' me we thought it was time to move. Fifteen years we've paid our rent *to* the day, and not a lick of paint have the landlord give it, an' we're past reachin' about doin' paperin' an' whitewashin' ourselves. I'm jus' movin' some o' these here flowers. They b'long to the missis, an' we've got a scrap of gyardin in the front where we can put 'em."

"I hope your new house is comfortable?"

"The gyardin's the worst part of it. In twenty years all the manure it have had is the half of a pig."

(The "half of a pig" represented to me a side of bacon, and I wondered how bad it was before anyone thought it necessary to bury it.)

"Is the house in better repair?"

"Oh yes, yes; it's pretty fair, the new house is, and sixpence a week cheaper, too."

I went to examine it for myself the next day. It was solidly built of rough stone, but the one living room was rather larger than a bathing machine, and quite as damp and draughty, and when the door was closed there was twilight at midday. The chimney was a black cavern of indefinite size; the fireplace so small, that when the potatoes were put on to boil, the kettle had to be suspended from a hook. I surreptitiously placed my hand across the oven, and found that I could easily span it, although I span less than nine inches. There was a tiny washhouse and one low bedroom overhead.

The old man caught a bad attack of pneumonia a few weeks later, and, while waiting to see the doctor one morning, I heard the family history, one of unbroken hardship and poverty, related with no resentment, and with only a touch of self-pity for " old, unhappy far-off things."

" My mother died when I was nine, and I got on as well as I could till I was thirteen. My father didn't marry again, and he wasn't not to say cruel, but he was pretty sour to us all, and I was the youngest by a long way. Then he found me a place at a farmhouse. It wasn't the place any mother would have let a child take. It was respectable enough, but the work was beyond me. My feet and hands used to be just a mass of chilblains, out feeding the pigs and working in the cowsheds, and doing all the scouring. I don't think I ever grew, not a mite, after I went there. I was afraid to leave, for I'd nowhere to go, and I knew father wouldn't take me back."

" Did you never go to school ? "

" I went for a bit, but they didn't teach on'y readin' an' sewin'. I can sew a bit still, don't you think ? " and she held out a half-finished sun-bonnet elaborately piped and gathered, the stitches rather large, but almost as even as if done by machine.

" When I got older I found myself a better place, and there I stayed till I was twenty-eight, when we got married. The missis was kind to me, for she knowed I'd a heap o' rough work to do. Often when she was mending clothes she'd mend mine. ' Mar'get,' she'd say, ' I've mended thee stockins and thee apern.' That's the way she'd talk. It's a way o' talkin' I don't never hear now, acept sometimes th'auld mon'll bring it out to me. When I showed un' the shawl you give me th'other day, he said : ' Eh, thou dost be blessed ! ' "

" And after you were married ? "

" I often think it's the work I done then as hurt me most. Young married women hadn't ought to go out to work, but we'd three childen, an' th'auld mon—it's truth I'm telling you—earnt *less'n* what he do now ! I couldn't get indoor work, charing and the like, and what should I have done with the childen if I had ? There's missises now at the farms that let women bring a couple o' childen with 'em, and have 'em set in the back kitchen, an' feed 'em too, and the rest can go to school an' be minded an' kep' warm for nothin' ; but missises wasn't put to it in those days to beg an' coax women

to come an' work for 'em! I had to take to field labour.
Th'other day I heerd a boy, he mus' a-been twelve,
ridin' past with a lady, and he called out, ' Mother, just
look, there's a *woman* workin' in that field!' as if he'd
never seen anything more s'prisin' in his life, and maybe
he hadn't, but it shows how times is changed. I've
often dragged a rake in the harvest field all day when
I wasn't as big as him, though a bit older. I used to
have to take the three childen with me, and set 'em
under a hedge, and make a kind of tent for 'em, and
there they'd stop, keepin' one another warm, Tom an'
Mary and Bessie, while I was weedin', or pickin' stones,
or whatever it might be. Gleanin' was the best time.
Tom could help a little with that, and I often gleaned
enough to last us all from harvest up to pretty nigh
Christmas. When they got old enough to profit, I sent
'em to school. It cost money then, but I meant 'em to
be scholars, and scholars they *are*. Yes, acept when I
was in my first place, that was my hardest time, from
the year I married until Tom could pretty well earn
his own keep."

As the old woman spoke, a scene rose before my mind
that I had observed from my breakfast-room window
for many mornings in succession : the Mary who had
cowered under wintry hedges some thirty-five years
previously, dressed as neatly as if every day were
Sunday with her, leading by the hand plump, extensively
curled and frilled, but rebellious and tearful Mary II.,
aged six, and consigning her to the care of the Infant
Schoolmistress, who led her the rest of the way to the

Kindergarten class. The child was then (I learnt on inquiry) led back by the teacher to the grandparents' house, where she had her dinner; her grandmother then took her to school again, where at four o'clock Mary 1st arrived to fetch her.

Both daughters had married well, and did a little to help their parents, but not much. Their only excuse is, that, owing to the hardships of their childhood and their mother's overwork, they have the nerves supposed to be the peculiar affliction of the idle rich, and spend a small fortune on expensive quack remedies. The son married rather above his station, and is partner in a small but flourishing business. He too is prematurely aged and broken. As far as I know—and the old people are touchingly ready to boast of all that their children do for them—I do not think he has ever given his parents the smallest assistance.

"There's on'y th'auld mon and me now," she continued, "and if anything was to happen to *he* I'd have to go to the Big House. I'd be feared to live here by myself, and they wouldn't let me neither. But I've good club money coming; there'll be eight pounds when I'm dead."

"Your husband must try and take a little more care of himself."

"I know th'auld mon didn't ought to work so hard, but he's no scholar, and he gets mis'ble when he's nothin' to do but sit by the fire. Else I daresay us could get relief, and with the club and the garden we'd manage. He'd ought to be able to raede, same as me, for his

father was none so poor; but he took against him, and
bound him out some'eres to work when he wasn't but
nine 'ear old, and he's done nothin' but work ever since.
I raedes to 'un, but he's gettin' deaf, and my voice is
weak with th'indygestun. But there, once Christmas
is over we'll do well enough. I do dread the frost.
It's a quarter of a mile across the medders to the well,
and when it's frozen, every step I do take I think I'll
slip and break my arm."

"But have you no rain water?"

"I've got *he*," pointing to an old forty-gallon oil cask;
"but the gentleman's horse next door he do have the
half of it."

I peeped in at the gentleman's horse's stable, and
satisfied myself that he was not living in undue luxury
of cleanliness or appointments. Whatever water the
poor animal had had must have gone down his gaunt
throat.

I met th'auld mon a few days ago, crawling stiffly
home in the dusk after a day's mangel heaving. He
had a heavy load of dry sticks on his back, and looked
like an over-burdened gnome. I commented angrily
on the conduct of the world in general, with a purely
private application to his son.

"We must all fill our place," he said gently, and
toiled on.

16

CHAPTER XII

SARAH has a husband who needs some keeping up to the mark, and eight children who adore her, and is the kind of person for whom neighbours and relatives send an urgent summons directly they are ill or in trouble. In fiction of an instructive tendency, Sarah's apron would be "spotless," her hearth "well swept," and every floor that she had anything to do with would be "fit to eat your dinner off." As a matter of fact, a large family and an actively charitable disposition, when combined with poverty, do not leave much time for attention to personal appearance, nor for meticulous house-keeping.

When, after getting breakfast for ten mouths, seeing her husband and eldest boy off to work, "starting" the seven other children to school, and "whisking round" bedrooms and kitchen, Sarah rushed three streets off to help some sick friend, her bonnet was often awry (if it was only the *next* street she probably wore her husband's old cap), and the apron that showed itself under the hastily fastened "dolman" was anything but clean. At a passing glance no one would have taken her for a pillar of society, and a gloomy person in a gloomy moment might have thought of the "submerged tenth," or at least of "the total ignorance of all house-wifely arts so common among the poor." Tithes of mint and cummin are not in her line, but she has a grand eye for the essential.

After working an hour or more for the invalid, Sarah would run home helter-skelter to cook the children's dinner. When they returned from school it would have been as undesirable as it was unnecessary for them to eat off the boards, and any attempt to see themselves in kettle or saucepan would have been a foredoomed failure. But what did they care as they tumbled eagerly in, four of them exclaiming, "Here's *me*, mother," and the others, "I *am* glad you're back. I was so afraid you'd have had to stop 'long of Mrs. Taylor. We do hate having dinner without you!"

Sarah does not stop to point a dismal moral, that it would be worse to be ill and have no dinner at all, but proceeds to help them all with an attention to their individual tastes which more than compensates for the plainness of the food. All through the meal at least three little voices at once are shouting, "Mother, what d'you think? Mother, listen while I tell you!" When she speaks they are silent, "because she is so funny." They never give any other reason, but it is easy to see that they have it in their hearts.

After dinner the younger ones go into the tiny yard to play, but the eldest, a boy and a girl, "help mother put the kitchen square," because she has promised to go Mrs. Taylor's again, "and clean up the place a bit and give a hand to the lady nurses."

Then every one of the seven must be "tidied" for school. Sarah's children are always wholesomely clean and generally kissable, but she has never yielded to the deadly vanity of making them "the cleanest in the whole class." Other poor little mortals are put on that slippery height, and kept there by dint of "fourteen pinnies in the wash every week of their lives," a constant drizzle of reproof and frequent hailstorms of slaps. Sarah saves up slaps and scoldings for the rare occasions when they are well earned, and delivers them with the vigour and efficiency that mark all her proceedings. "The day mother smacked me because—" "The day mother rowed me because—" are epochs in their lives.

"You'll be back to tea, *won't* you?" asks number six coaxingly, and there is a general chorus—

"Do, mother, *do* say you'll be back!"

Sarah does not wish to make works of charity hateful in their eyes, so she replies, as if she had thought of a far more charming plan—

"If I'm not in by five o'clock, the four little ones can have their faces and hands washed and go round to their grandma, and say will you please give them some tea because mother's gone to help poor Mrs. Taylor, and they'll do the same for *her* when they get bigger. And Katie can cut the bread for herself and Willy and Fanny, and they can each have a spoonful of jam, and Will shall put the door-key in his pocket, and you shall all three have tea 'long o' father and Tom."

"We can wait too, mother!" cry the little ones jealously, but Sarah only laughs; she knows that in three hours' time grandma's well-sweetened tea and kindly "fussing" will be irresistible. No special post of honour has been found for Fanny, and her mouth droops ominously. Luckily Sarah perceives it in time, re-ties her pinafore, and assures her that *she* is her lamb who is never a mite of trouble to nobody. A mendacious statement which Fanny tries to justify by winking away her tears, and they all set out cheerfully, walking with their mother to the top of the street, where their ways separate.

"Why do two nurses come to Mrs. Taylor?" asks number five, whose thirst for knowledge of a kind not provided in his "Standard" is insatiable.

"Oh, there'd be too much room if only one was to come." The reply is received, strictly according to age, as a witticism, a puzzle that needs rumination, or a fact much better established than any of the marvels related by teacher.

Instructions are repeated as to the precise message to be given to grandma, and the relative thickness of bread and jam, and the good-byes have all been exchanged, when Willy comes pelting after her, the big door-key in his pocket mercilessly thumping him as he runs: "Mother, if the superintendent's there, *do* give her that understudy of yours. It makes father laugh more than any bit you've got."

"Go 'long with you, Willy, you'll be late! She comes to see people does their work properly as they'd ought to, not to set laughin' as if she'd no more thought than your father and Tom."

"But I know she'd laugh like anything, you do it so queer."

"You be off! Why, the vicar might be her brother or her cousin, for all *you* know. People has to take more heed than that, you silly boy."

"But I *do* know, mother! There's a man told me her people was all 'wonders to fight.' He said they'd been eating salt meat a hundred years as *he* knew of, and that's why she can't abear it and tells people not to buy it."

"You hadn't ought to get talking about ladies with men like that. He can't be respectable at *all* with such a way of speaking."

"Why, *mother!* He lives in a house with a fore-court, and he's got two watches. His Sunday one's gold, and it's got his name in it, and he's been living right up for *years*."

Sarah cannot controvert such proofs of respectability, nor reconcile them with the indelicacy of bringing salt pork and fighting into connection with a lady's name, so she says, "You be off to school this minute!" with such a shade of authority in her voice that he obeys, only stopping when about ten yards off to shout over his shoulder—

"And he says he's often took off the lace and wore out their uniforms for 'em when the reggylations was changed so quick they hadn't time to do it for theirselves. He says it took him half a lifetime."

Ten minutes later, Sarah arrived on the scene of her charitable labours, a four-roomed house, which is the home of a middle-aged man and his wife, and their only daughter, a paralysed girl of twenty. The father is out all day at work, the mother is marked on the nurse's books as a severe surgical case, and has been confined to bed for ten weeks, but there are great hopes of her recovery, and she is as lively as Sarah herself. A month previously there had been a worse crisis in the family, for the daughter had caught a severe attack of influenza, and had to be nursed in the same room as her mother; while, even her feeble efforts at "keeping things going" being brought to an end, the dirt and confusion downstairs could scarcely be kept in check by Sarah's flying visits, much of which necessarily went in personal attentions to the two invalids, and cooking "a bit of something against your dad comes home."

To-day she gives a long and vigorous clean to the kitchen, and then leaves the girl to "set it to rights," while she goes up to the invalid, makes everything spick and span, collects all the articles the lady nurse is likely to want, and sits down to wait for her, and enjoy the long gossip with Mrs. Taylor which is her sole reward.

Nurse arrives, and as she is new to district work, the superintendent comes with her. Presently nurse goes downstairs to make lengthy preparations in the kitchen, and the invalid feels that some entertainment must be provided for the "leading man."

"Sarah, do give the superintendent that understudy of yours,—how you kep' the vicar downstairs when me and 'Lizabeth was both ill in bed."

" Well, miss, this is how it was. Mrs. Taylor and
'Lizabeth was both in bed, and I was seeing to 'em as
well's I could in between times, but in the circumstances
you can guess that nothing wasn't over and above
clean.   I'd brought Fanny with me, she'd cut her
finger so bad it wasn't much use for her to go to school
of an afternoon, so I set her just inside the door to
answer it, and not let no one in.   And neither she
wouldn't, not in an ordinary way, but I s'pose she
thought you'd got to let a parson in whether you
wanted to or not, so I didn't say nothing to her about
it.   Just as I'd begun to get things more comfortable,
but nothing you could call fit to be seen, we heard a
slow kind o' voice and a step along the downstairs
passage.

"'It's the vicar!' says Mrs. Taylor; 'don't you let
him upstairs, Sarah, whatever you do.   We're not going
to be seen by nobody.   Keep him out, whatever it
costs.   Don't spare to speak your mind if you must.
I won't have him in here at any price.'   So out of
the room I popped, and shut the door behind me.   My
apern was as black as could be, and my face—what's
it like now, Carryline?   Well, it was worse then, I'm
sure!   I got my foot on the top stair just as he got
his foot on the bottom one.

"'I hee-ar there are two in-va-lids in this how-ow-se.'

"'Yes, sir, there are,' I says, getting down three steps
while he got up two.

"'I should—ah—like to have a little conversation with
them.'

" ' Impossible, sir,' I says. ' Their temperature's a hundred and four. Nurse says they musn't be disturbed on *any* account.'

" ' I—ah—should so *much* like to see them.' This time he got up three steps while I only got down two, but I knew he'd never try to pass me with my apern as black as that, so I bore down on him, and worked him back till we reached the kitchen door, but, as bad luck would have it, the door was open.

" ' I couldn't let no one see them after what the nurse has said, sir.' He give a sort of sigh, and said : ' I should—ah—like to pray with you.' Well, I didn't feel I could deny him everything, but I can tell you I didn't like kneeling on that there floor even though my apern *was* past its best. He prayed for about ten minutes, and then he got up and said, " Ah, there are so many poo-er in my pah-rish that I find I can on-ly vis-it them *twice a year*.' Now, miss, you know the size of the parish, and how many's in it, and how many houses he'd behave like *that* in, so what d'you call it for a lie,—pretty stiff, eh ? "

Then Sarah helped the nurse clear away, and dashed home to get her husband's tea ready, and to convulse him with a representation of the superintendent's " way o' talking," and, by special request, giving a repetition of her understudy, with many details that the superintendent has suppressed,—and doubtless with many that were withheld from *her*.

CHAPTER XIII

SOME OF MY FRIENDS

THE SHOW PATIENT

THE Show Patient is to be found in nearly every large district. He is undoubtedly a sufferer, but there are moments when his victims can only regard him as a personal trial. How long he has been ill, no one seems to know; like the "oldest inhabitant," he probably exaggerates a little, and his wife "never crosses him" by discounting his statements, but at any rate he has always known "them nusses" ever since the branch was founded, and gives characters to the successive superintendents with the fluency of a seventh-standard boy maligning the Norman Kings. His favourite is "the one afore the last, a real lady *she* was, and a Christian too," shooting a baleful glance at the convicted heathen who stands by his bedside directing a probationer. "Many's the 'alf-sovereign she's give me."

"It is a melancholy change for you, Mr. Crampitt," she replies, with an unrelenting smile. She holds strong views on the subject of outdoor relief to married men; the patient has been on the books twelve years, and there are seven sickly children in the house. "Well,

Sooper, me and you and Mr. Bowring is the only ones as never could get on. Narchdeakin they *says* he is now. All I knows is, he wasn't a clergyman not at all when he was here, on'y a coorate. I says to my wife many a time, I says, I don't want no journeymen soul-savers here. If there's a job to be done, I like the master man for it. But we was better frien's afterwards, me an' 'im. I give him a Greek book I bought off a stall for tuppence, and told him if he'd rub up his learning it might help 'im on a bit, for I misdoubted he were as taught-up as the other chaps. Why, some of 'em's *learnt out* afore they're twenty! And so it *have* helped him, seemingly. There's a new coorate at Hall Saints', ain't there? Do he lodge with the same old dummon?'

The superintendent turns a deaf ear, and to sharpen her hearing he asks: "Is there going to be a rummidge sale to pay yer wages, same as there was last year? It do seem as if it got harder'n ever to raise the money!"

As soon as she leaves the house, she says to the probationer: "Do not supply him with any addresses. With his club money, and parish allowance, and what his wife earns at fine ironing, he is better off than if he were at work. The doctors attend him for nothing, the chemist lets him have everything half-price if the work-house supply falls short, the vicar of the parish is extravagantly generous to him, and there is hardly a sect or a church in the town from which he does not manage to extract money."

The Show Patient is generally a man, not because

women have not an even larger share of the ills that flesh is heir to, but because it is almost impossible to hold the position satisfactorily without the aid of a devoted wife. The district nurse is expected to call regularly and listen to an exposition of his view on things in general, but she is not often allowed the honour of attending him in a professional capacity. Commonly he prefers his wife's ministrations, for she can be forced either to slur the work over in twenty minutes, or spin it out to three hours, according to his fancy. Often he will shake his head with a melancholy sorry-to-dis-appoint-you air, and say: " No, nuss, there ain't nothin' you can do for *me*. I'm a doctor's job, I am. Well, yes, I '*ave* let Sooper see to me sometimes, but that was after the doctor had spoke to me confidenshul, and told me she'd learnt her tricks at the same shop as '*im*. And I knowed he wanted a nolliday, and he said he'd come back like a shot if I was anyways put about with her."

While refusing her services at reasonable hours, how-ever, he delights in calling her out at the latest possible time in the evening, or breaking in on her Sunday's rest. She knows perfectly well that when she gets to his house she will only be wanted to shake up a lotion bottle and put some on a rag, or to listen to a tirade against the chemist for not having sent any lotion to shake ; but bitter, indeed, will be his indignation and widespread his complaints if she does not arrive at the earliest possible moment after his summons.

I once suggested to the Show Patient who tacitly declined to give a farthing to the funds of the Association, that he might at least write a letter of thanks to the committee. "Yes," was the reply; "of course you'd like 'em to know as you'd done your duty."

A RULER OF DESTINY

Down a gloomy street where famous admirals lived in bygone days, down a narrower one where grey-haired mates, and captains of marines, and unprosperous pay-masters may have found their "foot on shore," halfway down a third that has lost all remembrance of better days, and at the end of a dingy court leading out of it, is a two-roomed house which I often visit. The tenant is a woman of eighty-four; she has no relatives left, no money of her own, for eight years she has been com-pletely bedridden, and it is more than twelve since she crossed her doorsill. Nevertheless, by sheer force of intellect and will, she is not only a householder, but the mistress of a most obedient servant, and a person who exerts powerful influence over other lives. She has a tiny income from a charitable society, and she allows a younger woman of meek and yielding disposition the use of one of the rooms on condition that she keeps the house clean, waits on the invalid, stands at attention during "the lady nurses'" visits, writes her letters, and, in brief, acts as charwoman, cook, maid, and companion. It is a complicated chronic case, and I attend chiefly to steer probationers through its manifold difficulties, but Mrs

C. always takes the burden of my entertainment on her shoulders with lofty courtesy.

"Auntie, show the superintendent my letter what I had yesterday. I call her 'auntie' and she calls me 'mother' *when we're alone*," she explains.

The letter was strangely unlike those generally handed to me to read, epistles stiff and empty at the beginning, affectionate and incoherent at the end, and with little but the address to mark one from the other. In fact, the letters I am asked to admire always remind me of a fifty years old story told me by a naval officer. A totally illiterate boatswain's mate went to the doctor and begged him to write a letter for him to his wife. The doctor consented, and after receiving instructions wrote it, read it over to him, and saw it safely despatched. Six months later the request was repeated.

"Well, what shall we say?" "Same as last time, sir, please. That done her very well."

The handwriting in itself was a surprise, for it was that of an educated man, and the whole tone of the composition puzzled me. I read it again from beginning to end, and still felt unable to make the intelligent comments that were evidently expected.

"Show the superintendent my two children," was the next command.

Two Russia leather frames with silver mounts were handed to me, one containing the photograph of an officer in uniform, the other of a graceful girl about twenty. Still no clue to the inward meaning of the letter. Young and generous hearts might well feel admiration and even love for such a brave old warrior, but how could a bedridden woman, some sixty years their senior, and not of their world, have earned the warm expressions of gratitude with which the letter closed ?

Later on I learnt the whole story, but as the actors are still living, and two of them are still very young, I can only give it in outline. A wife of nineteen and a husband of twenty-five, each "giving too little and asking too much," had made shipwreck of their happiness. The girl, separated thousands of miles from her husband, but separated far more widely by the bitterness of their final quarrel, sought relief in good works, one of which, suggested by a clergyman who knew something of human nature, consisted in regular visits to this dim courtyard room. The girl was an orphan, the woman had a mother's heart, plenty of strong common sense, and a knowledge of the world that reached beyond the blank wall blocking her only window. Week after week, and for many months, she varied her sermons on the one text, " My dearie, if you can't have things to your mind, bring your mind to the things as they are." The husband was suddenly ordered to England for a short time, and it was chiefly owing to this woman's influence that an interview took place and a lasting reconciliation was effected.

"Open the cupboard, auntie, and show the super-intendent the biscuit box the new curate sent me, and spread out the counterpane Captain —— knitted for me when he was getting over his wound. The light was so bad the last time she was here she didn't see it, not properly. I told you how he made it all himself, and brought it to me one evening tied up in brown paper? Auntie, that's my Tommy, let him in. Come here, my blessed; how should I live without you, though there *is* them that thinks nothing of you! No, nurse, those are not his paw marks on the pillow, and it's very naughty of you to say so! He always washes his feet before he climbs up, and he'd do it if he had a hundred feet, wouldn't you, my precious?"

Truly a wonderful old woman: soldier, sailor, priest, all lay their gifts before her, well knowing that her work is harder and her life more heroic than theirs.

FOR FORTY YEARS

A London artisan, born and bred in Hackney, never out of work in his life, married at twenty, happy in his wife and children, long since a grandfather, a churchwarden for a quarter of a century, why should he seem a tragic and an heroic figure?

For nearly forty years he has worked in the same half-underground room, and for thirty-five years of that time he has suffered from an agonising internal complaint. It developed so early, that no friendly society, no sick club of any description, would accept him as a member, and his whole life has been overshadowed by the fear of incapacitating illness. Mere pain is such a small evil in comparison, that he has almost ceased to take count of it. Five long illnesses have had to be met out of his savings. His skill and his integrity make him an invaluable workman, and each time his berth has been kept open for him, but no further consideration has ever been shown by his employers. Once, when he was pining with the strange yearning that he has for the country, and seemed on the verge of another breakdown, I suggested to his elder daughter that he should lengthen the August Bank Holiday to a week, and go away for change. The girl replied shrewdly: "They wouldn't give father the sack for being ill, not after his being with the old master so long, and the young master knowing he can go late to business half the time as long as father's there, but father can't take no libbaties. He knows he isn't everyone's money, not now. All the winter and a good bit of the summer they have to work by gaslight, and his sight isn't what it was. He says he trembles every time the master picks up a piece of his work, and he used to be so proud when anyone stopped to look at it. It was *him* that done the order they had for the King when he was Prince of Wales."

This is the man's daily life. At a quarter to seven, his wife, in order to allow him to rest until the last possible moment, brings him his breakfast in bed; at a quarter past he starts on a walk of nearly three miles to the workshop.

Whatever the weather is like, he must walk, for the motion of an omnibus or even a tram causes unbearable pain. In the evening his wife goes to meet him, timing

her departure according to the state of his health. As
the time draws near for his periodical collapse, she must
go the whole distance, so that he may have her arm to
lean on.

One morning, just before his last and almost fatal
illness, she implored him not to go to work,—she would
write, she would telegraph, she would send a messenger,
she would go herself and explain to the master, anything if he would only remain at home.

" I can't; I've got the key of the safe."

"They don't want any money before to - morrow
night."

" But I've got the key of the cupboard too, where
all the expensive materials are kept."

" Give them to me, and I'll take them to the master's
house. It wouldn't hinder the men an hour, if it
did that."

"I can't. I promised him I'd never let them out of
my hands for a moment."

" Then I must go with you."

They set off together, going even earlier than usual
to allow for his feebleness. It was half dark and
bitterly cold, and the streets were nearly empty. Step
by step he struggled on, but the effort grew more and
more intolerable. A homeless, half-starved lad crept
up, and, after following them silently for a few moments,
took the sick man's other arm in his. Within two
hundred yards of the workshop the sufferer fell in a
dead faint on the pavement. Not a soul was in sight.
Determined that at least his dying effort should not be

wasted, the distracted woman took the keys from his pocket and set off at a run. He had always been good to boys, and she said that it was not until hours after that it struck her that the lad might have stolen the helpless man's watch and the few shillings in his pocket, and disappeared silently as he came.

The master had fortunately just arrived, and she hurried back to her husband. In the meantime the ragged Samaritan had managed to stop a passing cab and rouse a chemist. Ten weeks' severe illness followed. "Once it was forty weeks," said his wife simply; "we spent every penny we had, for all the children was on our hands then, but we didn't have to pawn anything, for we'd close on fifty pounds when it started. Every time when it's over we have to begin saving up for the next bout. Oh, it might have been worse! There's always been work waiting for him as soon as ever he could do it. He's never known what it is to tramp round looking for work, and getting the door slammed in his face. He's a wonderful man for bearing up, but he takes things to heart so he'd never, never have bore *that*."

THE BROTHERS

John and Peter were unmarried agricultural labourers earning twelve shillings a week, and were the only surviving children of parents about thirty years their senior. All their lives had been spent together in a tumble-down cottage with a large garden. The father's health was always feeble, and he had been obliged to give up work much sooner than is usual in country districts, but as he managed to raise a sufficient supply of vegetables from the garden after it had been dug and roughly put in order by his sons, and as the mother was able to cook and clean and sew for the whole party, they lived very comfortably, until Peter met with an irreparable misfortune. He was occupied in hedging and ditching, and pricked his right eye with a thorn. The injury was at first neglected; when too late he was sent to hospital, and returned a few months later, hopelessly, incurably blind.

What was to be done? A weekly wage of twelve shillings would not suffice for the support of three men and a woman, and keep the sole wage-earner strong enough for hard work, and the Union happened to be one which, owing to old-time abuses, had a rooted objection to granting outdoor relief. The old parents settled the matter: it was hard for them to leave the cottage that had been their home for nearly fifty years, but they were over seventy now, they would still be together, and they would meet with some indulgence. They felt that it would be infinitely harder for their blind son to be taken from surroundings every inch of which were familiar to him, and among which he walked with a daily increasing boldness and certainty; and without hesitation or discussion, without a word of complaint, they moved to the hated Big House ten miles away.

Ever since then the two brothers have lived together. Peter can dig the potatoes, wash, peel, and cook them, clean the house, do the washing, and walk to the village shop to make the weekly purchases. The great pride of his life is to pick the fruit and concoct what he calls "a good keepin' jam," which he triumphantly exhibits to neighbouring housewives, who admire it with motherly deception, and remark to one another afterwards, "It's a mercy he can't *see* the stuff!" No outdoor relief can be obtained for him, and he owes his freedom and independence entirely to his brother.

Lately a still heavier burden has been added to John's hard lot. He has lost his work at the farm close by, and is obliged to walk to one four miles off. A cottage could be had there, but he pretends to make light of the distance. If anyone remonstrates, he lowers his voice (however far away from home he may be), and says: "Peter'd be *lost* if we was to move. As long as we're here, it's almost the same to him as if he had his sight."

THE LAST MONTHS OF HIS LIFE

He was a merchant seaman dying in a London hospital, and I saw more of him than of any patient before or since. He was nine months with us, and for nearly the whole of that time enjoyed the few small privileges that are attached to the melancholy distinction of being "the worst case in the ward."

He was a refined looking young fellow, with a slow and deliberate way of speaking, partly due to weakness, but chiefly to the conscious rejection of much of the language that must have been familiar to him during the previous eight or ten years; not a single nautical word or turn of speech was left: except for the accent, his expressions were those of an intelligent boy of the upper classes who has " been tumbled early " into a library of " good old English reading."

As a very small child he had been deserted by persons who could never be traced, and had been brought up by a charitable institution of which he retained most affectionate memories. His life at sea had been happy and fairly prosperous, for, though little more than a lad, he had saved £150. During a terrible storm he had been injured; his sufferings seemed trivial compared with those of some other mangled forms carried below that night, and he was overlooked until it was too late. When he came to us he had already been ill three months, and recovery was, humanly speaking, impossible. Incurable cases are generally dismissed at once, but he was homeless, his personality was attractive, the case was one of surgical interest, and he was allowed to remain until the end.

The hospital bore traces of age in some of its minor regulations, one being that each patient must have his own teapot, and supply himself with tea and sugar at his own expense. Patients on whom perhaps seventy shillings a week was expended for dressings alone, were deprived of these everyday comforts if they could not produce the necessary pence. Often the dying sailor would call me to his side, and whisper: "Sister, So-and-So has no money for tea or sugar." Then, with a cruel effort, his purse would be drawn from beneath his pillow. "Will you buy him some? He need not know where it comes from. He can think he gets it in with the rest. Only tell him to be careful. I mayn't be here as long as he is."

Like most really generous people, he was extremely sparing in personal expenditure. Just before he had realised that he would never walk again, I remember his telling me very seriously that he intended for the future to have his boots "made in threes," as he had been told it was an economical plan.

For some totally inadequate reason he had taken a nervous dislike to the sister-in-charge, and when in his rare moods of fretfulness would murmur: "Don't let her come near me, not even the tail of her gown!" As death drew near the groundless prejudice passed away, and, noticing her anxiously looking at him late one evening, and seeing her close by his bedside when he opened his eyes the next morning, he sighed out admiringly one of the few texts of Scripture that I have ever heard from a patient, "And they rest not day nor night."

EQUALITY OF SACRIFICE?

No one could have a greater horror of compulsory military service than I, but I sometimes come across families whose history silently reminds me, first, what an empire costs; and, secondly, how unequally the necessary sacrifices of life and health are distributed.

Seven years ago we were called in to nurse a dying boatswain. He had a comfortable pension and some savings, and was the kind of person who in an ordinary way would not have been on our books; but his illness was long and expensive, and his only daughter, who was nurse, companion, housekeeper, and servant, had entirely lost the use of one arm. I went often to the house, not that the excellent nurse "told off" to attend on him required any superintendence, but because conversation was his only pleasure, and her ignorance of all matters naval and military was so profound that she could not even make a good listener.

"She's an excellent person that you've sent me, miss, but I doubt if she knows one end of a ship from the other. If you could get at the bottom of it, I expect you'd find she's like the man up at Manchester, calls the bow the *thin end*."

I should not have come out with flying colours from any examination in seamanship, but, which was of far more consequence to him, I had known most of the gods of his idolatry, at any rate by reputation, and never mixed up the captain who gave half his pay to convert the Loo-Choo islanders with the commander who " never hardly swore, not nothing to speak of, except when he saw a missionary," and I was ready to accept the opinions of dead and gone admirals, on matters that they had never studied, with becoming gravity.

Some months later he died, and the daughter, having no means of support beyond his small savings, opened a kind of infant school for children in her own class of life. I do not know how far such a school would have satisfied H.M. Inspector, but few sights could have been prettier than the group of little dots with frilled pinafores and be-ribboned curls affectionately pressing round her; and a series of misfortunes happened to her brothers which soon compelled her to give it up and devote her whole attention to them.

The eldest son, a soldier, was invalided from South Africa, where he had witnessed some of the most terrible scenes of the whole campaign. The sister was warned that he was mentally affected, but courageously insisted on taking charge of him. Although not actually insane, he had lost all self-control, and the slightest and most involuntary provocation caused violent paroxysms of rage; not only was she made miserable by him, but we felt that her life was in actual danger. With great difficulty she was induced to see that the struggle must be given up; a special pension was obtained for him, and he was placed in a country cottage by himself, the doctors considering that with perfect quiet and outdoor occupation it would be safe to continue to leave him in freedom. Every week the devoted sister goes by train to see him, taking with her the provisions that she has cooked to assist his housekeeping.

Almost immediately after, the third brother, a sailor, was discharged the service on account of heart disease. He tried to find work on shore, but fell down in the street, was carried to her in a perfectly helpless condition, and nursed by her until his death. During his illness, the second brother, also a sailor, was drowned while on duty. He had been in the habit of making remittances to his sister, and the Admiralty therefore acknowledged her claim to a pension of five shillings a week.

At the end of the South African War the fourth brother left the army, and, having no trade, became a labourer at a pound a week, and made his home with his sister.

Thus, of the boatswain's four sons, none of whom would yet have reached middle age, two are dead, one is practically insane, and the fourth must remain a very poor man; while the health of the only daughter, always a delicate woman, has been irreparably injured by the efforts made on their behalf.

A DRUNKARD'S WIFE

She kept a box, and in it every day she dropped a penny for works of charity, "because God has been so good to me." My very soul rebelled as I looked at her, and thought of the life that she had led, and was leading, and must lead until death released her. How had God been good to her? Well, *she* knew. This is her history as I have learned it bit by bit during all the sharper crises of the last seven or eight years.

She married a man who could only have given her a bare pittance if he had tried, and who never did try; the best thing she experienced from him was neglect. They had six children, and the burden of supporting them fell almost entirely upon her. She did not, as a rule, have to provide her husband with food, he usually gave her about enough for the rent, and I think—mainly by spending them immediately— she generally succeeded in preventing him from robbing her of her earnings.

The man's occupation kept him away from the house a great deal, which gave her some chance of training her children properly, and enabled her to give ten or twelve hours a day to the peculiarly hard and monotonous sewing by which she earned their food and clothes. Never being certain when the husband would come, she dared not leave the house for a moment; night and day she must be there, not only to protect the children, whom he occasionally ill-treated, but the *home*. If she deserted her post for an hour, she knew she might return to find the place stripped of everything that could be sold or pawned.

Often she sat up waiting for him, with the three eldest children to guard her, until one o'clock in the morning. He generally arrived more than half drunk, and kicked his hat in at the door, saying: "If my hat's welcome, I am." The wife, with assumed gaiety, was obliged to kick the hat back to him, otherwise he would not enter. Sometimes they would succeed in getting him quietly to bed, but frequently, while the two eldest boys exerted their puny strength to hold him back from their mother, the third would rush out into the dark, not to call the police, but a childless woman who lived in the next street. At the first sound of the pitiful cry, "Come, do come, father's killing mother!" she would start up in her bed, fling on her clothes, and hurry back with him. Often for hours she stood between husband and wife, a frail protection, but one that he dared not thrust aside. He was never drunk enough to forget that, although she had left her hard-working husband asleep in the next street, he was nevertheless her protector, and any injury done to *her* would be dearly avenged.

After many years of this life, but while four of the children were too young to earn anything, the husband developed a fatal cancer. I can never forget the devotion with which she nursed him, the exquisite cleanliness and order of the sick-room. One detail will show the point to which her zeal was carried. I had requested, as we always do in such cases, that the counterpane should be replaced by a sheet which could be frequently changed. She complied, but that outer sheet was always *starched and ironed*. During the last few weeks of his life he consented to see a clergyman who worked with much devotion in that district, and died very peacefully.

The woman was free at last from his tyranny, but no half-forgotten victim of the Inquisition could have been released from his dungeon in a more shattered state. To this day, if she tries to go for a walk, she faints and has to be carried back; she cannot even summon up courage to cross the street, and practically still lives in her prison.

All her small savings had been put into a fraudulent concern. The day I read "Great exposure, entire swindle" on the placards, I remembered that that ten shillings a week was her all, and went at once to see her. I found that she had already returned to her old work, and not one word of complaint or self-pity was uttered.

Day after day, from morning till night, and sometimes half the night through, she sits sewing. My patients rarely speak to me of religion, but one day recently she said to me, "Though my body is here, my soul seems to be absolutely free. The older I grow, the closer and more perfect my communion with God becomes."

The sight of a few such homes as this excuses the wildest statement ever made by temperance lecturers, but in dealing with men of this type there is one weak point in teetotalism which is too commonly overlooked. According to its most ardent advocates, it is drink that makes men brutal, tyrannical, and selfish, and abstinence is the one thing necessary for reform. In my experience there are men who drink because they *are* brutal, tyrannical, and selfish. I have known homes that were very little happier after the pledge had been taken and kept; the bad qualities of the men simply took other and almost equally misery-making forms, stiffened by the addition of self-righteousness. I have come across instances where the wife of the "reformed" husband has been deliberately thrashed because she would not accept some of the fanatical opinions that he had embraced.

In one case recently brought under my notice, the ex-drunkard has become an enthusiast on the subject of moral suasion in the education of his boys: they are never to be scolded, never to be punished in any way whatever. I am well aware that punishment is by no means necessary for children, provided that they are fairly well disposed, that the general surroundings are good, and that the system is begun from the earliest days. I have known boys satisfactorily brought up even in the poorest homes with practically no punishment whatever. But to begin such a system suddenly with badly disposed boys living in bad surroundings is sheer madness. Not long ago, one of them, aged twelve, stole five shillings from his mother, remained out all day, and returned home late in the evening, having spent the last farthing. Very properly—in my opinion—she caned him soundly, but when the father heard of it he nearly murdered her. She barely escaped with her life.

There was no question of her having beaten the child cruelly, she had been far more distressed than angry, and a delicate, prematurely aged woman armed with a halfpenny cane is not likely to make too much impression through the jacket of a sturdy boy of twelve: her crime was in punishing him *at all*. Since then, whatever the children do, she has not dared to punish them in any way whatever; but I must add that this little villain is the only one of them who is " paltry " enough to take mean advantage of such an extraordinary state of domestic affairs.

The moral of this is,—well, it was expressed long ago by Horace Walpole,—"Unless one could cure men of being fools, it is of no purpose to cure them of any folly, as it is only making room for some other." The tale is not told to discourage temperance lecturers, but to warn them that, while the "pledge" is an excellent cure for men with weak heads and soft hearts, and wives who take the lead, a very great deal more is needed for the moralisation of the genuine drunkard.

PHILANTHROPY THAT FAILED

Twenty years ago, a little blind girl sat day by day in the sun outside her parents' house in a seaport town. A passing stranger pitied the gentle, helpless child, and sent her, entirely at his own expense, to be educated at a Home for the Blind. Unfortunately his knowledge was not equal to his charity, and he chose an old-fashioned school where little of anything was taught, and where no effort was made to develop the pupils physically, nor to make them move about independently. Ten years later she returned home with the soft, small hands of a child, a slight fragile frame, and complete incapacity for any kind of hard work.

The family consisted of the father, a man who at the best of times had never earned more than a guinea a week, and who now suffered from a chronic complaint which occasionally took an acute form; the mother, also in poor health; a sister of twenty-two, in service and engaged to be married; and a brother of about eleven. They received the girl kindly, and disguised from her as far as they could that she was a burden; but her over-refinement, her delicate health, and her almost entire lack of any suitable occupation, made the life a very hard and trying one.

Four or five years after her return, I was called in to nurse the father for a few weeks. I was much attracted by the girl, and touched by her innocent clinging to life, and her desire for a few of its pleasures, and I tried to find a friend for her among the many women of the leisured classes who had expressed a wish to help me in my work. Inexperienced in that branch of it, I thought that I had only to describe the girl's sad case, to mention the respectability of the parents, the cleanliness of the house, and the decency of the general surroundings, in order to have offers of assistance pressed on me. I could not truthfully have painted the girl's circumstances in any other colours, but I now recognise that strategically the form of my appeal was mistaken. If I could have said that the poverty of the family was due to drunkenness, that the girl was treated with harshness by her parents, and that her young brother was in the habit of throwing his boots at her head as a preliminary to making her clean them; if I had asserted that the well-drained little street was the nursery of typhoid and diphtheria, and the occasional resting-place of smallpox, and if I had dropped the suggestive hint that it was a place where the policeman dared not go, the results might have been different. As it was,—well, I made eight distinct attempts to get some lady to visit the girl for an hour twice a week, to read to her, and interest herself in her generally; I had hopes that she would be led on to the esplanade, or invited to sit in a sunny garden, or taken to hear the band play.

The first person to whom I made my application said that the distance was too great: I did not trouble to remind her that it was only half as far as the golf links; I only felt that among so many acquaintances I had made a foolish choice, and passed on. The second lady agreed to go, and did not do so. The third said that it was not in her parish, and "the vicar might not like it"; I assured her that he was far too sensible a man to look on her as a poacher, and if not, it was her duty to widen his views; but argument was useless. The fourth went once, behaved charmingly, raised many hopes, — and never went again. The fifth was merely a visitor in the town, and went just often enough to finish reading the treasured copy of *Mr. Barnes of New York* which had been left behind by the deeply regretted No. 4. The sixth person to whom I applied said that if the girl's mother was too busy to read to her, her brother ought to do it. In vain I explained that he was a restless growing lad of fourteen, already chained to indoor work for nine hours a day, that in the winter evenings he often tried to amuse his sister, but to expect it of him in the summer was to demand a thousand times more

18

than she looked for in her own sons and nephews ; she
remained of the same opinion : " We ought not to undertake what is plainly the duty of the girl's own family."
The principle was excellent, the application absurd.

But it was left for number seven to put the crowning
touch of exasperation.   She listened to all I had to say,
and then replied unctuously : " Oh, certainly ; I shall be
very glad indeed to go and speak a few words in season
to the poor young woman."

I recoiled at the arrogant audacity of the speech, and
said hastily—

" She does not need any ' words in season.'   She has
a strong sense of duty and religion, and her whole
family is thoroughly respectable.   What she wants is
someone who will read her *Three Men in a Boat*, or
The Adventures of Mrs. Lecks and Mrs. Aleshine, and
help her to forget herself and her troubles for an hour
or two.   She told me yesterday that she did not care to
be read stories about good little blind girls who died
young, or else supported their families in affluence.
One, unhappily for herself, she has not done, and the
other she can never do."

This was plain speaking, but when I next visited the
father I was greatly annoyed to find that it had not
been plain enough.   The lady had called at the house,
had kept this delicate girl on her knees until she nearly
fainted, and had then read her a sermon ; what it was
about, the poor child did not know, as she felt too ill to
make any attempt at listening.

Before I could learn what the eighth acquaintance

would do, the family affairs had reached a painful crisis. For many months the father had been unable to work, the club allowance had been reduced from ten shillings a week to six, and would shortly be permanently reduced to four, a sum insufficient to pay the rent. The boy's earnings were not yet enough to support himself, the mother could earn nothing, and indeed her time was fully taken up by the invalid. The daughter in service was to have been married a year previously, but had indefinitely postponed the marriage in order that she might continue to help her parents out of her wages. Her fiancé, although everything had been in readiness, had not only consented to this, but with the matter-of-course self-sacrifice of the poor which is so little known or noted, had helped them liberally himself. The father grew worse instead of better, the mother's health began to fail, and they were all obliged to recognise that the home must be broken up. The parents went to the workhouse, and the elder daughter married and took her brother to live with her until he should be entirely self-supporting.

Then I learnt what the eighth person would do. She was not rich, but she had many friends, and with incredible trouble and exertion she managed to guarantee a small income which opened the doors of a suitable Home for the Blind, where, the first few months of grief and depression once over, the girl has lived happily ever since, and, late in life as it was for her to benefit by modern systems of training, she is fortunately developing a little more physical strength and independence.

AN EARLY PASSAGE IN THE LIFE OF A HERO

"Well, I suppose he didn't thrash you for *nothing?*" said the mate of one of the smallest ocean-going vessels in existence, lying for a brief week of safety in a London dock. He was trying hard to maintain a judicial attitude, but he knew that his verdict had already been given against the absent father and in favour of the small boy in the big coat (the cuffs turned back almost reached his elbows, the skirts had been roughly jagged off with a knife) who stood with his grey eyes anxiously fixed on him.

"No, sir; he sent me on a message, and the circus was going through the town, and I followed, and forgot all about it until it was too late."

"And you lost the money?" struck in the only other man on deck, a grey-haired sailor with cheeks triumphantly pink through the coating of sunburn. The boy was too simple even to see the drift of the question.

"There wasn't any money. I said it was a message, not an errand."

"So you did, sonny,—so you did," agreed the mate, astonished at the failure of what he considered almost superhuman cunning in the line of cross-examination, but following up the hint his elderly insubordinate had furnished—

"And you've never taken any of his money?"

"I wouldn't ha' *dared!* And I don't know"—

reflectively—"that I ever wanted to. I always had plenty to eat, except sometimes when he'd locked me up and forgot me. Once it was three days."

"Three *days?*"

"Well, there was two nights in it anyway, sir. He'd locked me in the bedroom, and I hadn't even a drink of water, but the next morning I pushed the lock back with the heel of my boot. You know, some locks *does* go like that?"

The mate nodded, and his attention wandered for a moment. Was it possible that locks were still made like that? And it must be twenty years ago!

"Then I got into the kitchen and had a drink. There was nearly half a loaf. I was afraid to touch it at first, but when it came about dinner-time I cut off a thin slice I thought he wouldn't miss, and I kept cutting till there wasn't any left. I went back in the bedroom then. It was evening the next day when he came. He ran up in a hurry, and didn't seem to notice the door not being locked, and gave me lots for supper. He didn't lick me not for a good ten days after that. I don't know where he'd been. There was a boy said he'd been in prison."

"What did you say to that?"

"I punched his head, and said it wasn't no business of *his.*"

"How big was the boy?"

"About as big as me."

"This is serious," said the mate, shaking his head.

"Why, long before you're as old as Jenkins there,

you'd be telling the truth neat, and where should we all be then ? I can't remember that I ever thrashed a boy who wasn't at least half as big again as myself. If no one else was there, they were generally twice as big."

" He *might* ha' been a bit bigger'n me, but his birthday's the same month. We'll both be twelve in December."

" How long ago was this ? "

" Last summer."

" And he's been knocking you about ever since ? Why didn't you run away before ? "

" I didn't think of it, sir."

" Ah, not till you read that book,—let me see, what was it called ?—where the boy knocked the school-master down and ran away to sea, and the mate killed the captain, and the shark killed the mate, and the pirates killed most of the crew, and the hurricane killed the pirates, and then the boy navigated the ship single-handed ? "

" No, sir; the boy was in America to *start* with, and he ran away on land."

" And there were Red Indians ? Well, it all comes to the same thing. And when you'd seen as much of the circus as you could see for nothing, you went home, and your father thrashed you ? "

" I thought he'd have killed me, sir. When it got dark I let myself down out of the window. I couldn't get my own coat, so I took his. I set off for London, and I've been walking ever since, begging my food and sleeping under haystacks."

" But why to London ? "

"Because of the ships."

"Let me see; that was Monday, and this is Thursday. Now, if it was anything you could *call* a thrashing, there'd be marks left, eh?"

"I don't know, sir; you can't always tell by the feel. Sometimes it hurts a lot and don't bruise you much, and sometimes it's the other way."

The mate smiled reminiscently. He had had a tolerably easy time as a boy, but his father had been a firm believer in what he called "mod'rate chas*tise*ment."

"We'll have a look, and if there are no marks, well" —remembering an occasion when he had borrowed his mother's hand-glass and had been bitterly disappointed at the poor result in bruises, for it really *was* a stinger! —"well, anyway you shall stop aboard of us to-night. Take your coat off, and turn round to the light." The boy obeyed him. Jenkins came closer, and peered through the gathering dusk.

"Strike a match!" said the mate. The old man did so, going on one knee, and sheltering the flickering light with his knotted blue-and-brown hand.

The men's eyes met; each waited for the other to speak, and there was a stormy silence. ("I've only one thing to say against the mate," the old salt told a crony later on; "if he feel he can't do justice to a thing, he don't even try.")

"Wrap it round you again, sonny. Gently does it. That's the ticket. Take him below, Jenkins, and give him some supper. Grog?—I don't know but what he oughtn't to have it, but I want him to keep awake till the captain comes. Ointment?—If it were fresh, but most of it's like the labels in the museums, 'Age unknown; probably of great antiquity.' Pick him out a clean shirt, my wash is on my bunk. No, not a jumper, you idiot—a linen shirt."

"D'you think the captain'll let me stop?" the boy asked anxiously, before he had swallowed two mouthfuls.

"Nogus vogus," said the man soothingly; "you get on with your vittles. There ain't much done *here* but what the mate has the ordering of."

An hour later the mate led the boy into the little cabin. The captain had just left home, and was naturally in a gloomy frame of mind, the only relief to which was to be found in opposing the mate. He shook his head ominously.

"I've seen ropes' ends, and I've seen boys, and I've never seen any good come of putting cushions between 'em."

"D'you call *that* rope-ending, and done last Monday?" asked the mate fiercely, turning the glare of the unshaded lamp on the boy's back.

"You might have let me have my supper first," said the captain, with sick disgust.

"D'you call that rope's-ending?" demanded the mate, in the tones of a person whose strength lies in sticking to the point.

"Well, no! Not unless there was a devil at *one* end of it, and a powerful devil at that. Keep the little beggar if you want him. Tell the men to make use of him if they can, but anyone who lays a finger on him this side of a month will have *me* to settle with. Better keep him out of sight. I doubt if he's eleven."

"Twelve next December, he says."

"Well, I don't know the law, and I don't want to. Keep him out of sight, that's all. If anyone says we arn't in the right of it, I don't envy him his share of the Day of Judgment."

This is an early passage in the life of a hero, and the only one that he can be prevailed on to relate.

HEPHZIBAH'S BOYS

When I first knew Hephzibah, she was a plump, fair-haired girl with very clean aprons and very dowdy caps, and lived in a pretty suburban house in the position of "gen'ral where a nurse is kep'." She was the bosom friend of a certain S'fia who held a rather less respons-ible position in my own family, and both from the voluble S'fia and the girl's young mistress I heard so much of her industry, good sense, and sweet temper, that I was more than grieved when I came across her seven or eight years later as the wife of a drunken and quarrelsome bricklayer, and mother of four of the most restless, disobedient, obstinate, violent, and generally unmanageable boys that ever fell to the lot of mortal mother.

Her attitude to her husband was one of unbroken amiability, but backed by a dogged refusal to take the support of the family upon her own shoulders. She made her home with his parents, a skilled artisan in bad health, with a semi-invalid wife. They had a cottage of their own, and in return for the daughter-in-law's services allowed their son and his family to live with them rent free. Beyond this Hephzibah would not go. "Of course it's *really* me that keeps a roof over our heads, and many a time the children would go hungry to bed if their grandfather didn't give them more than half his supper. He always will have them sit up to table with him, however late it is when he gets back from work, and they're too small to hide it when they haven't had enough. But for all that my husband sees, *he's got their living to earn,* and as long as he knows that he won't sink real LOW. There may be more money one week than another, and a cruel pinch the next, but he won't give up working altogether as I've known some men do, and he *may* take a turn. I've known men give up drink before now, but I never knew one give up living on his wife if he once began it."

No one reproached Hephzibah for her drunken husband, not even her mother-in-law, but for the turbulence of her boys she was held entirely responsible. The whole neighbourhood was convinced that if she would only "take an' *smack* 'em," all would be well. But though distressed by criticism, Hephzibah felt unable to follow the advice, and it was not merely by the natural gentleness of her disposition that she was restrained. She had had a terrifying experience with her eldest boy. One day he had strained her patience to breaking-point, and she threatened to whip him. The boy, who was not yet four years old, snatched up a knife from the dinner-table and rushed at her with savage fury. She was horrorstruck at the child's blind passion, and from that moment refused to slap the children or to allow anyone else to do it. " While I was beating one devil out," she said, "I should be beating three devils in."

In those days I read much about heredity, degeneration, and all the rest of it, and when I heard this story and reflected on the early death of two of the grandparents, the bad health of the two surviving ones, and the drunken habits of the father, the words "instinctive criminal" were very near my lips. What I actually said, however, was: "They may be so troublesome simply because they are stronger and cleverer than the children round them, and living in narrow streets there is no outlet for their energy. Take them to the park as often as you can, and when they are old enough to go to school it will work off part of their spare strength. At any rate, if they are so unlike your neighbours' children, you must be right to try a different way of bringing them up."

S'fia, now the childless wife of a remarkably tame shopman, and connected with her by marriage, was her severest critic. With the frankness which is the distinguishing features of " In-laws," she would often remark, " Hephzibah, if you don't teach them who's master, they'll be fit for nothing but an Informatory."

Ten years or more slipped away; I heard nothing of

Hephzibah, but I never saw an exceptionally trouble-some boy without thinking of her. S'fia's husband had moved into a small county town, and S'fia took a good-sized house in the outskirts and let lodgings. One day I noticed two lads of about sixteen and eighteen with bicycles, cameras, and luncheon bag coming out of her garden. They were healthy-looking young fellows, broad shouldered and well set up, but something about them reminded me irresistibly of London. Soon after, I met S'fia, and asked who they were.

"Why, I s'pose, m'm, you wouldn't remember Hephzibah's boys, them awful little ruffians that their mother used to spoil so, to *my* thinking? It's the two eldest, Tom and Frank, come down to lodge with me for a fortnight. All of them seemed to take a turn for the better direckly they went to school, and I can't tell you what Standards they wasn't in before they was no age at all, and Tom had the silver watch for good conduct. We couldn't none of us help laughing about it, for he was always the worst Turk of the lot. Well, when Tom was turned thirteen his mother tried all one holidays to find work for him, and she couldn't do it nohow, so she said to him: "I can't have you running the streets. Tuesday morning you'll just go back to school till I *have* found it." Tom didn't say anything, but on the Monday he asked her for his best clothes and his watch, and she let him have them without a word,—which I'm pretty sure *I* shouldn't have done. He went to the schoolmaster and asked for a stifficate, and then he walked off after a place he'd seen in a newspaper, something a chalk above anything Hephzibah had thought of. Forty boys was after it, and he was about the only one that went with no one to speak up for him. At first the gentleman didn't seem to think much of him, but when he'd seen the watch and asked who ironed his shirt front for him, he said that settled it. Tom's been there ever since, and he's had five rises a'ready. Frank's getting on just as well. The other two is still at school, but they earn seven shillings a week between them tying up parcels at a grocer's. They found the work for theirselves, and Hephzibah wouldn't say nothing against it, because she said it *was* better than running the roads, and the air wasn't any worse than they'd get at home."

" Have their tempers improved ? "

" Why, you wouldn't find a better hearted boy than Tom, look where you might. What d'you s'pose he wanted to do for father ? Father's been ailing a long time, and he came down by the same train as them, but *their* tickets is for a fortnight, and father's was only a four-day excursion. When it come to the third day, I said he was looking so much better that he'd ought to stop longer, and I was sure the master wouldn't mind, not s'long as he sent word, but father said he couldn't afford to throw his ticket away and pay the full fare back. Tom akshally wanted father to have *his* ticket, and he'd have gone back himself by the excursion. Of course father wouldn't accept of it. He knew the boy had been saving up for a year, and he'd nothing to go back to but that stuffy little house."

" And what of Hephzibah's husband ? "

" He took the pledge seven years ago, and he's kep' it, which was more than anyone looked for. His health's bad now, and he can't earn much, but Hephzibah don't make a trouble out of that, s'long's he earns what he can and there's peace in the house. The boys is doing so well they don't want for money."

" Why do they still live in that small house ? It must be sadly overcrowded with those four great boys."

" Well, sometimes Hephzibah feels they ought to move to give the boys more room, but the grandfather is worse in his health than ever. Often he don't earn a week's wages in a month, and if Hephzibah weren't there he couldn't hardly manage. She likes to think of her boys, but she says it don't do to forget that there was a time when they owed a very great deal to their grandparents."

" But if Hephzibah took a larger house, they could let or sell their own, and live with her."

" Ah, but it wouldn't be *theirs*. Hephzibah thinks of their feelings."

I know nothing of Hephzibah's parents, except that her mother " never allowed her to be shortened," and so, although born and bred in a street turning off one that turns off the Old Kent Road, she has never been robbed of any of the syllables that are her due. Perhaps in this pregnant fact believers in heredity may find some explanation of the success of Hephzibah's sons.

THE LIGHT OF THEIR EYES

My little friend Fanny lives with her parents and four grown-up brothers and sisters in a street which of late years has fallen on evil days, and is most commonly known as Thieves' Row. I do not think that even a minority of the inhabitants have done anything to deserve that title, but, taken as a whole, they are dirty, drunken, and disorderly. The A.'s occupancy, however, dates from the time when the street was called by "its chrissened name," and they are exceedingly respectable people. "Birds of a feather flock together" is one of the truest of proverbs, as we constantly prove in district work, but there are many exceptions: the A.'s remain where they are, not only because they shrink from the effort and expense of moving, but because they are positively attached to the tiny four-roomed house which is the only home that even the eldest of the children has ever known.

Fanny's early life was outwardly like that of most of her little neighbours, except that meals were more regularly supplied, while slaps and scoldings were a negligible quantity. She played in the streets and in the recreation ground, and sometimes saw the sea— although it was nearly a whole mile distant. She went to the Board School, was a regular attendant at an unusually efficient Sunday school, and at thirteen entered a factory. In a very short time—I believe it was measured by days—the work brought to light some unsuspected weakness of nerve or frame, and she suddenly fell helpless on the floor, paralysed from the waist downwards. She was carried home, and, except for a short and resultless visit to a hospital, has never left her bed since.

All her life Fanny had been loved, but from that moment onwards she has been unceasingly adored. To those who know the jealously exclusive habits of the respectable poor, no further proof is needed than this: ever since her illness began the doors have always been open to every one, gentle or simple, who could do anything to afford the child the smallest pleasure of any kind whatever. The curates bring her flowers and all the news of the parish; the church sisters teach her delightfully complicated patterns of crochet, and bring her just the story books that she loves,—tales of school life, and vigorous, mischief-loving girls; two young girls visit her constantly, or write to her when in the country or abroad, telling her freely of all their doings, confident of the sympathetic insight that makes even the strangest and most distant things vividly real to her. Twice a day for two years a long succession of nurses and probationers have visited her, and I have never yet known one who, out of love and pity for the child, and admiration of her sweet courage, did not go in some way beyond the ordinary routine to try and give her pleasure. One probationer — Fanny did not tell me of it until long after, from honourable fears that it might in some occult way hinder her promotion— danced the cake-walk in the few spare feet at the foot of the little chain bed; one nurse always brought an amusing book in her pocket, and would read her a page while waiting for the kettle to boil; another, when off duty, carried her camera to the house and photographed the room.

Once a young naval officer was brought to the house, and his visit is marked for ever as a red-letter day in Fanny's memory, for he brought a large parcel from which came sounds of life. When the wrappings were unfastened, a brass birdcage was disclosed, tenanted by a canary. It was hung up between the white curtains that shut out the sordid street, and from that moment she has never felt alone.

Only one visitor has failed to please. A lady arrived one day, and sat down at the head of her bed, and read her chapter after chapter of the Bible for a solid hour. The poor child was stupefied, first with the effort of trying to follow a strange voice when she could not see the speaker, and then, when she was too tired to try any longer, with the actual noise. A severe headache followed, and the next time the lady called the mother must be excused for holding one hand firmly on the front door, and the other on the door of the sick room, and stating positively, though Fanny's gay laugh had been ringing out not two minutes before, that her little daughter was too ill to see visitors.

There has been one great day in the child's life, one most triumphant episode for the whole family, one glorious excitement provided by her for the whole neighbourhood. There was an evening confirmation to be held at the old parish church. Fanny, at her earnest desire, had been prepared, and the doctor's opinion was asked as to the possibility of her attendance. "Impossible!" was the verdict. The disappointment was so bitter, that the favourite boy curate, whose photograph always stood on her mantelpiece, appealed to the vicar to see what could be done. The vicar wrote to the bishop, laying the whole case before him, and the bishop replied that he would confirm the child privately in her own room.

Was ever room so much scrubbed? Were ever curtains so much starched? At five o'clock on a dark winter's afternoon, the bishop's carriage drove up. Wooden posts blocked the entrance to the street, and he was obliged to alight and walk down it in full canonicals, attended by the vicar and two curates, one of whom remained on the doorstep to keep order, for a dense crowd had rapidly collected. Every scrap of furniture except the bed had been removed, and that left just standing room for the three clergymen, the parents, a son and the two grown-up daughters. The bishop greeted the candidate with a few gentle words, and was about to begin the service, when the child whispered an anxious request to the vicar: "Would the bishop wait just a quarter of an hour until her other brother, a labourer, came in from his work?" Tired and busy as the bishop was, and with an exceptionally long and fatiguing service in front of him that evening, he would not allow any shadow of disappointment to fall on this one great day. A chair was brought, and he sat down and talked to her and her parents until the brother arrived. When the service was over, he was escorted to his carriage by excited but respectful crowds, leaving behind him an ineffaceable memory of gracious courtesy.

When we began visiting her two years ago, Fanny lived in the front room on the ground floor. There was no chimney, and the bed was placed as far as possible from the window, for a reason which did not at once suggest itself to me. As evening fell it was necessary to bolt the window and fasten the shutters, to give the poor child a sense of security when drunken brawls began in the street, while every inch that she could be removed from it reduced the amount of foul language that fell on her ears. Visiting her recently, after a few months' absence, I found the mother so seriously ill that the front room and the chain mattress had had to be given up to her, and Fanny had been moved to a chair bedstead in the kitchen, which measures nine feet by eight.

But no loss without a gain: formerly the kitchen was not only dirty, but often the scene of wrangles that disturbed her through the thin wall. Now everything that it contains is exquisitely clean; "anything would do" for the tired factory hands, but where their darling is there must be no speck of dust, and no one could be cruel enough to cloud her bright face by quarrelling in her presence. She did not utter a word of complaint over the change, but told me joyfully, "Now I'm in the kitchen I can do such lots of work; I help wash up, and I polish the lamp glasses."

The mother shut in the front room said sadly: "I have not seen my Fanny's face since October. [They are not six feet apart.] I don't know what I should do if ever there came a day when I could not hear her dear voice call out, 'Good-morning, mother; are you better to-day?'"

My little friend is not too good to live. When she heard that the boy curate had hurt his knee playing football, she said, "Now he will have an opportunity to practise the patience that he preaches to *me;*" and when she was told—probably his fellow-curate was drawing the long bow to amuse her—how badly he bore up under his sufferings, she laughed gleefully.

REPULSION

"Every house there has its skeleton," said an old naval officer, waving a lean brown hand towards a dingy row of Early Georgian houses which has pointed the moral and adorned the tale of a long line of teetotal lecturers. It does still, although in these comparatively sober days the street, instead of being an almost unbroken line of drinking dens, is sparsely punctuated by licensed public-houses with a steadily dwindling custom.

"I suppose so," I said absently, thinking of a pitiable case I was about to attend, shut in by those grimy brick walls. "I mean *real* ones," he said. "There was no 'continuous service' for more than a hundred years after those were built, and no proper system of paying the men. They used to be discharged at the end of a seven years' commission with all their pay in their pockets. They went into the houses to have a drink, fell asleep, and woke—somewhere else! If these houses were pulled down, you would find skeletons built into the chimneys, and behind the cupboards, and under every cellar floor. Ah, you don't believe it, but it's true. Of course, nurses have no nerves? Worse things than ghosts knocking about, eh? There might be mice! Women are a jolly sight more afraid of *them* than of ghosts. Now, is that a sign of a good conscience or of a more material nature? What's wrong with your patient here?"

I evaded the question: if it is wrong to sadden the young needlessly, it must be at least equally so to sadden the old, and he went off cheerfully convinced that I was "fussing after" a case of measles, or something else "better left to nature."

I crossed over to the public-house at the corner, glad that my jovial old friend could not see me, and glad too of the side door which gave entrance to the passage leading to my patient's room. In this neighbourhood the traditional love of nurses for "a quartern o' gin" is firmly believed in, and I did not wish to give it such a substantial confirmation as being seen pass through a bar.

The patient, who was entirely dependent upon his

parents, was a man of forty, who had been blind and a helpless cripple for twelve years. He could speak and move his head slightly, and had the partial use of his left arm and of two fingers of the left hand. His intellect was perfectly clear, there was nothing repulsive in his appearance, and his room had been papered and painted and entirely re-furnished by some charitable friends.

Apparently there was everything in the man's circumstances to call forth pity, and nothing to excite disgust or abhorrence. And yet, such is the eternal mystery of attraction and repulsion, no patient I ever had on my books caused me more trouble. No one wished to visit him: not the trustiest staff-nurse, not the most enthusiastic probationer, not the steadiest most matter-of-course worker in the Home. Nurse after nurse, women who uncomplainingly attended the worst cases of cancer in the filthiest houses, or who spent their days going from one little victim of diphtheria or typhoid to another, would come to me privately, and, with faces of shuddering repulsion, ask: " Must I go and see F———? I would rather do *anything* else!" None of them could explain why, but the repugnance was so strong and so general, that although I am considered a hard task-mistress, I was forced to compromise: each nurse had to pay a certain number of visits, and if possible I accompanied her. Often I had to go alone.

Not only human beings felt the repulsion. There were two cats in the house, and, knowing how much he was left by himself, and seeing numerous rat-holes, I tried to induce them to make friends with him. Notwithstanding the fact that strong affection usually exists between these animals and chronic patients, neither of them ever entered the room voluntarily, or could be induced to remain there. A lady who was in the habit of visiting him, and who found conversation with him intensely difficult, one day took her dog with her, a friendly, high-spirited Irish terrier. To her extreme annoyance, the animal shrank away in abject terror, and if he had not had a strong leader on he would have torn wildly out of the house.

One of the ladies who had refurnished the man's room taught him to read the Braille system, and I induced a friend, who had been taken several times to see him while visiting the town, to learn it also and write to him regularly. She did so, and persevered up to the time of his death, but she told me frankly: "I always write to him on the 27th of the month, and although I cannot tell you how it is, in the whole course of the year I never do anything that I dislike a hundredth part so much. The effort even affects my sleep. Yet all the time I am full of pity for him, and disgusted with my unwillingness. Do the nurses ever complain, or seem to shrink from waiting on him?"

She appeared strangely relieved to know that she was not alone in her sin.

The sufferer's grandfather, and possibly his great-grandfather, had occupied the same house, and carried on the same trade. What a tale of horror Edgar Poe could have woven from these disjointed fragments.

THE LAST PASSAGE IN THE LIFE OF A HERO

Civilians in a seaport town have often complained bitterly to me because seamen gunners after twenty-one years' service are given a pension. " Other men have to work till they drop dead." I often reply: " Did these men when they were young take their life in their hands and risk it for their country ? You see the men who have lived to draw a pension, you do not see or think of those who died of yellow fever on one ocean, or cholera on another, or who left all of them that was mortal in the The White Man's Grave. You do not even think of those who in the plain course of their duty have received injuries, or contracted diseases, compared with which death is indeed a light affliction."

For many years we visited one of these victims. Scientists decided that he had received the germs of an obscure Asiatic disease through some small wounds in his hands. The details are too terrible for description; his hands and feet were enormously swollen and quite useless to him, the spine became fixed like a log of wood, lockjaw supervened, and he could only be fed with a tube passed through a gap where one of his teeth had been removed.

From year's end to year's end he lay upon a small hospital bed placed under the window of a room scarcely ten feet square. He had the thoughtful, earnest look which characterises all the better class of sailors, but there was more in his face than that,—contentment, peace, and often the vivid flash of unquenchable humour. No one entering the neatly kept room, and receiving his cheerful greeting, could ever realise the sufferings of the tortured body beneath the snowy counterpane, and no word of complaint ever passed his lips. The nearest approach to one that I heard from him was the quotation, with eyes full of meaning, of a scrap of Marcus Aurelius which had somehow reached that narrow side street—

"Bring your will to your fate, and suit your mind to your circumstances, and love those people heartily that it is your fortune to be engaged with."

Not long after, an event occurred which threw a halo of importance over the entire family, and greatly consoled the wife's heart. The doctor, feeling unable to give even the slightest alleviation to the case, invited four of his colleagues to meet him in that tiny room. Four carriages drove up, the neighbours rushed to door or window to view the unusual sight, and when a paragraph appeared in the evening paper, stating that A. M. of such and such an address was suffering from a disease "that baffled medical science," even the most distant relatives felt proud of him.

It was a disease in which doctor and nurse alike were useless, unless they would simply leave ordinary routine duties out of the question, and give what time they could spare to his amusement. The man's intellect was extraordinarily clear, and he took the deepest interest in public matters. All through the South African War a large map was pinned at the foot of his bed, and he followed every detail of the campaign. The flag captain's wife had given him a convenient reading stand, the nearest publican sent him on the *Standard*, and he would study the page in front of him until one of his children came and changed it for him. Another great interest in life was the composition of verses. He would turn one over in his mind until satisfied with it, and then call his eldest son and dictate it to him. I was allowed to see the exercise-book that contained most of them. They were full of manly, sensible advice to his children, but I was most touched by the constant recurrence of the prayer, " Be good to your mother when I am gone."

He told me one day that the greatest joy of his life was music, and that two of his first wife's sons often came to play the banjo to him. I was trying to find out something that he would really like to have, and after much questioning learnt that the banjo was out of order and had always been " a poor thing." I told one of his many rich friends, and a new instrument was soon hanging in his room, ready for any visitor who could play on it. One of these visitors was a former shipmate who had lost his sight during a thunderstorm on the East Coast. He was coming downstairs with his wife at the moment, and she was killed by his side. £500 was collected for the sufferer, and my patient never wearied of telling what excitement the arrival of the millionaire had caused in the neighbourhood; how many pressing offers of marriage he had received, and the wrath and disappointment of the bride elect when she learnt, rather too late, that the donors of the money had firmly tied it up for the first wife's two children.

One day he told me: "Lady B—— was here yesterday. We did laugh. I think if your melly-fluous voice had been here to join us, the roof would have come off. She said the King was coming to have his dinner with her in the evening, but she didn't seem to be taking it to heart at all. I suppose it was to be just in a friendly way, like! I remember when Prince —— used to dine with Admiral ——, he used to say, 'If he comes by himself we'll have a beef steak and onions, that's what the old boy likes; but if anyone else comes, we'll have to have a thundering blow-out.' What laughs the officers used to have in those days over the things the men 'ud take it into their heads to do just when there was any pa'ticler company. You know, mess-servanting wasn't the reg'lar business that it is now. There was one admiral, and he couldn't bear to see 'em waiting at table in their ordinary clothes, so he dressed out his whole dozen to suit his fancy, and then he invited every captain in the fleet to his house to a big dinner. One of them was an earl when he was at home, same as Lady B.'s husband, so he wasn't a bit took aback when he saw twelve men in a private uny-form. He just took it as a matter o' course. But presently he wanted a bit of bread. I daresay you've been to one of them dinners yourself, admiral [his usual name for me], but if you haven't, it'd fair surprise you to see the bread they'll eat, enough to break the cook's heart if he knew it. Anyone would think they were trying to wipe the taste

of his messes out of their mouth. So he turned to the
nearest of the dozen, which he was a red marine under
his new clothes, 'Bread, please,' says he. Joey didn't
take no notice, but stood there with his eyes straight
ahead and his little fingers glued to his trouser seams,
'*Bread*, please, says the earl, speaking a bit sharper;
'I asked you before.' Up went the back of Joey's hand
to his forehead with a slap, 'Beg pardin, sir; I was *told
off for the petaties.*' Luckily the earl's manners was
pretty good. He never even smiled, but when they was
walking down to the boats, how they roared! Once the
same admiral give a party when he was abroad, and he
wouldn't have no ladies, because he'd took a fit of saving,
and he thought it would come cheaper. Well, the first
thing happened was that some of the young officers was
so dull that they broke into the refreshment room two
hours sooner than anyone was meant to, and drank up
the wine that was to ha' lasted the whole evening.
Naturally after that they got jackacting and fighting.
Before midnight, a dozen or more, old and young, was so
drunk they *couldn't* go back to their ships. Five of 'em
slep' under the billiard table. The admiral he was so
disgusted he couldn't sleep, and early in the morning he
went out in his garden, and up comes a commander in
nothing but a cocked hat and a shirt, saluting him as
bold as brass. Of course the admiral couldn't see him,
so he doubled back to the house pretty quick. The
servants had been up early too, making out lists of wine
and breakages. When the admiral saw the totals, he
come up all he'd ever said against ladies in all his born

days, and swore he'd never give a bull-party again as long as he lived."

Gradually, after many, many years of suffering, he became weaker, and one hot summer's day the long-looked-for order of release arrived. He had always cherished a secret wish for a military funeral, and a few days later a gun-carriage covered with the Union-jack, accompanied by a firing party and a troop of old friends who had been shipmates "when all the world was young," stood outside his door, and the procession moved slowly away to a grave within sound of the waves that he loved and had so long missed. Three volleys were fired, the bugler sounded "The Last Post," and the veterans returned to their homes, satisfied that a brave man had met with due honour. An anchor rests on his grave, with the inscription: "Well done, good and faithful soldier."

It may be asked, What was the religion of your hero? Any sect might be proud of him, but to which he belonged I simply do not know. Nominally he was an Anglican, but he never spoke of such matters. It may be my wickedness, or it may be theirs, but my patients rarely quote texts to me, or say anything that would sound well in a missionary report or at a revival meeting. When he was dying, his one great anxiety was to live until the month's pension was due, and the few days beyond it rendered necessary by the position of his name on the list. Men are paid in alphabetical succession, and it might well happen that the "M's" were not reached until the third of the month. The last words of many a naval and military man are—

"Doctor, nurse, pray do what you can to keep me here till the 1st, so that my poor wife won't lose the money." Even in the extremest agony they hold it cowardice to die one hour too soon.

THE SERGEANT'S WIDOW

"Yes, my friends didn't like me marrying a soldier," said the sergeant's widow, "but it was a great mercy I *did*. Why, I get a shilling every week from the s'ciety,—there's the order on the chimley-piece now. It goes a long way in groceries. It makes all the difference in the world to me, that shilling."

She spoke with such genuine satisfaction of the provision thus made for her by the deceased warrior, that it did not strike me until long afterwards, and apparently it had never struck her, that such a pretty and capable girl as she must have been could easily have married a civilian, who might have left her five shillings a week of his own, instead of a minute claim on a charity.

Mrs. K. is not far short of eighty, and has been living by herself in a single room for nearly twenty years. The house where she passed most of them was called a "Building," but that is a mere modern affectation, for it contains none of the comforts and conveniences which (to the poor at any rate) are implied by that term. I am no archæologist, but I should be inclined to think that it had at one time been a monastery school, and then, eighty or a hundred years ago, was roughly adapted to its present purpose. Many of the inmates were far from desirable neighbours, but she had a good door with a strong lock on it, and her one window was large, and commanded a view of a middle-class street. Another widow, active and considerably younger, lived in the next apartment, and could be summoned at any time by a sharp knock on the wall. Mrs. K. could manage to lock and unlock her door without leaving her bed, so that, even when her chronic complaint took an acute form and prevented her from moving, I thought her perfectly safe, until one day she told me tales of broad-daylight visits from rats which alarmed me more for her safety than her neighbours' quarrels and "language."

"Oh, I'm all right as long as I have my dear pussy," she said cheerfully. "He never leaves me at night, and only in the daytime just for an hour or two over to the stables. Cats is always welcome in a stable, so no one does him any harm. I leave the window open at the bottom, and he climbs in and out, and crosses the road where it's *respectable*. He wouldn't be safe the way you come."

I was somewhat reassured, and, to use a phrase common among my patients, "I come up all as ever I'd said" against cats, and especially cats in a sick-room, and made no adverse comments even when I found Benny stretched full length on the bed, ecstatically kneading the clean pillow-case. His most faithful guardianship lasted for four years, and then came to a sudden and needless end. Some alterations were being made in the stableyard that he visited daily for recreation and to decrease the cost of his keep. ("He never asks me for nothing but a spoonful or two of milk twice a day," his mistress had often told me.) Unfortunately a heap of broken bricks was left on the ground, and out of sheer idleness one of the lads picked up a piece and flung it at Benny. I believe he only meant to "scare" him, but the missile was too heavy and the aim too exact. Benny, as the poor old widow expressed it, "fell down then and there, and never spoke again."

It was impossible to replace him : firstly, because a decent period of mourning was needed ; and, secondly, because few cats had intellect enough for the post. As the only practicable alternative, Mrs. K. at last resolved to leave the rat-haunted building, and took the "front room" of a respectable young couple who could not afford to furnish it, and were glad to reduce their rent. One great charm of the new house is that it is "almost touching a pillar post." I was slightly puzzled, thinking that her correspondence could not be large, but she explained—

"Just think what it saves me ! I write a card to the grocer, and in comes all my groceries for a week ; another to the butcher, and there's my bit of meat. The bread and milk comes without telling, so there's

all my errands done for two ha'pennies. Now, there's
not a child that 'ud run an errand for less than a
penny, and even if they was willing, their parents
wouldn't let 'em; and if I wanted six or seven bits of
things, as one does, I should have to pay more."

"Greedy little things! And then it goes in
sweets?"

"Oh no; whatever they earns they have to give
their mother, and perhaps she'll give 'em a penny out
of it on Saturdays."

"And what becomes of it?"

"Oh, respectable people don't never *spend* what
school children earns, unless they're rather put to it
at the time. It goes into the savings bank for 'em, or
into a Boot Club, or a Meat Club, or something of that
kind. Boot Clubs is the best. There's no *charity* about
it. Seven-and-sixpence would buy a good stout lasting
pair of boy's boots in any shop if the mother had it
ready to pay. But when there's many of them it's very
likely she hasn't, so she gives four shillings and sixpence,
and the boots is to pieces in no time. 'Sides, the Boot
Clubs teaches boys what boots costs, and they're more
careful. No; I wouldn't grudge 'em the pennies for
errands if I had them, but now I can't do much sewing
I have to count rather closely."

Yet only the other day, when a lady wrote to her
from a distant part of England, and told her of a
certain old man in the workhouse with not a relative
in the world left, her letter in reply enclosed three
postage stamps and the request, " Please keep these and

20

give threepence to the old gentleman to buy newspapers or tobacco. Gentlemen like a pipe."

Her own passion is for newspapers. As a rule, she is contented with yesterday's at a heavy reduction, but all through the South African War the "latest editions" were bought recklessly. Her interest in the present conflict is deep, her horror of the belligerents, whom she rather inaptly calls Rush-ons, is intense. "I pray every night for the poor dear Japs. I feel that they have need of it." This abhorrence of Russians is probably a legacy from her deceased husband, but I have only been favoured with one anecdote in reference to him.

She was "on the strength," but lived outside the barracks, and one night, very early in their married life, he came home drunk and beat her, but was fortunately too drunk to do the slender little creature much harm. She did what all successful matrons tell me must be done, "took it in time." She waited until he had fallen into a heavy sleep, and then sewed him up firmly in a stout sheet. When he woke up sufficiently recovered "to know what was for his *good*," she took a stick and thrashed him soundly. Three hours after, not finding him sufficiently subdued, and her arm aching too much to continue the discipline satisfactorily, she called in one of her brothers, who beat him until she said "enough." (The mummified soldier had been saying it for some time.) He never struck his wife again, and as he became a sergeant and remained one until he died, I conclude that he also gave up the immoderate use of strong drink.

A soldier's wife, even at the present day, is in a worse position than other women if her husband should be inclined to drink, because she is more bound to *conceal* his misdeeds, and she thus loses the check that public opinion would be to him. If a complaint of his conduct reached the colonel, heavy punishment would follow, but it might come in the form of reduced pay, and seriously affect the small amount that ever reaches the wife. When, however, a man's drunkenness only affects a man's private life, colonels will sometimes take the law into their own hands : the husband is given a trifle for pocket money, all the rest of the pay is handed over to the wife, and the delinquent has to attend so many extra roll-calls that he is perforce kept sober at all times.

HIS THIRD WIFE

The husband was a man of the highest respectability, the little house was well furnished throughout, and in spite of the wife's illness there was not a speck of dirt to be seen in any part of it.

It was a surgical case of no great severity, and the patient was always in good spirits and eager for conversation. The husband was most kind and attentive, but, noticing another woman's photograph on the mantelpiece, I asked—

" What number are you, Mrs. Jervis ? "

" Number three," she said laughingly,—" and he's *my* number two."

I had always wished to know why widowers prefer marrying widows, and I thought this was a good opportunity of obtaining the opinion of an expert gratis. She was a woman of considerable education as well as experience, and this is what she told me—

"The reason why widows can always get married again, however many young spinsters there may be to choose from, is this, widows understand the conditions of married life, and they do not expect affection. They know that the man has none left to give. The heart loves but once. My second husband is the best man in the world; we study one another, we are kind to one another's children and grandchildren, and we are happy together, but his heart is with *her*, and mine is with a man who raised a pewter pot to his lips far too often."

"How did you come to marry Mr. Jervis?"

"Well, my children were both out in the world, and I was beginning to feel almost as much alone as if I had never had any. I had been housekeeper for four years to a gentleman who worked a great deal among the poor. He was very delicate, and it used to take all my time trying to keep his strength up for what he *would* do. Well, Mr. Jervis wanted a wife, and he heard of me. He inquired into my character, and said to himself: 'If that gentleman could put up with her for four years she can't be a bad sort.' And then he asked me to share all he had. I said to the gentleman: 'I'm thinking of getting married, sir.' He said: 'Caroline, it's a good match. Don't let me stand in

your way.' I said : 'Sir, you must let me do the best
I can for you first.' So I found him another housekeeper, and taught her all his ways, and then me and
Mr. Jervis got married, and neither of us has ever
regretted it.

One winter we nursed a pensioner dying of dropsy.
The wife, a woman of about sixty-five, but in vigorous
health, waited on him with great devotion, and seemed
heart-broken when he died. The pension having ceased,
she sold off all her furniture except what was necessary
for a single room, and lived on an allowance of thirty
shillings a month made her by a sailor son. I saw her
several times after the funeral, in deep mourning and a
most depressed state of mind.

Six months later I came across her, joy in her face,
violets in her bonnet. I guessed that this meant
matrimony, but I waited to be told. With peals of
laughter she related how a widower "with a good
home" had wanted someone to look after him and
his children, and how he asked, "Will you?" and she
replied, "Well, I thank you, sir!" (making a little bob
curtsey to illustrate her state of mind).

"And now," she said joyfully, "I've forty children
and grandchildren, all told, and I'm as happy as the
day is long."

Then her eye fell on my uniform : it reminded her of
the husband of her youth. The smile faded from her
face for a moment, and she said, with a pitiful droop of
her mouth, " *You cannot live by the dead.*"

THE TWO EXCEPTIONS

My patients, with only two exceptions, have all belonged to the poor. One of these was brought into the accident ward of a London hospital, a terribly battered and muddy object. His main injury, a fracture, had been already attended to, and, with the help of a senior medical student, we cut off his clothing and got him into bed. Just as we did so he gave a heavy groan, and seemed about to collapse.

"All right, old chappie,—all right! You'll be better soon," said the future specialist cheerfully.

The apparently dying man opened his eyes, and in the coldest of clerical voices replied—

"Young man, I am a canon of my cathedral, and I am not accustomed to such a form of address."

He would have been still more mortified if he had heard the timid question whispered to me by a lady pupil: "Sister, is he drunk?"

When he left he presented the ward with an easy-chair, and later on he wrote a sermon in which grateful reference was made to us all, and sent us printed copies. It had been impossible for us to give him a private room, and as far as I knew no special attention had been shown him, so I thought it very forgiving of him, little guessing what balm in Gilead he had found. Years after, a former lady pupil, who was the daughter of a Church dignitary, and had "kept of them tame," confessed gleefully: "Sister, you are supposed to see everything, but you never suspected! I used to put up a screen and make him buttered toast."

The second was also the victim of a street accident. He only remained with us three days, during which he examined the literature of the ward rather closely. A week or two later he sent us a donation of twenty books. I heard that they were beautifully printed and bound, and hoped that some of the more educated of the men would derive great pleasure from them. Unluckily he had wandered too far from the style of fiction commonly admitted into hospitals. For some weeks it was impossible to get the volumes out of the house-surgeon's sitting-room, and then it proved impossible to let them into the wards. But he meant well, and I cannot wonder at the contemptuous irritation with which he had inspected our library.

Fortunately his brief stay did not coincide with the visits of a lady who read *Froggy's Little Brother* aloud in the men's wards. They used to listen decorously while she was there, and roar with laughter as soon as she was gone. Perhaps I ought to have told her, but she enjoyed herself thoroughly,—and so did they.

The most dissatisfied patient I ever met was, as might reasonably be expected, a doctor. I had nothing to do with nursing him, but I listened to his complaints for an hour. First and foremost, he had been " starved."

" Could you have eaten more ? "

" Eaten more ! I could have *stolen* it if there had

been any chance, but they kept me in a cell. They called it a private room."

"Did you complain to the medical staff before leaving?"

"You don't suppose you can keep a man on toast and water for two months and then have him spoiling for a fight? I told the sister in charge what I thought of them, and I hope she repeated it to them."

"Most probably not. Was she apologetic?"

"She said, 'We flatter ourselves we know something about fever.' I said, 'So do I, *now!*' and then I skipped off to the P. & O. and began eating. I ate for twenty-four hours straight on end, and I've been eating ever since."

Printed by MORRISON & GIBB LIMITED, *Edinburgh*